Resistance and Reconstruction

RESISTANCE
AND
RECONSTRUCTION

Messages During China's Six Years of War
1937 — 1943

By

GENERALISSIMO CHIANG KAI-SHEK

Essay Index Reprint Series

BOOKS FOR LIBRARIES PRESS
FREEPORT, NEW YORK

STANDARD BOOK NUMBER:

8369-1597-6

LIBRARY OF CONGRESS CATALOC CARD NUMBER:

71-111819

PRINTED IN THE UNITED STATES OF AMERICA

CONTENTS

III. *CHINA FIGHTS AND BUILDS* (1940-1941)

IV. *CHINA FIGHTS ON WITH ALLIES* (1941-1943)

A NOTE ON THE TRANSLATION

GENERALISSIMO CHIANG KAI-SHEK'S speeches are translated into English and made available to the press as soon as they are given, through Central News Agency and the Chinese Ministry of Information. The present work is compiled from new translations of the Chinese texts. Dr. Albert French Lutley of Chengtu is responsible for the translations included in the first section, "China Resists Japan." Dr. Frank Wilson Price, translator of Sun Yat-sen's *San Min Chu I,* is responsible for the second section, "China Fights On." Mr. Ma Pin-ho of Chungking translated the speeches that make up the last two sections, "China Fights and Builds" and "China Fights On with Allies."

FOREWORD

O N JULY 7, 1943, China will have entered her seventh year of armed resistance against Japan. The story of China's war, now a part of the world war, has been told by many and in various ways, but it will be an understatement to say that, of all people, Generalissimo Chiang Kai-shek is the one best qualified to tell it.

In this volume the leader of the Chinese people tells in his own words how they have been fighting and standing ground against a world aggressor, what has happened so far in China's War of Resistance, and why his nation has been fighting and is today continuing to fight. This is not a book written with the benefit of hindsight, when the smoke has been cleared from the battlefield. It is a book made up of what the Generalissimo thought and what he said, from day to day and from month to month, during the past six years of leading a nation in life-and-death struggle. The words contained in it are the product of war's each excruciating moment. They are given as weapons to his people when real weapons at times seem so scarce. They are part of the living record of this war, indeed, the sum and substance of the war itself.

Ten days after the Marco Polo Bridge Incident, Generalissimo Chiang Kai-shek solemnly defined to the nation the limit of China's endurance and took up the challenge to fight for freedom against the greatest odds. At the beginning of 1943, when the United Nations had completed their first year of joint endeavor, he rose again to inform his people of a new and hard-won status for China and of the new responsibilities that go with it.

In almost every speech made by Generalissimo Chiang between July 17, 1937, and January 12, 1943—the first and last items in this volume —the theme of "Resistance and Reconstruction" is stressed. The dual chord was sounded from the start, in the first two messages he delivered after the outbreak of war; it has reverberated ever since in his utterances and it has been proclaimed China's national program during and after the war.

What lesser men are apt to repeat glibly, Generalissimo Chiang believes with his whole heart, soul and mind. It has been justly observed that a leader of men is simply one who sees more clearly and feels more deeply than others. That armed resistance and national reconstruction are the *sine qua non* of China's final victory over Japan has now become a commonplace. Generalissimo Chiang's merit is that in him this commonplace is transformed into an inspiration and faith by his passionate advocacy of it.

Words forged in the white heat of hostilities, printed as they were delivered, may appear repetitious, but the repetitions in Generalissimo Chiang's wartime messages are necessary because they embody truths which we must not forget for one single moment at our peril. Though addressing himself primarily to his fellow countrymen, Generalissimo Chiang had occasion to speak to America, to Britain, to India, to Australia, to the world at large—even to the Japanese people. At times he is the resolute soldier, the able executive, the steadfast Christian, the champion of a united front long before such came into existence, or the stern reformer denouncing political and social weaknesses in his own country. Again he is the world statesman, giving at every turn a correct prognosis of world events, or interpreting China's hopes and ideals for a new cooperative international order based on law and justice.

Through all the vicissitudes of the war, Generalissimo Chiang's confidence in China's ultimate victory has remained unshaken, and he has been able to communicate his faith and courage to the people of China through his speeches, writings and actions.

To keep the present work within the bounds of a readable book, selections are made from the vast amount of material available. In due time the complete and collected state papers of Generalissimo Chiang Kai-shek will be published for the English-reading world. Meanwhile, the reader will find all the major speeches brought into focus in the present volume, covering each year of China's war from 1937 to 1943, without damage to unity and continuity.

The items gathered here are arranged in chronological order though, in the nature of the war's progress, they fall conveniently into four general sections. The first section covers the period during which China defied Japan and surprised the world with her heroic stand at Shanghai and where ever the enemy struck. The second stage of the war was keynoted by the Commander-in-Chief when, after Japan's pyrrhic victory at Nanking, he declared simply: "We prefer to fight on." The outbreak of war in Europe served only to strengthen China's convictions by underscoring their universal application. In the third section, the problems of China's rebuilding are more and more discussed, with emphasis on both the material and the spiritual bases of prolonged resistance. And the epic of the war moves inexorably on to its next stage where China was destined, after Pearl Harbor, to be joined by other freedom-loving nations in the common struggle for world peace and justice which has only just begun.

With the exception of a few pieces in the last section, none of the speeches collected here has been published in America in its full text, in the press or anywhere else. It may therefore be said that, though the substance of this book has been almost six years in the making, it is here uncovered for the English reader virtually for the first time and as an organized whole.

CHING-LIN HSIA

New York City
June 1, 1943.

A GLOSSARY OF TERMS

MUKDEN INCIDENT—the Japanese attack at Mukden, capital of Liaoning Province, on September 18, 1931, marking the beginning of Japan's invasion of China in Manchuria, and now recognized as the act of aggression that started the Second World War.

THE NORTHEASTERN PROVINCES—the Provinces of Liaoning, Kirin and Heilungkiang, in the northeastern corner of China, commonly known in Chinese as the Three Eastern Provinces or the Northeast, and known to the West as Manchuria. Since the Japanese first invaded and occupied these provinces and, in 1933, the adjacent Province of Jehol, they have been called collectively the Four Northeastern Provinces.

TANGKU AGREEMENT—the so-called Tangku Truce of May 31, 1933, concluded for the suspension of hostilities which, resulting from the Japanese invasion of Manchuria and Jehol, had extended into Peiping and Tientsin areas. Both China and Japan undertook to withdraw their troops, the Chinese from the territory between the Great Wall and the Peiping area ; the Japanese to the Great Wall. The agreement, exacted by *force majeure,* was objectionable to the Chinese. It promised renewed Japanese aggression in provisions for the Japanese Army "at any time to use aeroplanes or other means to verify the carrying out" of Chinese troop withdrawals and for a Chinese police force in the demilitarized zone "not hostile to Japanese feelings."

LUKOUCHIAO INCIDENT—the Japanese attack near Peiping on July 7, 1937, that marked the beginning of China's War of Resistance. Lukouchiao is known to the West as Marco Polo Bridge.

WUHAN—collective name for the three cities, Hankow, Wuchang and Hanyang, on the Yangtze River in Hupeh Province, center of China's resistance for the period between the fall of Nanking on December 13, 1937, and the evacuation of Hankow on October 25, 1938.

THE REVOLUTION—designating the Revolution started by Dr. Sun Yat-sen. In 1912 it succeeded in overthrowing the Manchu Dynasty and establishing the Chinese Republic. The continuity of the Revolution is seen in subsequent efforts to bring about complete achievement of

xiii

Dr. Sun's revolutionary goals—the Northern Expedition led by Generalissimo Chiang Kai-shek in 1926 is known as the Nationalist Revolution; the present War of Resistance against Japanese aggression is considered another stage in the Revolution.

TSUNGLI—Dr. Sun Yat-sen (1866-1925), Father of the Chinese Republic, referred to by Generalissimo Chiang as the Leader (of the Nationalist Party).

SAN MIN CHU I—Dr. Sun's revolutionary aims and the basic doctrine of the Chinese Republic: *Min Tsu Chu I* (The Principle of Nationalism), *Min Chuan Chu I* (The Principle of Democracy), and *Min Sheng Chu I* (The Principle of People's Livelihood).

KUOMINTANG—the Nationalist Party, founded by Dr. Sun Yat-sen in 1893 and now under the leadership of Generalissimo Chiang Kai-shek as *Tsungtsai* (Director-General). The Party is dedicated to the task of achieving China's Revolution and the realization of *San Min Chu I*.

THE NEW LIFE MOVEMENT—founded in 1934 by Generalissimo and Madame Chiang to rejuvenate the nation through promotion of a regular life guided by the four ancient Chinese virtues: *Li* (Propriety), *I* (Justice), *Lien* (Integrity) and *Ch'ih* (Conscientiousness).

HSIEN—the basic unit in the new system for local administration promulgated by the Government in 1939, translated County or District. China's 28 provinces are divided into 1,934 *hsien,* more than half of which have been reorganized into autonomous administrative units under the new system.

PAO-CHIA SYSTEM—an ancient Chinese system of registration and mutual guarantee under which households are organized for local administration and self-defense.

PEOPLE'S POLITICAL COUNCIL—a wartime representative assembly organized because the war had made it impossible for the Government to convoke the scheduled National People's Assembly and it was necessary to rally the nation's talents for the formulation and execution of national policies. The First People's Political Council began its sessions at Hankow in July, 1938. The Third People's Political Council, inaugurated in Chungking in October, 1942, was composed of 240 members, about two thirds of whom were elected from the provincial and municipal People's Political Councils.

HWANG TI—literally the Yellow Emperor, legendary founder of the Chinese civilization who is credited with fighting successfully against the barbarians.

A

CHRONOLOGY

of

CHINA'S WAR OF RESISTANCE

and the

WAR MESSAGES OF GENERALISSIMO CHIANG KAI-SHEK

1937–1943

PRELUDE

Sept. 18, 1931—Japan invaded China's Three Northeastern Provinces (Manchuria).

Jan. 7, 1932—U.S. sent "Non-Recognition Note" to China and Japan.

Jan. 28, 1932—Japan attacked Shanghai.

Feb. 24, 1933—League of Nations adopted Lytton Report and pledged its members not to recognize puppet state of "Manchukuo."

FIRST YEAR

July 7, 1937—Japanese troops opened fire on Chinese Army at Lukouchiao (Marco Polo Bridge), outskirts of Peiping.

July 17, 1937—*The Limit of China's Endurance.* Address to the nation's leaders at Lushan, Kiangsi.

July 18, 1937—*On National Reconstruction.* Address to the Summer Training Corps at Lushan, Kiangsi.

July 1937—*Drive Out the Invader.* Message to the nation's armed forces after the Japanese capture of Peiping and Tientsin.

Aug. 13, 1937—Fighting broke out in Shanghai.

NOTE: Selected speeches of Generalissimo Chiang during the past six years are listed in italics and related to the leading events of the war.

Aug. 21, 1937—China and Soviet Russia signed non-aggression pact.
Sept. 21, 1937—The "Government of the Soviet Republic of China" dissolved itself. The Chinese Communist Party pledged support of the National Government.
Sept. 24, 1937—*National Solidarity*. Statement in connection with the Chinese Communist Party's declaration for the United Front.
Oct. 5, 1937—President Roosevelt delivered "quarantine the aggressors" speech.
Oct. 6, 1937—League of Nations adopted resolution calling Nine-Power Treaty Conference. U.S. State Department issued statement condemning Japan as invader of China and violator of Nine-Power Treaty and Kellogg Pact.
Oct. 9, 1937—*Fight to Win*. Broadcast on the even of the "Double Tenth" National Holiday.
Nov. 6, 1937—Japan joined Germany, Italy in anti-Comintern Pact.
Nov. 12, 1937—Shanghai fell.
Nov. 15, 1937—Fifteen nations at Brussels Conference of Nine-Power Treaty signatories adopted resolution condemning Japan.
Nov. 20, 1937—China moved its capital from Nanking to Chungking.
Dec. 12, 1937—Japanese planes sank U.S. gunboat "Panay" in the Yangtze River.
Dec. 13, 1937—Nanking taken by Japanese troops who plundered the city, perpetrated wholesale atrocities.
Dec. 16, 1937—*After the Fall of Nanking*. Message to the nation from Field Headquarters.
Dec. 20, 1937—"Scorched Earth Policy", first carried out systematically in Tsingtao.
April 2, 1938—People's Political Council created.
April 8, 1938—Japanese army routed in Battle of Taierhchwang, exploding myth of its invincibility.
May 20, 1938—Chinese planes "bombed" Japanese cities with leaflets. Japanese claimed occupation of Hsuchow.
June 6, 1938—Fall of Kaifeng, capital of Honan Province.
June 12, 1938—Fall of Anking, capital of Anhwei Province.
June 19, 1938—Japanese checked in Honan by Yellow River flood.
July 6, 1938—*China's Path to Victory*. Address at inaugural session of People's Political Council.

SECOND YEAR

Feb. 10, 1939—Hainan Island occupied by Japan.

Feb. 21, 1939—*China's March Towards Democracy*. Closing address to the third session of People's Political Council. ·

March 8, 1939—London announced £5,000,000 credit to China.

March 15, 1939—German troops entered Prague; Czechoslovakia fell.

March 27, 1939—Nanchang fell.

March 29, 1939—Republican Spain surrendered to Franco after 3 years of war.

March 31, 1939—Japan annexed Spratly Islands, about 700 miles west of Manila, 300 miles south of Saigon and 1,000 miles from Hongkong.

April   7, 1939—Italy invaded and later conquered Albania.

April 17, 1939—*Spiritual Mobilization and Victory*. Radio message to the people of China.

May   1, 1939—*The Citizen's Pact*. Address at inauguration of Spiritual Mobilization Movement.

May   3, 1939—Chungking heavily raided by Japanese bombers.

May 16, 1939—*Bombing of Civilians and Open Towns*. Message to the nation.

June 14, 1939—Japan started blockade of British and French concessions in Tientsin.

June 22, 1939—Japanese forces occupied the port of Swatow.

June 24, 1939—Announcement made of Sino-Soviet trade agreement based on principles of mutuality and reciprocity.

THIRD YEAR

July   7, 1939—Second anniversary of war.
 Prepare for Victory. Message to the Chinese armed forces and civilians.
 A Common Front Against Aggression. Message to friendly Powers.
 Resistance in the Enemy's Rear. Message to the Chinese people in war zones and occupied areas.

July 23, 1939—Anglo-Japanese agreement signed.

July 24, 1939—*No Far Eastern Munich*. Address at weekly assembly of National Government.

July 26, 1939—U.S. denounced American-Japanese trade treaty.

July 29, 1939—*Appeal to Britain*. Statement to the *News Chronicle*, London.

Aug.   13, 1939—*Mission of the People of Shanghai*. Message sent on the 2nd anniversary of the beginning of hostilities in the Shanghai area.

Aug.   22, 1939—Germany signed non-aggression pact with Soviet Union.

Aug.   23, 1939—Chungking gave Jawaharlal Nehru warm welcome.

Sept.   1, 1939—German troops invaded Poland.

Sept.   3, 1939—England and France at war with Germany.

Sept.   9, 1939—*China and the European War*. Opening address at fourth session of People's Political Council.

Sept.   18, 1939—*Rights and Obligations of the Chinese People*. Closing address at fourth session of People's Political Council.

Oct.   10, 1939—*The People's War*. Message to the nation on 28th anniversary of Chinese Republic.

Oct.   16, 1939—China scored great victory at Changsha.

Nov.   25, 1939—Nanning, Kwangsi Province, devastated by fire from enemy bombings.

Dec.   29, 1939—Japanese offensive in North Kwangtung halted.

Jan.   21, 1940—Japan-Wang Ching-wei secret agreement exposed.

Feb.   18, 1940—*New Life in Wartime*. Broadcast to the nation on 6th anniversary of New Life Movement.

Feb.   20, 1940—*The Educator's Mission in China Today*. Message to the principals of all schools and colleges.

March 7, 1940—Second U.S. commercial loan of $20,000,000 to China.

March 22, 1940—*The Responsibilities of Modern Journalists*. Message to journalism graduates of Central Political Academy.

March 25, 1940—China recaptured Wuyuan in western Suiyuan.

March 30, 1940—Wang Ching-wei's puppet government set up in Nanking, refused recognition by Secretary Hull. President Lin Sen ordered Wang's arrest.

April   1, 1940—*No Relaxation of Our Efforts*. Opening address to fifth session of People's Political Council.

April   9, 1940—German troops occupied Denmark; invaded Norway.

April   10, 1940—People's Political Council closed with adoption of Revised Bill of the Draft Constitution.
       People in Government. Closing address to fifth session of People's Political Council.

May   1, 1940—*The Way to Local Autonomy*. Address at Szechwan Training Academy.

May   10, 1940—Germany invaded Holland, Belgium, Luxembourg.

May 25, 1940—Chinese troops broke out of Chungtiao Mountains, Shensi.

June 4, 1940—British troops evacuated Dunkirk.

June 10, 1940—Japan took Ichang, westernmost point of invasion on Yangtze.

June 20, 1940—France gave in to Japan on Indo-China.

June 22, 1940—France signed armistice with Germany.

FOURTH YEAR

July 7, 1940—Third anniversary of war.

July 17, 1940—Britain under Churchill's new government yielded to Japanese demands and closed Burma Road for three months.

July 27, 1940—China concluded new trade treaty with Russia.

Sept. 9, 1940—Chungking proclaimed the auxiliary capital.

Sept. 18, 1940—*Manchuria: Hell on Earth.* Message on 9th anniversary of Japan's invasion of Manchuria.

Sept. 23, 1940—Japanese army marched into French Indo-China.

Sept. 25, 1940—Third U.S. commercial loan to China of $25,000,000.

Sept. 27, 1940—Japan signed triple military alliance pact with Germany and Italy.

Oct. 10, 1940—*The International Role of the Republic.* Message on the 29th anniversary of the Chinese Republic.

Oct. 16, 1940—U.S. embargoed all forms of iron and steel to Japan.

Oct. 18, 1940—Japan's attempt to secure a "negotiated peace" failed and Britain reopened Burma Road.

Oct. 28, 1940—China recaptured Nanning, Kwangsi Province.

Nov. 30, 1940—U.S. extended to China $100,000,000 credits, half for general purposes, half for currency stabilization.
Hull disapproved Japan's recognition of Wang Ching-wei.

Dec. 10, 1940—London announced new loan of £10,000,000 to China.

Jan. 12, 1941—Chungking announced a third China-Soviet trade pact.

Jan. 27, 1941—*The Function of Revolutionary Discipline.* Speech at weekly assembly of the National Government.

March 1, 1941—*National Defense First.* Speech at inaugural session of Second People's Political Council.

March 6, 1941—*Again National Solidarity.* Report to People's Political Council explaining the Government's attitude to-
ward the demands of the Chinese Communist Party.

March 11, 1941—President Roosevelt signed Lend-Lease Bill.

April 6, 1941—Germany invaded Yugoslavia.

April 13, 1941—Russia and Japan signed a four-point neutrality pact.

April 27, 1941—Greece fell.

May 10, 1941—*Bonds Between China and America.* Address at farewell dinner to Ambassador Nelson T. Johnson.

May 31, 1941—Hull-Quo exchange of letters stated U.S. intention of
relinquishing extraterritorial rights and other special
privileges in China.

June 16, 1941—*A Balanced Development in National Finances.* Address at the Third National Financial Conference.

June 22, 1941—Russia invaded by Germany.

July 1, 1941—Chungking severed diplomatic relations with Berlin
and Rome after Axis recognition of Wang Ching-wei
regime.

FIFTH YEAR

July 7, 1941—Fourth anniversary of war.

July 14, 1941—British-Chinese notes reaffirmed Britain's willingness
to abolish extraterritoriality.

July 25, 1941—Washington froze all Japanese assets in America.
Britain took similar action a day later.

Aug. 14, 1941—Roosevelt and Churchill proclaimed Atlantic Charter
and eight-point peace program.

Sept. 15, 1941—30,000 puppet Nanking troops mutinied.

Sept. 18, 1941—*The Northeast and Territorial Integrity.* Message on
10th anniversary of Japanese occupation of Man-
churia.

Oct. 1, 1941—Chinese scored big victory in Second Battle of Changsha.

Oct. 11, 1941—Chinese reoccupied Ichang, forced to abandon it two
days later after enemy's use of poison gas.

Oct. 22, 1941—*Engineers' Role in National Crisis.* Message to meeting of Association of Chinese Engineers.

Nov. 1, 1941—Chinese reoccupied Chengchow.

Nov. 17, 1941—Roosevelt conferred with Kurusu.

America's Chance to Strike at Japan. Opening ad-

xxii

April 30, 1942—Lashio fell.

May 15, 1942—Japan opened new drive in Chekiang Province to destroy Allied air bases in China.

May 17, 1942—Chinese checked Japanese attempt to invade Yunnan Province via Burma Road.

May 19, 1942—Chungking spokesman issued urgent appeal to U.S. for bombers and pursuit planes.

May 31, 1942—*Morale plus Equipment.* Broadcast to America on Army Hour program.

June 27, 1942—Japan took Lishui in Chekiang Province, the last of three important bomb-Japan bases.

June 29, 1942—Japanese routed from Shansi-Honan border.

July 4, 1942—A.V.G. reorganized as United States Army Air Force in China.

SIXTH YEAR

July 7, 1942—Fifth anniversary of war.
China's War, a World War. Broadcast to the Chinese people and army.

Aug. 11, 1942—U.S. Air Force in China raided five major Japanese bases at Canton, Hankow, Nanchang, Hsienning and Yochow.

Aug. 29, 1942—Chinese retook Chuhsien and Lishui, climaxing a series of victories in counter-offensive along the Kiangsi-Chekiang railway.

Oct. 3, 1942—*A Friend from Distant Lands.* Speech at dinner to welcome Wendell L. Willkie.

Oct. 9, 1942—U.S. and Britain announced readiness to negotiate for abolition of extraterritorial rights in China.

Oct. 10, 1942—*Loyalty and Reciprocity.* Message to the nation on 31st anniversary of the Chinese Republic.

Oct. 22, 1942—*National and Allied Cooperation.* Opening address at the Third People's Political Council.

Oct. 23, 1942—U.S. Air Force in China bombed Linsi and Kailan coal mines near Tientsin in North China.

Oct. 31, 1942—*From Equality to Ideal Unity.* Closing address at Third People's Political Council.

Nov. 12, 1942—*From Men's Oldest Parliament.* Speech at dinner to welcome the British Parliamentary Mission.

I
China Resists Japan
(1937-1938)

The Limit of China's Endurance

JUST when China was exerting every effort to preserve peace with other nations and to secure internal unity, the Lukouchiao Incident suddenly burst upon us. Not only was our whole nation thrown into a state of profound indignation, but world opinion also was deeply shocked. The consequences of this incident threatened not only the very existence of China, but the peace and prosperity of mankind. You, who have upon your hearts our nation's difficulties, are naturally very anxious over this incident; therefore I want to take this opportunity to set forth simply but clearly certain significant points in relation to it.

In the first place, the Chinese have ever been a peace-loving race. The internal policy of the National Government has always been directed toward our own survival as a nation, and our foreign policy toward the corporate survival of the family of nations. In February of this year [1937], at the Plenary Session of the Central Executive Committee of the Kuomintang, a Manifesto was issued in which these points were even more clearly emphasized. For the last two years the National Government, in its policy toward Japan, has consistently followed these principles, in the hope that the confusion caused by Japan's arbitrary actions might be overcome, and all problems might be dealt with through recognized diplomatic channels, so that a just settlement could be reached. The facts show how earnest have been our efforts both within the country and abroad.

I feel strongly that if we are to meet this national crisis, we must first of all realize the position of our own country. We are a weak nation; therefore it is all the more necessary that we should have a true estimate of our strength. Peace is an absolute essential for the reconstruction of the nation. It is for this reason that for the past few years we have striven hard to maintain peace with other nations, in spite of all the injustice and suffering that has been our lot. In my report on foreign affairs at the Fifth Plenary Session of the Kuomintang the

An address at a gathering of Chinese leaders from various walks of life at Lushan (Kuling), Kiangsi, July 17, 1937, ten days after the Lukouchiao Incident which precipitated the war.

3

year before last, I stated that while there was the slightest hope for peace, we would not abandon it: so long as we had not reached the limit of endurance, we would not talk lightly of sacrifice. The explanation of the meaning of the phrase, "the limit of endurance," given at the Central Executive Session in February of this year showed plainly our love of peace and our anxiety to maintain it.

Since we are a weak country, there is only one thing to do when we reach the limit of endurance: we must throw every ounce of energy into the struggle for our national existence and independence. When that is done, neither time nor circumstances will permit our stopping midway to seek peace. We should realize that the only condition of which it would be possible to secure peace after war has once begun would be complete surrender, which would mean the complete annihilation of our race. Let our people realize to the full the meaning of "the limit of endurance," and the extent of sacrifice implied. For, once that stage is reached, we can only sacrifice and fight to the bitter end. Only a determination to sacrifice ourselves to the uttermost can bring us ultimate victory. Should we hesitate, however, and vainly hope for ease and safety, we shall tumble into an abyss from which there will be no hope of escape even though we endure "a myriad ages of suffering."

Secondly, there may be people who imagine that the Lukouchiao Incident was a sudden and unpremeditated event. But for the past month there have been statements coming from the other side [Japan], either directly through the press or through diplomatic channels, which to us were all omens that an incident was imminent. Furthermore, the night before the incident occurred, various reports were circulated to the effect that the Japanese were going to expand the Tangku Agreement, enlarge the bogus East Hopei Government, drive out the 29th Army, and force the resignation of General Sung Cheh-yuan. There were countless other reports of similar demands too numerous to mention. From this, it can easily be seen that the Lukouchiao Incident was not a sudden or accidental development. Rather we must realize from what has transpired in connection with this incident, that the other side has been most assiduous in its designs against us, and that peace, therefore, cannot be easily secured.

At the present moment the only way to maintain peace and to avoid trouble would be to allow the Japanese armies to come and go without let or hindrance within our country. Our own troops, on the other hand, would have to put up with all kinds of restrictions and would not be allowed to take up positions freely on their own territory. They would even have to allow the Japanese to fire upon them without being

4

able to return the fire! There is an old saying, "He is the sacrificial knife and bowl, and I am the sacrificial meat and fish." We are about to reach this most terrible condition. No country in the world with the slightest semblance of self-respect could possibly accept such humiliation.

The four Northeastern Provinces have already been lost to us for six years. Following this loss came the Tangku Agreement, and now the area of conflict has spread to Lukouchiao at the very gates of Peiping. If we should allow Lukouchiao to be occupied by force, the result would be that Peiping, which was our ancient capital for five hundred years, and which is the political, cultural and strategic center of all north China, would become a second Mukden. And if Peiping becomes a second Mukden, Hopei and Chahar will share the fate of the four Northeastern Provinces. What, then, will prevent Nanking from becoming a second Peiping? The developments at Lukouchiao therefore raise problems involving the existence of the nation as a whole. Whether they can be amicably settled or not will determine whether we have reached the "limit of endurance."

Thirdly, if it should turn out that we have reached the limit, and a conflict is unavoidable, then we cannot do otherwise than resist and be prepared for the supreme sacrifice. But our attitude will be simply one of resistance: we have not sought war; it will have been enforced upon us. We will resist because there is no other possible way of meeting the situation, when the limit of endurance is reached. All our people must have confidence in the National Government, and realize that it is in the process of making comprehensive preparations for the defense of the country. We are a weak nation, and our policy is to maintain peace; it is impossible for us to seek war. We are weak yet we must fight for the life of our race, and shoulder the historic responsibilities handed down to us by our fathers and all the generations before us. When there is no alternative, we shall have to resist. Let us realize, however, that once the war has begun, there will be no opportunity for a weak nation to seek a compromise. If we allow one inch more of our territory to be lost, or our sovereignty to be again infringed, we shall be guilty of committing an unpardonable offense against our race. There will then be no way left but to throw all the resources of our nation into a grim struggle for ultimate victory.

Fourth, whether the Lukouchiao Incident will grow into a war between China and Japan depends entirely on the attitude of the Japanese Government. Whether or not there is any hope for peace between China and Japan depends entirely upon the actions of the Japanese

Army. We shall continue to hope for a peaceful solution through diplomatic means, until the very last moment before hope of peace is finally abandoned.

We take our stand on these four clear principles:

1. Any settlement reached must not infringe upon China's territorial integrity and sovereign rights.

2. The status of the Hopei and Chahar Political Council must not be subjected to any illegal alteration.

3. Local officials appointed by the Central Government, such as General Sung Cheh-yuan, the Chairman of the Hopei and Chahar Political Council, may not be removed or changed as a result of outside pressure.

4. There shall be no restrictions vis-a-vis the position now held by the 29th Army.

These principles constitute the minimum basis for diplomatic negotiations in view of the weakness of our nation. If Japan would only place herself in our position, and take a wide view of the interests of the peoples on the East; if she does not wish to force our two countries into hostilities, and does not want to make them enemies forever, then she ought not to dismiss lightly these conditions which are the minimum that can be considered. To sum up: the National Government in relation to the Lukouchiao Incident has followed a consistent policy and adopted a consistent attitude. We must maintain this position and policy with all our strength.

We hope for peace, but we do not seek an easy path to peace; we prepare for war but we do not want war. When we reach the point where the whole nation must take up arms, then we know we shall have to sacrifice to the very end without the slightest hope of avoiding suffering by some sudden turn of fortune. Once the battle is joined there can be no distinction between north and south, or between old and young. Everyone, everywhere, will have to shoulder the responsibility for protecting the country and for resisting the foe. Everyone will have to give everything that he has. Knowing this, the Government is exercising great caution as it approaches the grave crisis. Let the whole nation with calmness and discipline prepare for self-defense. At this moment when the issue of peace and war hangs in the balance, only our united efforts to maintain strict discipline and order can save the nation. When you return to your home districts I trust that you will pass this message on to all the people, so that they may understand clearly the present situation and be absolutely loyal to the state. I am counting earnestly upon you.

6

On National Reconstruction

I WISH to give you a systematic, comprehensive exposition of the National Reconstruction Movement at the graduation exercises today. I do this in order that you may better understand the meaning and purpose of the movement, the driving forces behind it, and the steps we must take and methods we must use in order that it may accomplish its task. Only as we see clearly what national reconstruction really is can we determine the direction it should take. Only as we appreciate the motivating spirit of national reconstruction and the distinctive character which the movement should everywhere manifest can we extend quickly the work of reconstruction and achieve large and successful results.

We want to build a new China upon the foundation of the Three Principles of the People; that is the central aim in National Reconstruction. The Three Principles given us by Dr. Sun Yat-sen are the highest principles of social revolution and national salvation. They will bring China to a position of political and economic equality in the community of nations and will assure China a permanent place in the world. If we want to build a new nation we must carry out the principles of national independence, democracy, and economic welfare for all the people.

I. *The Aims of National Reconstruction*

1. Racial and National Independence. We must focus the total strength of our people upon the task of elevating our position as a race and nation. We must get rid of all aggression and oppression and build a truly independent China.

2. Democracy and Equality. If we are to give the people of China complete self-government we must first solve the problem of livelihood for all, and give real freedom to the races within China. If the foundations of democracy are secure, then true equality can be achieved.

3. Economic Freedom and Prosperity. This means that the living

An address to the first graduating class of the Summer Training Corps at Lushan, Kiangsi, July 18, 1937.

7

needs of all the people must be equally and fully supplied without any unwarranted restrictions or deprivations.

In order to reach these three goals we must revive the spirit of self-confidence, the power of self-government, and the creative abilities which have in the past characterized our race.

1. Self-confidence. We must teach our people the greatness of China's historical culture. In our educational program we must stress Chinese history and geography so that all may know and appreciate China's civilization of five thousand years and the far-flung boundaries of our ancient race. This will engender a greater faith in our own future. We must elevate the national consciousness of our people so that they will put the nation above self. We must develop a firm confidence in our own national strength; we must not blindly worship foreign culture and disregard our own. Let us believe that our revolution will succeed and that our national spirit can be revived.

2. Self-government. In ancient China self-government was highly developed both in community life and in personal life. The custom of mutual protection and assistance was widespread. The organization and regulations of local self-government were clearly defined and strictly applied. Individual self-control was even more strongly emphasized. Now we must revive this old power of self-government in order to realize the equalities of modern democracy. Let us raise the intellectual and economic level of the people, develop their political powers, and in practical ways train them for administration of their own affairs and for exercising the four rights of initiative, referendum, suffrage, and recall. Then the "sovereignty of the people" will have a sure foundation.

3. Creative Abilities. The civilization and inventions of ancient China were superior to those of other countries. Our poverty and weakness today are due to the loss of our old creative power. If we are to accomplish the material reconstruction of our country and solve the living problems of our people, we must revive the ancient wisdom and abilities of our race and at the same time absorb all we can of modern scientific knowledge and skill.

II. *Reconstruction Starts with Economic Improvement*

This is what Dr. Sun Yat-sen declared emphatically in his *Outline of National Reconstruction*. And in his lectures on the *Principle of the People's Livelihood* Dr. Sun clearly showed that livelihood or economic welfare is the central problem of history; in fact, the people's livelihood may be considered the central theme of the whole Three

8

Principles. The Principle of Nationalism aims at the establishment of national and racial independence, and thus removes the obstacles to economic welfare; the Principle of Democracy aims at establishment of popular sovereignty, and thus enables the people to solve their own economic problems. According to the definition of Dr. Sun, the third Principle includes four things: the daily life of the people; the existence and welfare of society; the economic policy of the state; and the perpetuation of our race. The people's livelihood is therefore of central importance in the reconstruction of the nation.

Theoretically the Principle of Livelihood seems to cover a very broad and general field. Actually its main problems are those related to the daily necessities of the people—food, clothing, shelter, and communications. All of the economic activities of humanity may be called efforts to supply these basic necessities.

The Principle of Livelihood aims at widespread and equitable supply of such necessities to our people. However, we know that living standards are limited by material conditions. Therefore, in order to provide more adequately for our people we must increase production, and in order to equalize economic advantages we must solve the problem of distribution. We must make production our prime objective, and at the same time we must work for equitable distribution. I wish to propose the following national economic policy based upon Dr. Sun's *Outline of National Reconstruction* and the concrete, immediate needs of the nation at this time:

1. Equalization of Land Ownership. We must survey all the land, determine clearly property boundaries, promulgate land laws, and tax the land according to its assessed value. Land is the most important economic problem of our people. A satisfactory solution to this problem will mean the elimination of such evils as land monopoly, usurpation and expropriation of property, and inequalities in land distribution. It will also lead to the goal of "every peasant tilling his own land."

2. Prevention of Capitalistic Monopolies, and Imposition of Graded Taxes. Dr. Sun Yat-sen's proposal of "regulated capital" favors private business, but at the same time restricts private capital because of its tendency to create monopolies over living necessities. For preventing the over-expansion of private capital no plan will be more effective than a graded system of taxation, including inheritance taxes, income taxes, and taxes on all other sources of capital income. Daily necessities should not be taxed; they should be subject, however, to limitation in quantity.

3. Cooperation Between Labor and Capital, and Regulation of

Wages. In a country like ours with backward methods of production, we should never permit disputes between labor and capital to obstruct our productive program. We want close cooperation between capital and labor in order to intensify production and in order to promote the highest welfare of the nation and people. When conflicts occur they should be submitted to compulsory arbitration, so that production will not be adversely affected.

4. Development of State Capital, and Protection of Private Business. In order to improve living conditions of the poor and weak classes we must greatly increase production. For independent enterprises and those which private capital cannot handle, and for large-scale projects related to our national economic program we shall need to develop state capital. At the same time we must protect private business, so that all property will contribute to production.

5. Cooperation Between Government and People in Solving Problems of Production and Distribution. Cooperation is an urgent necessity in dealing with food, clothing, shelter, communications, and other economic needs and problems.

III. *Three Essential Factors in Reconstruction.*

There are three essential factors in all human activity: spirit, materials, and action. Our tremendous and difficult task of national reconstruction depends for its success on all these factors. We must raise the spirit or morale of our people; we must increase the use of our material resources; and we must extend the range and effectiveness of our action. The three factors are closely interrelated, and each must be given consideration if we are to achieve large results and complete the work of national reconstruction. The philosophy of our reconstruction movement leans neither toward the spiritual nor the material, but recognizes the equal necessity and importance of both. Moreover, spiritual and material forces must be related to definite action; otherwise they are ineffective. I believe in a philosophy of action, action which is easy when the fundamental material and spiritual conditions, the conditions of knowledge and wisdom, have been met.

1. Spiritual Factors. We must advance the New Life Movement, the chief aims of which are to change the moral atmosphere, to build civic character, to eliminate bad social customs, and to develop a vital and healthy social organism. The principles of *Li I Lien Ch'ih* [Propriety, Justice, Integrity, Conscientiousness] must be applied to our daily life. In all our doings we should maintain high standards of orderliness, cleanliness, simplicity, speed, and thoroughness. The New Life Move-

ment is really a kind of spiritual revolution. We had lost our national spirit for a long time and we still lack almost all the essential qualities for building a new nation. So let us push the New Life Movement, revive the ancient virtues of our race, reform our social customs, and stir up the people; then we can develop the powerful morale needed for successful reconstruction.

2. Material Factors. We must promote economic reconstruction on a national scale. We are in sore need of materials for large-scale national reconstruction; this lack of material resources causes poverty and weakness among our people and makes it difficult for us to revive our nation. The goal of national economic reconstruction is the full and best use of our manpower and of our material resources and products; in other words, "use human resources to the limit, open up the earth's treasures, supply the needs of all, let goods flow freely, and enrich the material life of all the people." China is not lacking in resources of the soil nor in material products, but the resources are not well developed and the products are not well used. We must awaken all the people to united effort and actively promote economic reconstruction, if we are to solve our problem of material scarcity.

3. Action—Push the Labor Service Movement. Without some form of wide-range, positive action we cannot link together our spiritual revival and our plan for increase of materials and goods, nor can we hope to tear up the inter-twined and deeply-rooted evils in our society and bring about the rapid reconstruction of our national life. We must urge action upon our fellow-citizens and get them all to undertake some definite labor for the state. Let all set a high value upon service. Let all do their part in the labor service movement. We expect schools, public institutions and army units, general social organizations and homes to help continuously in promotion and supervision, until labor service for the state becomes a nation-wide movement.

IV. *How to Begin Reconstruction*

Next I wish to discuss with you how we may launch our program of national reconstruction. Reconstruction is so vast a subject that unless we grasp its essential points and proceed from these we are in danger of wasting our energy. Two good starting points are: the small geographical units within the state political organization in which we can further the cause of self-government, and the various social organizations within the state in which educational and training methods can be employed to develop the strength and morale of the people.

1. According to *The Outline of National Reconstruction,* the Gov-

ernment during the period of political tutelage should help the people prepare for self-government by taking part in local affairs and by laying the foundations of democracy. Dr. Sun Yat-sen in his *Outline of National Reconstruction* and *Methods of Initiating Local Self-Government* gave detailed instructions regarding the local government enterprises and activities. I shall revise his list somewhat to meet the concrete needs and situations of today. The Government should make provision in local districts for the following: a census of families; land survey and registration; police protection (including the *pao-chia* or mutual guarantee system); development of communications; extension of educational facilities; reclamation of waste land and reforestation; water conservancy (including improvement of waterways and irrigation, repair of dykes, digging of irrigation ditches and wells, dredging of rivers, etc.); promotion of cooperative enterprises (through various kinds of cooperative societies—producers', consumers', credit, transportation, etc.).

2. For the success of national reconstruction it is essential that we have a strong and active citizenry able to make a definite contribution to reconstruction of the people. This involves a four-fold program of *Kuan Chiao Yang Wei* [Management, Education, Maintenance, Defense]. These have been largely matters of government administration, but if we are to have active, well-developed citizens we must consider them also matters involving education and training.

Kuan. In the past, China has neglected the important science of management. In our dealings with men, with business matters, with the earth and with things, we need to know the principles of efficient control. With men and affairs, for example, we have what we call direction, supervision, delegation of responsibilities, transfer of office, examination, and such. In relation to the earth and material objects and forces strict control is also necessary in order to prevent careless use and depreciation in value, the waste of the earth's products, and the loss of important materials. In western countries scientific management has become a special field of study. Without such training the Chinese people do not realize the importance of careful management and control. As a result we do not know how to be strict and exact; we do not know how to make reasonable distribution and use of our resources. Consequently there is much waste and extravagance. It is impossible to estimate the amount of land and goods that is foolishly wasted each year through lack of good management. If we want our people to become strong we must teach them management and control, not only instructing them in the principles, but also training them through concrete projects.

Chiao. A good program of education is essential to our program of national salvation and reconstruction, and to the cultivation of the people's strength. In all grades of education we must put more emphasis upon practical knowledge. In the past our education has been too much in the clouds; it has not kept its feet on the ground. We forget that the most practical and useful knowledge has to do with simple, everyday things. Some of us who have received a higher education are lacking in certain elementary knowledge and skills and are ignorant of ordinary facts. No wonder that it is difficult to secure a large number of experts in various fields. If we want to cultivate the strength of the people we must give them a good foundation of common knowledge. Then they will be able to shoulder the definite responsibilities of citizens.

Yang. Maintenance aims at economic improvement and better living conditions for the people. It naturally requires training in methods of production. From the standpoint of the state this means the development of public property and business; from the standpoint of the individual, the increase of productive power. Reconstruction in a country as poor as ours cannot succeed without greatly increased production on the part of all citizens. Therefore we must everywhere and under all conditions educate the people in improved methods of production and in the habit of hard work. We must help them get rid of their lazy and dependent ways and to become strong and self-reliant. Our nation should become self-sufficient at least in agricultural and industrial production.

Wei. If we are to become a free and independent nation we must cultivate the power of self-defense among our people. On a small scale this means protection of communities and neighborhoods; on a large scale, defense of the nation. In our training program we must lay major emphasis upon national defense. To this end we should elevate the national consciousness, foster a willingness to struggle and sacrifice, and inculcate habits of discipline and order.

If we carry out as a people all that I have been saying, then we shall certainly achieve our four-fold objective: "Abilities of men, products of the earth, goods on the market, and business activity all utilized to the limit." National reconstruction will then have completed its first stage.

V. *The Driving Force in National Reconstruction*

Any great enterprise must have a powerful inner driving force. This is true of national reconstruction. Our task is so tremendous, aims and methods are so varied and complex, the position of our nation is so difficult, and the former foundations were so weak that we cannot hope to carry out rapidly our mission of reconstruction by ordinary effort alone. We need a powerful driving force, and it is this I wish to speak about in closing. This driving force will be our contribution to the spiritual training of our people, and to the cultivation of strong national morale without which we cannot hope to unite or to fulfill our duty at this time.

The driving force we need is none other than the ancient moral principles of our race: *Chung Hsiao Jen Ai Hsin I Ho P'ing* [Loyalty, Filial Devotion, Kindness, Love, Faithfulness, Justice, Harmony, and Peace]. Central among these are Kindness and Love. These virtues have been China's ethical heritage for millenniums; they have become a part of the very thought and life of many of our people. We may say that they are characteristics of the Sons of Hwang Ti. All we need to do now is to revive these age-long principles and to restore them to their former influence and power; then we shall have a mighty driving force for our National Reconstruction Movement.

A touchstone of our actions, as we follow these old moral principles, is *Ch'eng* [Sincerity]. *Ch'eng* means a sincere and determined purpose, absolute loyalty to our cause, so that we do not falter or turn back, but give all our energy to the task before us. It means that we must not cease to make ourselves strong and capable: what we do not know we must faithfully learn; what we have learned we must faithfully do. Our ancient sages said, "Gold and hard rock will break open for the man of sincere devotion."

Another important standard of action is *Yen* [Strictness or Severity]. We must be strict in self-discipline, strict in managing affairs, avoiding all falseness and deceit, setting our wills against all laxness, and seeking perfection in all our work. *Yen* is also manifested in the inward qualities of *Chih Jen Hsin Yung* [Knowledge, Generosity, Trustworthiness, and Courage], and in our outward behavior according to the principles of *Li I Lien Ch'ih* [Propriety, Justice, Integrity, Conscientiousness]. With such a character we shall be fearless and strong, we shall not bow to any outward pressure, and we shall always maintain dignity and self-respect. The man with stern self-discipline will be real and thorough in all he does; he will bury himself in his tasks and show definite results. He will not be afraid of difficulties; he will stand upon his own feet; he will be open and above board in his actions. In all his work for his country he will be loyal and public-spirited, without a trace of selfish greed. He will put society above self, and work for the welfare of all. He will obey faithfully the laws made for the common good. On the one hand, he will make himself strong and worthy; on the other hand, he will cooperate unselfishly with others in service to the state. "Nothing is impossible to the man of fixed purpose." With such men in our nation—patriotic, unselfish, loyal, stern—we can sweep away all obstacles before us, establish a free and democratic state for the welfare of all, and accomplish the task of national reconstruction.

Drive Out the Invader

FOLLOWING recent developments at Lukouchiao, the Japanese have by low and treacherous methods seized our cities, Peiping and Tientsin, and have killed many of our fellow-countrymen. There is no end to the humiliation and insults that they have heaped upon us. To think about it makes the heart sick. Since the Mukden incident on September 18, 1931, the more indignities we have borne, the more we have yielded, the more violent has Japanese oppression become. Give them an inch and they take a foot. Now we have reached the point when we can endure it no longer; we will give way no more. The whole nation must rise as one man and fight these Japanese bandits until we have destroyed them, and our own life is secure.

We soldiers in normal times are fed and supplied by the blood and sweat of our fellow-countrymen. How eager we should now be to show ourselves brave and faithful and to fulfill our duty of protecting the people. As Commander-in-Chief I must carry the entire responsibility for the lives of my soldiers and the safety of the state. Naturally I must put forth my maximum effort and keep a firm grip on the fundamental conditions of victory. You, too, must do your part. Victory is assured, if only all our troops will obey orders wholeheartedly. We shall certainly defeat these Japanese robbers, and wipe out our humiliation. Now that we have hurled defiance at Japan and are going to fight to the death, I must bring to your close attention the following very important points.

1. *We must resolve to sacrifice to the limit.*

You must realize that the Japanese have been able to rob us of our territory by clever opportunism. You must also realize that unless they receive some heavy blows, they certainly will not stop their policy of aggression. Since the whole nation now is unitedly resisting the invaders, they will be sure (for the sake of face) to put out their maximum effort into the fight. Now that the war has started, it is sure to last long; if it does not end in the destruction of the Japanese, it will end in ours. We must therefore mobilize all our resources for this life-and-death struggle. We must all be of one mind and fight to the death. Victory or defeat depends on the spirit shown. If I do not fear enemy he is sure to

A message to the armed forces of the nation at the end of July, 1937, after the Japanese captured Peiping and Tientsin.

fear me. Those who are afraid are sure to be defeated, while those who are not afraid are sure to win. Although our military equipment is not equal to that of the enemy, yet if we retain the revolutionary spirit that is ready for any sacrifice and keeps loyal and brave to the end, and in that spirit go forward against the foe, there will be no question of Japan's defeat. The Japanese are only good at opportunist moves; they are unwilling to face any real sacrifice.

2. *We must firmly believe that final victory is ours.*

Since the Japanese invaders reached the interior of our country, where they are unfamiliar with the terrain and are confronted on all sides by our fellow-countrymen, hostile to them, they find they can hardly advance. Consequently they are all imbued with a spirit of fear—fear of death—and an unwillingness to sacrifice themselves. Their progress now is very slow; they are afraid to advance quickly. They can only use their planes and big guns to bombard us heavily, hoping to terrify us and make us retreat, and thus avoid the necessity of a real battle. If we will resolve to fight to the last and stubbornly resist all aggression, fearing neither suffering, nor hardship, nor even death itself; if we husband our ammunition, take careful aim, defend all positions to the last, and wear down the invader's strength, then without question the victory will be ours. If there is no panic or confusion as the battle draws near, if, when we have suffered some losses or have met with temporary reverses, we make good use of the weak points of the Japanese—their unwillingness to sacrifice themselves, their fear of advancing too quickly,—if we calmly reinforce our position and carry on the struggle, then we shall most certainly win in the end.

3. *We must make full use of our mental powers and take the initiative.*

In the history of war, general strategy and tactics have naturally been the responsibility of the highest authority, the Commander-in-Chief and his Staff. But the officers of each unit must on their own initiative study the situation before them and implement the orders of headquarters, for example, in matters that concern local topography, the details of the enemy's condition and of our own, the organization of guerrillas, and the use of spies. Ways and means of meeting emergencies caused by the loss of contact in the thick of the fight, or by the breakdown of communications when orders can no longer get through, must be devised by the officers of each unit, using their own mental powers to secure the victory. All officers from army, division, and brigade commanders down to the subalterns must learn to take the initiative.

4. *Soldiers and civilians must be united in a common bond of love and sincerity.*

In any war victory is assured if the support of the people is obtained. This particular War of Resistance should arouse the people everywhere throughout our land to exert all their strength and to risk their very lives against the enemy. But if we expect the ordinary people and the soldiers wholeheartedly to unite their efforts, if we expect them to work in perfect harmony and to help each other, then you soldiers must first show your genuine love for the people and win their trust and confidence. As for ways of showing your love and sincerity, they are many. When it is necessary to conscript labor, always demonstrate your sympathy with those you have to conscript, and do not overwork them so that they murmur and complain. When you meet women, old folks, or children who have met with misfortune, help them to the limit of your powers; treat them as though they were members of your own family. When you talk with civilians in war areas or near the front, make clear to them that the nation has reached a crisis in its history, a time of extreme danger; and that since they are part of the Chinese nation, it is their duty to rise as one body, destroy the enemy, and save their country. In any case you must, wherever you are, help the civilian population, instruct them and guide them, protect them and save them, and so give evidence of your love and sincerity. If you sympathize with them in their sufferings, and share in their joys and sorrows, then soldiers and civilians will form a closely knit body, and the civilians will naturally be glad to help. There will be no cause for traitors to spring up, and the enemy will meet with defeat everywhere.

5. *We must stubbornly hold our ground: there must be no retreat, only advance.*

It is the essence of our revolutionary spirit that we know only advance, not retreat. The success of our revolution in the past has been due to this two-fold principle: advance, but never retreat. The principle is even more necessary in this war against the Japanese invader. If we can carry it out, then the brave need not be anxious, and those who fear to die and want to retreat will not dare to do so. The Japanese, relying on their superior armament, will bombard us heavily in the hope of forcing us to retreat so that they can advance. But if our soldiers stand firm as a rock, and stubbornly hold their positions in the spirit of "advance but never retreat;" if they wait until the enemy gets near, then break through his lines and engage him in hand-to-hand fighting, airplanes and heavy guns will be of no use to the enemy, and the long experience of our troops will bring us final victory. If any soldiers, before being ordered to do so by the Commander-in-Chief, retire of their own accord, they will be punished individually and collectively, because they undermine the morale and do grave injury to the state; they should be treated exactly like traitors, for they have "let the wolf into the fold, and guided the tiger to his prey." If an officer or soldier meets anyone who has retreated without the Generalissimo's orders, he should not spare him, but put him to death as a traitor. We each of us must die one day, but our death should be a worthy one, a glorious one. Rather than be put to death under military law for retreating without orders, leaving an infamous name for all time, would it not be far better to make the supreme sacrifice at the front and leave a fragrant memory down the centuries? The National Government at the present moment is considering an order setting forth rewards for those who hold stubbornly to important positions. Anyone who resolutely defends an important position and refuses to retreat, will be promoted three ranks; his father and grandfather will be honored as well as himself, and similarly his children and grandchildren. So you must hold your positions, firmly refusing to retreat, bringing glory to the nation and winning an honorable name for yourselves. But anyone who of his own accord and without orders retires from his post will be treated as a traitor and shot without mercy.

These are the five most important conditions for driving out the Japanese invader and for resurrecting our nation. I shall have other important pronouncements to make in due course. Meanwhile, remember that since September 18, 1931, when we lost the four Northeastern Provinces, we have been through much bitter suffering and have lost a great deal of territory. How can we for one moment forget this deep humiliation? Why have we patiently endured Japan's insults during all these years, not returning curses for curses or blows for blows? Because we wanted to settle our internal problems in order to have strength to resist to the end. If we are to resist to the end, the whole country must be united, ready for any sacrifice, willing to fight the Japanese to the death.

We are all descendants of Hwang Ti who have sworn allegiance to the Revolution. Should we not fight to the last and so pay our country what we owe her? Only thus can we be worthy of our great leader, Dr. Sun Yat-sen, and of the heroes who have laid down their lives before us. Only thus can we preserve the spacious land and glorious heritage passed down to us by our ancestors. Only thus can we requite our parents and teachers for the faithful instruction and the training that they have given us. Only thus can we be true to the generations that follow us.

Soldiers! The supreme moment has come. With one heart and purpose advance. Refuse to retreat. Drive out the unspeakably evil invaders and bring about the rebirth of our nation.

National Solidarity

THE aim of the Nationalist Revolution is to seek freedom and equality for China. Dr. Sun Yat-sen said that the *San Min Chu I* are fundamental principles of national salvation. He earnestly hoped that all our people would strive with one heart to save the state from its perils. Unfortunately, during the past ten years not all of our countrymen have had a sincere and unwavering faith in the Three Principles of the People, nor have they fully realized the magnitude of the crisis confronting our country. The course of the Revolution in its efforts at national reconstruction has been blocked by many obstacles. The result has been waste in our national resources, widespread suffering among the people, increasing humiliations from outside, and growing dangers to the state.

During the past few years the National Government has been calling ceaselessly upon the nation to achieve genuine internal solidarity, and to face unitedly the national crisis. Those who have in the past doubted the Three Principles of the People have now realized the paramount importance of our national interests, and have buried their differences for the sake of internal unity. The Chinese people today fully realize that they must survive together or perish together, and that the interests of the nation must take precedence over the interests of individuals or groups.

The Manifesto recently issued by the Chinese Communist Party is an outstanding instance of the triumph of national sentiment over every other consideration. The various decisions embodied in the Manifesto, such as the abandonment of a policy of violence, the cessation of Communist propaganda, the abolition of the Chinese Soviet Government, and the disbandment of the Red Army are all essential conditions for mobilizing our national strength in order that we may meet the menace from without and guarantee our own national existence.

These decisions agree with the spirit of the Manifesto and resolutions adopted by the Third Plenary Session of the Kuomintang. The Communist Party's Manifesto declares that the Chinese Communists are

A statement on September 24, 1937, in connection with the Manifesto on the United Front issued by the Chinese Communist Party.

willing to strive to carry out the Three Principles. This is ample proof that China today has only one objective in its war efforts.

In our revolution we are struggling not for personal ambitions or opinions, but for the realization of the Three Principles of the People. Especially during this period of national crisis, when the fate of China lies in the balance, we ought not to argue over the past, but should try as a nation to make a new start. We should earnestly strive to unite, so that as a united nation we may safeguard the continued existence of the Republic.

If a citizen believes in the Three Principles and works actively for the salvation of the state, the Government should not concern itself with his past, but should give him opportunity to prove his loyalty in service to the Republic. Likewise, the Government will gladly accept the services of any political organization provided it is sincerely working for the nation's salvation, and is willing under the banner of our national revolution to join with us in our struggle against aggression.

The Chinese Communist Party, by surrendering its prejudices, has clearly recognized the vital importance of our national independence and welfare. I sincerely hope that all members of the Communist Party will faithfully and unitedly put into practice the various decisions reached, and under the unified military command that is directing our resistance, will offer their services to the state, fighting shoulder to shoulder with the rest of the nation for the successful completion of the Nationalist Revolution.

In conclusion, I may say that the foundation of the Chinese state rests firmly on the Three Principles first expounded by Dr. Sun Yatsen. This foundation is one that cannot be shaken or changed. Now that the entire nation is awakened and solidly united, it will boldly follow the unswerving policy of the Government, and will mobilize its entire resources to resist the tyrannical Japanese and save the state from its imminent peril.

Enlightened people the world over now realize that China is fighting not merely for her own survival, but also for world peace and for international faith and justice.

Fight to Win

THIS year our national anniversary falls at a time of grave peril and great difficulty for our nation, but a time, also, of supreme importance in the resurgent life of our people. We are at the moment suffering from the invasion of a cruel foe; an invasion carried out with unparalleled ferocity. The nation today is engaged in a bitter struggle. All our people are endeavoring by sacrifice of flesh and blood—yea, of their very lives—to secure the survival of the state. In this war of resistance, the warm patriotism of our fellow-Chinese overseas, and the courage and enthusiasm of all our citizens is more than enough to inspire and encourage us, and to convince us that out of this period of trial and suffering we shall be able to achieve the revival of our nation.

As we approach this glorious anniversary, I have a few important things to say to you, my fellow-countrymen.

First of all, we must realize that we are fighting this war of self-defense in order to save ourselves from annihilation—to snatch life out of death. Moreover, we shall have to pass through extraordinary perils and difficulties before we can win the final victory. We must thoroughly wake up, my fellow-countrymen, and continue our initial efforts in a spirit of still greater courage and sacrifice. This war will not be finished in six months or a year, nor any similarly short time. We must face the fact that our hardships will increase every day. We must fully prepare to meet difficulties ten times more severe than those we are undergoing today. Only the determination to sacrifice to the very limit will enable us to reach our goal and to secure the survival of our race.

Our brave troops at the front, by their self-denying efforts, have dealt the enemy very heavy blows, and have revealed his weak points one by one. They have won the unbounded sympathy of the world. Recently the nations have come to a fresh realization of the vital impor-

A broadcast from Nanking on October 9, 1937, on the eve of the "Double Tenth" National Holiday which marked the twenty-sixth anniversary of the birth of the Chinese Republic.

tance of maintaining international justice and righteousness, and of honoring treaties and international law. Gradually they have begun to make more grave and decided pronouncements on the issues involved, so that justice is again raising its head. This is definitely the result of the spirit shown by our soldiers at the front—their heroism and their determination to check the enemy. But there has been another important reason—the unity and solidarity of our nation. During the past twenty years the world has been watching the spectacle of a nation divided against itself, with its strength sadly dissipated. But today our nation is united. Never before has it shown such a spirit of unity and cooperation; never before has it been able to resist a foe with such wholehearted determination. Today we are one in purpose and spirit. This solidarity is adding greatly to the power and results of the sacrificial efforts of our troops. More than this, our new unity has resulted in unbounded sympathy and support from the nations of the world.

We must remember that real victory will be won only by a long persevering struggle, not by any lucky accident. International sympathy, though greatly encouraging to us, should not be allowed to foster a spirit of reliance upon others. We must first help ourselves; only then will others help us.

Let our people cultivate a willingness to face unprecedented suffering, to begrudge no sacrifice, to fight undaunted and unyielding to the end. Let us overcome all perils, and endure suffering and hardship. Let us through this war train and discipline ourselves, transform our race, and create new life for our nation.

Secondly, we must not only maintain our unity to the end, but continually strengthen our solidarity. We have already proved the enormous strength that comes from national unity. Now we must go on to the point where, retreating or advancing, living or dying, we are absolutely one. We must be united in danger as well as in peace, in calamity as well as in prosperity. Seeking only the highest interests of the nation we must maintain absolute discipline and cultivate strict obedience, so that we may win the final victory. Only thus can we prove ourselves worthy of the soldiers who have laid down their lives; only thus can we repay the sympathy of the friendly Powers.

Thirdly, we must have a firm faith in final victory. This war is not simply for the survival of our own race, it is a struggle for justice among men, and for international faith and righteousness. The Japanese started this war to satisfy their lust for aggression. They have not only destroyed international faith and justice, but have become the enemy of all mankind. Such an inhuman and unjust war of aggression, such an unwarranted attack upon another country cannot but end in defeat and ruin. There is an old saying: "In war a righteous cause is strength, but an unjust cause is weakness"; and again: "Many come to the aid of the man who has right on his side, but none helps the man who flouts all moral principles." This war has already shown that the Japanese, in spirit and in reality, are defeated, and that their end is at hand. If we but sacrifice to the end, our cause will certainly triumph.

I have said before that the first task of our national revolution was the achievement of internal unity; and that the second was the realization of national independence. These two tasks are in essence one. At the present moment our revolution is in the second stage. It is now meeting a very severe test, yet complete success is not far off. Nothing can now stop our united nation as it marches forward under the standard of the Three Principles.

As for me, entrusted with a great task by the Central Government, and sustained by the expectations of the whole nation, I must seek to carry out the will of my fellow-countrymen. I must lead the army forward, every soldier determined to be faithful and courageous and to fight to the end. I have responsibilities that cannot be evaded in relation to the state, the nation, the troops under me, and the political testament of our great Leader. I long ago made up my mind to spend and be spent even unto death to repay all that I owe to the Party, the nation, and my fellow-countrymen. I hope that you will all, men and women, old and young, offer to the state your strength and your resources, and under the guidance of the National Government will fulfill your responsibilities as one man, pressing on with the great task before us. We must first concentrate all our powers of resistance before we can drive out the invading hordes, and make it possible for our nation to stand on an equality with the other nations of the world.

Fellow-countrymen! we have behind us five thousand years of history and culture; we have the resources of four million square miles of territory; we have a population of 450,000,000—the greatest in the world. We may be sure that so great a nation cannot be destroyed, if only we are animated by a spirit of self-sacrifice and are willing to fight on. You all recall the last admonition of our great Leader: "Peace—Struggle—Save China." We must not only save ourselves; we must save the world. This is the spirit of Christ—His spirit of self-sacrifice, of love, and of peace. This is a truth that can never be destroyed. We must realize that our struggle today has as its basis our determination to establish permanent peace. This is the only road that will bring salvation to the state, the nation, mankind, and ourselves. In all history

24

there is no case of the survival of any nation that was unwilling to make sacrifices, and there is no instance of peace being won without a struggle; if there is, it is only in the case of those willing to be enslaved, bound hand and foot under the control of others. Only in such a condition of slavery can the stupid dream of peace without struggle be realized.

The nearer our War of Resistance draws to its close, the greater will be the sacrifices demanded of us, and the heavier will be our responsibilities. But a glorious future awaits us at the end of this dark road, if only we will exert our full energy and press ever forward. Our people, whether at the front or in the rear, must lay aside all thoughts of careless ease, and all ideas of avoiding trouble. We must persevere continuously, our enthusiasm growing as the conflict lengthens. All in official position must be willing to give without stint, and to be examples of fortitude and perseverance to all the people. The outcome of this fight will determine the destiny of our nation for generations to come. We must, therefore, sacrifice everything in order that we may secure permanent peace and prosperity for our people and our nation.

Fellow-countrymen! On this all important national anniversary may every Chinese citizen make it his or her firm resolve to imitate the revolutionary heroes of the past decades, and to follow in the footsteps of the soldiers at the front who have laid down their lives. If we rise as one man and struggle valiantly for the sake of our nation, then victory is assured and a bright and glorious future will dawn for the Republic of China. Finally, let all on this day humbly pay respect to the memory of the soldiers and civilians who have paid the supreme sacrifice, and remember with deep affection the loved ones they have left behind.

After the Fall of Nanking

SINCE the beginning of this war, our total casualties in dead and wounded at the front have been more than three hundred thousand. The loss of civilian lives and property is beyond computation. Such heavy sacrifice is unprecedented in China's history of opposition to foreign aggressors. As Commander-in-Chief I have been forced to bring these losses upon our nation and people. I accept the responsibility, but it is a responsibility that could not be evaded. My mental anguish has been a thousand-fold more acute than the suffering of the soldiers and civilians who have died; it will last as long as I live. Only by dedication of my whole self, body and soul, and by unwavering determination to resist to the bitter end in order to secure ultimate victory for the nation, can I repay what I owe to the Party and to the State, and bring consolation to my fellow-countrymen.

Japan's aggression in China has followed two lines of strategy: one we call "swallowing like a whale" (that is, seizing great areas of territory, as it were at one gulp), and the other "nibbling like a silk-worm" (that is, slowly but steadily encroaching on our country and our rights). By violent means Japan has now occupied Nanking. From now on she will with increasing ferocity carry out her design of subduing the whole of China. Facts prove that she is now like a whale swallowing great areas at one gulp, and not simply nibbling at Chinese territory. But what China has to fear is the nibbling process, not the "swallowing in one gulp." The danger of being "swallowed in one gulp" is easily seen, whereas the process of being "nibbled away" is gradual and difficult to detect. Should Japan pursue the policy of slowly "nibbling like a silk-worm," and lull us into a false sense of security until we are unconscious of our danger, it would be difficult to avoid becoming easy-going and careless, and consequently slack about requiting the enemy. China would then be gradually dismembered and destroyed.

In face of the great crisis confronting us at this moment, there is no use in looking back with vain regrets. If we look ahead to the final out-

A message to the nation from Field Headquarters on December 16, 1937, after the fall of Nanking.

come of the whole struggle, we may say that the present situation is definitely favorable to China. The basis of our confidence in China's ultimate success in prolonged resistance is not to be found in Nanking, nor in the big cities or municipalities, but in the villages, and in the widespread and unshaken determination of the people. Let our fellow-countrymen realize that there is no possible way of avoiding Japan's wanton aggression; let fathers inform their children, and elder brothers encourage the younger ones; then, animated by general hatred of the enemy, our people will erect defenses everywhere. Throughout the 4,000,000 square miles of Chinese territory, strong fortifications, both visible and invisible, will be erected, and the enemy will receive a mortal blow.

In the present situation you must not be swayed by temporary victories or reverses. Rather should you seek to understand the true meaning of prolonged resistance, and hold firmly to your belief in the ultimate triumph of our cause.

Let me mention briefly a few points for your encouragement. First, the present armed resistance against Japan is an inevitable stage in the progress of China's national revolution. Externally China desires independence, internally she seeks to maintain her existence as a nation; China therefore strives to loose the bonds that bind her people, and to complete the establishment of a new state. This war with all its bitter suffering was bound to come sooner or later. Our war is a war of the Three Principles of the People against the brutal forces of imperialism. It is a war against aggression waged by a people whose land has been invaded, a war for survival and independence. It is a very different struggle from the ordinary international war between equally powerful states. Although we knew from the beginning that we were greatly inferior to our enemy in arms, equipment, and material resources, yet, because of our revolutionary spirit, we never considered that as a reason for dismay or surrender.

A study of the history of nations teaches us that no revolution involving the reconstruction of the state can be accomplished overnight. The more numerous the dangers and obstacles encountered, the richer will be the harvest of victory. If each encounter only heightens our morale, and if each reverse only makes us more determined, then the clearing away of all obstacles will signalize the day of final victory.

The present Japanese invasion of China has for its chief objectives not merely the occupation of our territory, the massacre of our people, and the destruction of our culture and civilization, but also the eradication of our Three Principles, and the suppression of our revolutionary spirit. So long as this revolutionary spirit exists, our nation cannot be destroyed. The reverses we have suffered so far have not been of a decisive nature. But if we voluntarily submit, our spirit will collapse, and the nation will inevitably be ruined. The humiliation we shall then have to endure—a life of slavery, a life no better than that of a beast of burden—will be infinitely more painful than all the sufferings of the present war.

Fellow-countrymen, you must realize that no nation can free itself from oppression, and bring its revolution to a successful completion, without paying a high price. The more we are willing to suffer today, the more we shall achieve tomorrow. Great as the sacrifices are, let us bear them for the sake of our nation and people and of the generations that will follow us. Suffering cannot be avoided and it must not be refused. This is what prolonged resistance really means.

In the second place, if we realize that China at the present stage of its revolutionary development must fight this war to the very end, then no matter how the present situation may change, we will only press forward, and not on any account stop halfway or surrender. To fight on may not bring us any guarantee of victory, but to capitulate is to court certain disaster. We prefer, therefore, to fight on even though we are defeated, feeling sure that there will come a time when defeat can be turned into victory. But if we submit, there is no hope of our rising again as a nation. If our status as an independent nation is lost, the enemy's methods of crushing and carving up our country will become even more ruthless and tyrannical, and we shall not be able to stand up even after "a myriad ages of suffering." We shall perish forever.

The final outcome of a war is often determined by the degree of initiative shown on each side. Hostilities have already lasted five months. The enemy's original plan and hope was to subdue us without having to fight. But from first to last our answer has been to fight back; we have refused to submit. As long as we can hold out, the enemy will never be able to reach his goal.

The deeper the Japanese penetrate into the interior, the more they will be forced to the defensive. If they want to occupy the whole four million square miles of Chinese territory, and destroy our four hundred million people, what an enormous army they will have to place in the field! If all our people resolve neither to submit nor to be dismayed; if as one falls, another takes his place; if everywhere and always we put up strong resistance, then the time must come when Japan's military strength will be completely exhausted, and China will be completely victorious.

Thirdly, Japan's present aggression in China is really the initial phase of her plan for world conquest. Since the very beginning of this struggle China has made clear her two-fold purpose: first, to maintain her own national existence and independence; and secondly, to secure international peace and justice. Although during the past few months international sanctions have not been enforced against Japan, the question as to who is in the right and who is in the wrong, from the point of view of international justice, has been made manifest to the whole world.

We have boldly taken up this great cause. Now we must support it with all our strength, no matter how the international situation develops. So long as justice survives in the world, we can be sure that our objectives will some day be realized. However long the road ahead may be, we must not for a moment slacken our effort. With the mandate I have received from the Party and the Government I can only go forward. Let us all go forward; let us never retreat. May you all encourage each other to stand firm in this hour of our nation's greatest peril.

China's Path to Victory

I T IS a great privilege for me to be able to attend this great gathering today—the inaugural session of the People's Political Council. That you members of the Council have all been able to meet together here at this time, when the enemy forces are advancing deep into our country and cruelly oppressing our people, is an event of tremendous significance in the history of the Republic. Now that we are in the midst of our War of Resistance and our program of national reconstruction, the work of this People's Political Council is especially important. And so I want to take the opportunity afforded by the opening session to present a few ideas for your consideration.

It is a year now since we took up arms in self-defense. There used to be a great deal of criticism by some people with regard to our War of Resistance. The criticism was chiefly to the effect that we had mobilized only our military forces, and had failed to rally the nation's political strength and to mobilize all the people for direct participation in the war. This view was frequently heard expressed in our own country. But now the People's Political Council has been formed, the situation is different. You, the members of the Council, are all respected leaders in your various localities. You will certainly be able to give both the civilian population and the soldiers at the front greater encouragement and comfort than they have had in the past, and thus increase our powers of resistance and confidence in final victory.

Abroad, especially among our enemies the Japanese imperialists, there is still the idea that only China's military forces are resisting the invader, and that the rest of the nation is socially and politically just as it was before; that is, disorganized and disunited. In their opinion, China cannot be described as waging war on a national scale in the modern sense of the word. That is why the Japanese dared to invade our country and to oppress our people. They were sure that they could defeat and absorb China. But from the time we started nation-wide resistance, their plans for the destruction of our nation and the extermination of our race have been completely exposed and frustrated.

An address at the inaugural session of the People's Political Council in Hankow, July 6, 1938.

An even heavier blow can be dealt the invader by the People's Political Council, the opening session of which is being held here today. The Council gathers into one body the talent of the whole nation, the most learned and the most experienced and those of the highest character from every party and class and organization. Such a gathering of men and women, as they bring their full intellectual powers to bear on our problems, and give concrete expression to the country's united determination to support the Government in the war, can give the enemy a tremendous shock. For the chief reason why the Japanese dare to despise us and plan the destruction of our nation is not our military weakness, but what they have seen of lack of cohesion within the nation and lack of unity in the government, and their feeling that we had not developed any adequate basis for a modern state. They thought, therefore, that they could defeat us, even if they used only a small part of their armed forces.

Before the war the Japanese thought the Chinese army would not be able to withstand one assault of their troops. But facts today prove that we can not only withstand the invader, but also steadily wear him down. Further, we have shown by our organization and actions that we are politically united in this war, so that the enemy has been obliged to change his conception of China's strength; he realizes now that all our national resources have been concentrated under the government to meet the invasion. This has been a fatal blow to the enemy. The chief significance of this Council and its central purpose is found in the mobilization of all our strength as a people to fight the invader to the death, to secure victory, and to accomplish our national program of reconstruction.

To attain these objectives, however, we must first complete two fundamental tasks:

In the first place, the inauguration of the People's Political Council, at a time when the nation is engaged in a desperate struggle for its existence, is designed to meet the pressing needs of this great emergency. During this extraordinary period the Council is charged with especially heavy responsibilities. We may say that the particular function of this Council is the prosecution of the war and the rebuilding of the nation. All our deliberations and all our work must be directed towards bringing the war to a victorious conclusion, and towards furthering the speedy completion of our national reconstruction. We must unitedly and effectively exert our full strength; we must develop our resources to the utmost so that we can attain our objectives. The first task that must be completed is the strengthening of our national solidarity. If we can solidly unite, then, even though we are a weak country, we shall be able to meet the strongest foe. But even the strongest country without internal unity can be invaded and ultimately destroyed. In this period, therefore, of national resistance and reconstruction there is nothing so vital as strengthening the bonds of national unity. I hope that each of you will do your best to strengthen the spirit and unify the will of the whole nation until the hearts of all our four hundred and fifty million people beat as one. I hope you will help to direct all the resources of the country toward finishing quickly the tremendous task of national defense and reconstruction. Whatever recommendations may come up for discussion, and whatever resolutions you may pass, let your one object be to complete this task.

Secondly, we must lay the foundation for democracy in China. The chairman has just pointed out that the People's Political Council is not a temporary conference. Rather it is the means by which, during this period of resistance, we should lay the foundation of a true and permanent form of democratic government. How can this be done? To begin with, I hope that you will set up a model of democratic procedure in this Council. What is democracy? Democracy is liberty—a liberty which maintains strict discipline, and makes law its guarantee and the basis of its exercise. This alone is true liberty; this alone can produce true democracy.

Especially at this time of crisis, when the fate of the whole nation is hanging in the balance, true democratic liberty is to be found, not in the liberty of the individual or of any small group, but in the sacrifice of individual and group liberty in order to win freedom for the whole nation. If we want to obtain this freedom we must recognize the position in which the nation, and we ourselves as individuals, are placed today, and the demands of the present time and circumstances. Only thus can we make our laws effective, defend our country successfully, and set up a model democratic government. Only thus can we lay the basis of national liberty. We must have real democratic ideals and spirit if we are to carry out the mission of this Political Council.

The Republic has now been established for twenty-seven years. Looking back over this period, we see that although we have had so-called popular assemblies, we have not become a state with a real democratic constitution. On the contrary, because of various corrupt practices in the past, the nation has been divided and chaotic, and therefore very weak. As a result we have been subjected to the humiliation of this invasion by the Japanese. Of course the People's Political Council is not a parliament, but warned by the failure of the democratic procedure of previous popular assemblies, you should strive hard to lay the foundation of a truly democratic government. This is another of the important duties resting on your shoulders in connection with our national reconstruction.

If from now on we are going to lay the foundation of democracy in China, then all you who are members of the People's Political Council must set an example yourselves, and guide the people so that everyone does his duty and shoulders his responsibility. Everyone must obey the laws and strive for the good of the state as a whole, that we may win the final victory.

In short, if the People's Political Council henceforth is to bear the responsibility of resistance and reconstruction, and bring them both to a successful conclusion, then it is essential that the interests of the state and the nation be placed before everything else. In all recommendations, discussions, and resolutions, and in our own words and actions as individuals, we must give first consideration to the needs of the state and the nation, and make the successful conclusion of the war our prime objective. I hope you will all with firm union of hearts and in one solid front face bravely the national emergency. I hope that sincerity, frankness, and justice will mark all your actions, and that all the resolutions passed by the Council will be aimed at meeting the needs of the war and reconstruction period, so that you may fulfill the great mission entrusted to you at this time. I wish the People's Political Council every success.

Japan: Enemy of Humanity

TODAY is the first anniversary of China's War of Resistance against the aggression of Japanese imperialism. On behalf of the four hundred and fifty million Chinese, soldiers and civilians, who are fighting in the cause of justice, I want to express my sincere and unbounded gratitude to all friendly Powers and to all individual friends of China who have helped us in our struggle.

From the seventeenth year of the Republic [1928], which saw the unification of China, until now, we have consistently followed the principles laid down by our late Leader, Dr. Sun Yat-sen, in his *San Min Chu I* and in all the other writings he has left us. We have taken these as a basis for our national reconstruction. Internally, our efforts have been directed toward the revival of our nation. Externally, our policy has been, in collaboration with other nations, to strive for the maintenance of justice in the world, and to make our contribution to civilization and the welfare of mankind. For ten years we have not relaxed our efforts. This fact is well known to all friends of China whether nations or individuals.

And yet, the Japanese, driven by their mad idea of world conquest and believing that to conquer the world they must first conquer China, have subjected our country to increasing violence and oppression, endeavoring to undermine our national revolution and to prevent our national unification. Countless examples can be given of their infamous plans and treacherous designs.

Let us examine the history of Sino-Japanese negotiations during the past six years. Is not every case a clear proof of the disregard of justice by Japanese imperialists, and of their wilful violation of international law? The Mukden Incident on September 18, 1931, was part and parcel of Japan's premeditated plan. With a lightning stroke Japan seized our Northeastern Provinces and enslaved thirty million of our fellow-countrymen. It was like "the roar of thunder that comes so quickly there is no time to cover one's ears." This violent and illegal action shook the

A message to friendly nations on the first anniversary of China's War of Resistance, July 7, 1938.

34

world. But China was willing to endure patiently this oppression, and after the battle of the Great Wall signed the Tangku Agreement, hoping that Japan would awaken to her own folly.

Cruelty has become second nature to the Japanese militarists, and their greed and savagery have steadily grown. The fact that China was becoming increasingly unified and stable and was making such great strides forward in reconstruction, stuck like a thorn in Japan's side, so that Japanese militarists "could neither sleep nor eat." When they gained an inch they proceeded to take a foot, and oppressed our people unceasingly. A year ago today they carried things to an extreme. They began illegal manoeuvres, attacking by night our garrison at Lukouchiao near Peiping, and thus picked a quarrel with us for no reason at all. They followed this up by a large-scale attack on Shanghai with their sea, air, and land forces.

China, with her five thousand years of history, her vast territory and her enormous population, stands like a mountain peak among the nations of the world. Her contribution to the civilization of mankind is imperishable. She has been a keen lover of peace; she has had a deep respect for international justice. In this the whole country has been united, and the whole world knows it. But there is a limit to the aggression to which we will submit. We cannot submit when our existence as a nation, the territorial integrity of our country, and the independence and sovereignty of our State are at stake, and when international justice and respect for treaties are involved. It was, therefore, with greatest determination that we began our sacred War of Resistance against these mad Japanese imperialists, who ignore justice and tear up treaties, and who dream of conquering China as a prelude to conquering the world. We have already dealt the aggressor some hard blows.

Entrusted as I have been by the Party and the nation with the grave responsibility of leadership, sustained by the sincere support of the people, and encouraged by the hopes placed in me by friendly nations, I certainly shall not try to shift the responsibility to others. I have in the past often stated my sworn resolve to rid our land entirely of the invader, to complete the reconstruction of new China, and, in concert with other friendly nations, to strive toward a new era of prosperity for all mankind, and of peace throughout the world.

I have been actively engaged for a whole year in carrying out this mission. Let me review the most significant and memorable events of this period. Beginning from Peiping and Tientsin, the Japanese have carried hostilities into Chahar and Suiyuan, into Shansi and Shantung, and then into Kiangsu, Chekiang, Hunan, and Anhwei. Superficially it would seem as though the invaders have occupied a vast area, as large as Europe, but actually all that they hold are one or two lines of communications, and a few strategic points. When the Japanese seized such and such a point, or line of communication, it by no means fell like a ripe plum into their hands; they captured these places only by using their powers to the very limit, even to the point of exhaustion, and they paid a very high price for their successes.

The indomitable will that animates all of our people in this war against aggression must be well known to all friendly Powers; there is no need for me to dwell upon it. What I do want to emphasize is the barbarism of the Japanese militarists, a barbarism which would wipe out those basic human qualities that Heaven has implanted in man. This barbarism affects the whole future of mankind, and cannot be passed by. Since we began our resistance to the enemy countless industries and vast quantities of raw material, at the front and in the occupied areas, have been totally destroyed, and young men and girls, women and children, the old and the weak, have been subjected to unspeakable horrors, to rape and plunder and burning and death. The Japanese air force has continued unceasingly to attack our open cities and undefended countryside, and taking as its special targets our cultural, educational, and philanthropic institutions and our residential areas, has constantly rained bombs upon them. Not only so, but wherever Japanese fury has reached, the institutions and industries carried on for many years by nationals of friendly nations have been reduced to ashes.

Take, for example, the open city of Canton. Recently for more than half a month it has been bombed continually day and night—and with what results? Several thousands of ordinary folk have not merely heard the sound of exploding bombs, but have been blown to pieces. Officials and nationals of all the friendly Powers have conducted investigations on the spot, or have taken photographs of the bombings. The terrible scenes, unprecedented in world history, have made their blood run cold. They have described in detail what they have witnessed, in order to expose the true character of this barbarous nation. If the savage cruelty of these Japanese bandits perpetrated in the name of civilization is allowed to continue unchecked and unpunished, then the world will never know permanent peace or justice, and we shall be left with an indelible stain upon our consciences.

When China began her resistance to aggression Japan, relying on the quality of the military equipment she had accumulated over several decades, believed that the conquest of China would be a matter of but two or three weeks at the most. With this idea the Japanese government deceived their people and enticed them into carrying out blindly their policy of destruction. Who would have thought that in the one area of Shanghai alone we should have held up the enemy for more than three months; while during the months that followed, in Kiangsu, Chekiang, Shansi, and Shantung the Japanese would everywhere meet with stubborn resistance from our troops?

If we seek the reason for this, it is to be found in the fact that all the people—men and women, old and young—have been deeply influenced by the Three Principles of the People, and by our new national consciousness, so that every one is willing to undergo suffering and hardship, and to fulfill his duties to the uttermost, in order to win life out of death. Another reason is the warm sympathy and help of friendly nations —both governments and private citizens—which has found practical expression in frequent denunciations of Japanese aggression, in boycott of Japanese goods, in refusal to transport Japanese merchandise, and in denial of business facilities and credits to Japanese industrialists. The vigorous demonstrations and other activities of the world-wide Anti-Aggression Movement shows the deep disgust and resentment of the members of this organization. In all these ways, by moral sanctions and by material restrictions, Japan has been made to feel the pinch. Fierce and barbarous as she is, Japan has in a moment, in the twinkling of an eye, been brought to realize that her guilt can no longer be concealed. As for the comfort and help sent to the people of China, in the form of medical supplies and material assistance, we are more than grateful, and cannot express our thanks too often.

At the present juncture when their troops are exhausted, and they have "drained the pond to catch the fish," the Japanese are sure to resort to more violent measures. But China has from the very beginning been prepared to face any sacrifice that is necessary, and to persevere in the struggle without flinching or wavering. At the same time, we cannot but sincerely hope that all the friendly nations will, in accordance with the warm sympathy expressed in the past, take effective measures to stop this enemy of humanity, so that justice and peace may be established throughout the world. We eagerly expect that the friendly Powers who signed the League Covenant, the Paris Pact, and the Nine Power Treaty, will carry out their treaty obligations. The League of Nations has repeatedly passed resolutions urging each state separately to give all possible aid to China. I am sure that each of the friendly nations will honestly carry out its treaty responsibilities, and put into effect the League's resolutions, so that a stop may be put to Japanese aggression.

Right will ultimately be victorious; this is my own unshakable faith, and it is the faith of our whole nation. The recent convocation of the People's Political Council, the putting into effect of compulsory military service, and the rapid progress in internal reconstruction, all prove the unity of the Chinese people, and the progress that has been and is being made towards a modern democratic state. Our powers of resistance have been correspondingly increased.

In the future our people and our soldiers will be even more determined to press on boldly against the foe. We shall never change our policy of resistance until the invading Japanese troops have been completely withdrawn, and until China's territorial and administrative integrity have been fully restored. Our people are deeply conscious of the great responsibility that is theirs, not only to their own nation, but to the world. In this fight with a cruel enemy, the one who is loyal never looks back. I say categorically that until international righteousness has been established, and the sanctity of treaties is respected, China will not cease fighting. Look at all the outrageous and inhuman brutalities inflicted by the Japanese on our people. So far from terrifying them or forcing them to submit, these brutalities have only increased the determination of our people to resist. This fact alone is sufficient to prove that China's powers of resistance are inexhaustible.

Friendly nations and opponents of aggression : Peace is indivisible, isolation is impossible. So long as Japan's aggression is not checked, so long will it be impossible to have peace in the Far East, or in the world at large. The maintenance of international justice and the sanctity of treaties, the preservation of the happiness of mankind and of its cultural heritage, are the common responsibility of all human beings. I am quite sure that all our good friends of the friendly nations and all opponents of aggression are fully aware of this common responsibility, and that they also know what are the best ways to unite our efforts for the attainment of our common goal. On my part, I will continue to lead my four hundred and fifty million fellow-countrymen forward in the fight against aggression, so that we may all together reach our objective. I have taken the opportunity of this anniversary to share with you some of my thoughts. I ask you to give serious consideration to what I have said.

To the People of Japan

A YEAR has passed since the Sino-Japanese conflict began. Though, for fear of the militarists, you cannot give vent to your sentiments, you must have viewed the past events with a heavy heart. Had your War Department not boasted to you that Japan could conquer China without a battle? Had they not also told you after the war started, that the conflict would be promptly concluded? But now, are you not required to prepare for a long war? As the Japanese militarists go deeper and deeper into the bog, they repeatedly change their art of hoodwinking you. Think of it! How many of your brothers, sons and nephews have become ghosts on the Continent? How many of your young women have become widows and how many of your children have become orphans? But what have you gained from the war? Take the case of the four Northeastern Provinces; your militarists have occupied them for several years, yet what have you got other than your share of the enormous burden of war expenditure?

Nothing has left the "Soul of Yamato" and "Bushido," of both of which your country had been so proud. Poisonous gases are relentlessly used. Opium and narcotics are publicly sold. International treaties and principles of justice are trampled under the feet of your invading army. Wherever your troops went, there was looting and burning of property. They massacred innocent civilians and wounded soldiers. They slung these poor creatures together by the hundreds and mowed them down with machine-gun fire. In some instances, they drove scores of people into a room and set fire to it. At other times they made competitions among themselves to see who killed most simply for fun. Your air force has extended its activities to our undefended cities far behind the fighting lines and rain bombs on them. Your airmen seemed to have gone mad every time they went on their deadly mission. The objects of their bombing were defenseless civilians, and cultural, educational and charity institutions. My friends, you must have known that our military planes have flown around your principal cities. But we only conveyed to you our

Delivered on July 7, 1938, the first anniversary of the Lukouchiao Incident and the outbreak of war.

39

sympathy, not destructive bombs. Just imagine what harm would have been done on the cities of Tokio, Osaka or Kobe, and the universities there, if the Chinese air force should have let fall the same number of bombs as your planes have poured on the city of Canton.

There is one more thing which it pains me to mention but which I cannot help mentioning. This is the shameful behavior of your troops toward our women, whom they first violated and then brutally killed. Such actions of the Japanese troops are not only a disgrace to Japan but will leave a most ugly blot in the history of mankind.

My friends, if you will not rise in time to denounce your militarists and check their aggression, the future of your country will be gloomy indeed. Dear friends, before it is too late, you should force your militarists to reexamine their aggressive policy towards China. Ask them: What is the meaning of invading China? What is the object of this campaign? How much, after all, has Japan so far gained from the war? How much have they already lost? Can the war result in the conquest of China, the stabilization of East Asia? Can Japan oust the white people from East Asia and become the mistress of the Pacific herself? My friends, just think what your country has reaped since this war of aggression began, and who are making all these sacrifices. Ponder over these questions, my friends, and you will see that our War of Resistance is not only for our own salvation but for yours too.

Thus, apart from self-defense and self-preservation, our war carries also the purpose of bringing about a state of happiness for the good of both the Chinese and Japanese peoples. Hence your truculent militarists are the enemy not only of China but also of the whole of the Japanese people. From the very beginning of the conflict, we have regarded as our enemy only your militarists but not the people of Japan, people like yourselves. The army and the people of China have always looked upon you, who love peace but are mercilessly oppressed by the militarists, as friends whose interests coincide with theirs. They are therefore full of warm sympathy for you and entertain great expectations of you.

Our Own Soil, Our Own People

SINCE the Manchuria Incident of September 18, 1931, two million square kilometers of Chinese territory with an aggregate population of 150,000,000 have been overrun, wholly or partially, by the Japanese aggressor. These vast tracts of territory are our own soil, and these millions of people our own people. This is certainly a shame and disgrace unprecedented in the history of the Chinese nation.

The atrocities committed by the Japanese in the occupied areas are more horrible than any perpetrated during the end of the Sung, or the Ming Dynasty. With their endless atrocities of indiscriminate bombing, killing, slaughtering, pillaging and raping, the Japanese invaders have broken the black record in the history of mankind. But these are not all. For, in addition to these brutalities, the Japanese have been adopting wholesale drugging and enslaving policies. They have driven our compatriots to fight for them at the battlefronts in pursuance of their pernicious principle of making Chinese kill Chinese. They have also kidnapped large numbers of Chinese children in the occupied areas, and sent them to Japan to teach them to fight against their own kin. Evidently, the Japanese are determined not only to annex the Chinese territory but also to exterminate the Chinese race.

On this occasion of the first anniversary of the outbreak of hostilities at Shanghai, it pains me to think of my compatriots seething in the fire of unbearable oppression and being subjected to both the harsh and the refined forms of cruelty. In attempting to exterminate our race, the Japanese have resorted to every pernicious means that they can think of. Witness the rigid control of educational policies, the suppression of our language, the dissemination of "the rule of right and the soil of happiness" propaganda, the compulsion to adopt enslaving textbooks, the issuing of bogus "banknotes" and the forcible allotment of bonds so as to extract the last drop of blood from our compatriots.

Above all, what makes one gnash one's teeth in anger is their mean and malicious policy of drugging. According to a Japanese official com-

A message to the people in Japanese-occupied areas delivered August 13, 1938, on the first anniversary of the outbreak of hostilities at Shanghai.

muniqué issued last year, registered opium addicts in the four North-eastern Provinces numbered 13,000,000, representing more than one-third of the total population there. In North China, heroin, morphine, cocaine, and other drugs are produced on large scales, besides opium. In the Japanese Concession in Tientsin, more than a thousand "firms" are selling these narcotics, and more than two hundred factories, employing 10,000 workmen, are engaged day and night in producing these murder-ous drugs. Beyond the north bank of the Yellow River, in the lower reaches of the Yangtze, in the south of Fukien, in the north of Kiangsu—in a word, wherever the Japanese have set their foot, the places are soon flooded with narcotics.

One thing I wish to tell my compatriots is that though both our Army and people have suffered great distress and sacrifices, yet throughout the thirteen months' struggle, victory has been always with us. Up to now, we have gained the upper hand over the Japanese in at least four re-spects: strategic, political, spiritual, and diplomatic.

The Japanese planned originally to fight "a short war with a swift conclusion," while we, a prolonged one in order to exhaust the enemy's strength and thus to win the final victory in a last decisive battle. It is obvious, however, that Japan's hope of a short war has been entirely shattered. They have failed every time after occupying one of our prin-cipal cities to gain the point in their wild dream of making our people submit without further struggle. On the contrary, the farther they pene-trate into China, the stronger is our resistance and the greater their losses. In other words, as the war-fronts extend, the strength of our resistance will increase, whereas our enemy's exhaustion will be aggra-vated.

The Japanese are determined to annex our country not only by fight-ing a short war but also by splitting up our people, making them fight one group against another. But this plan, like the above one, has also failed. The Chinese people have never been more united and consolidated than they are at the present moment. Notwithstanding that the Japanese bribe some shameless hooligans and rowdies to set up puppet govern-ments here and there, their meanness only serves to intensify the indig-nation of our compatriots in the occupied areas. Their policies of coercion and temptation have failed of all effect, while our resistance has been daily strengthened.

The firm stand made by us has astounded observers in every part of the world. Through this War of Resistance, the Chinese people have burst the mythical bubble of Japanese invincibility and gained self-confi-dence. We are no longer afraid of the Japanese, but firmly believe that we shall gain the ultimate victory. Our grim determination to resist is not to be shaken by any trials or hardships whatsoever. This is a sure sign of the general awakening of our people.

With regard to the world, our War of Resistance, being fought for the cause of world peace and justice, has enhanced immeasurably the strength of the world peace forces. For this reason, there is no single person in all the peace-loving countries but sympathizes with us. China's status among the family of nations is being daily elevated just as Japan's is daily sinking.

It is only thirteen months since the war broke out, and yet, within this short period, we have gained in these four different respects. In short, we are sure of our success whether in the strategic, the political, the spiritual, or the diplomatic field. This testifies to the correctness of my former statement, "As the war goes on, we shall grow stronger; while the enemy, weaker."

II
China Fights On
(1938-1940)

Our Power of Resistance Grows Stronger

MY DEAR FELLOW-COUNTRYMEN, as you commemorate today the twenty-seventh anniversary of the founding of our Republic, you will call to mind the events of the fifteen months since our War of Resistance began and you will feel immeasurably heartened by the successes that we have already achieved. A year ago today some of you were still wavering; but now the faith and the determination of the whole nation are unmistakable and unshakable. Friendly states have come to understand more clearly the meaning of our defensive struggle, and even our enemy has been forced to admit that our power of resistance grows stronger all the time. In Japan they are now saying that there must be a "new understanding and new evaluation of China," and the Japanese militarists are being forced to warn the Japanese people that they must "prepare to fight for a hundred years." During our year and more of resistance, the national consciousness of our people—men and women, young and old—has been awakened, and new life, full of hope and glorious possibilities, has begun to surge through the nation.

During the past year the international situation has been extremely complex, yet the general trend has been toward condemnation of the use of force and toward maintenance of peace. Such a development has been due in part to China's strong resistance against aggression. Future historians will, I believe, regard our War of Resistance as the most significant event in this period of world history, since by our enormous sacrifices we are contributing not only to the good of the Chinese nation but also to the welfare of all mankind. From now on, however, we must struggle even harder and must be ready for even greater sacrifices, in order that justice may be accomplished. The aims of our struggle are simple and clear. If we succeed we shall not only be able to build a new China but we shall also contribute immeasurably to the peace of the world.

Just now the immediate objective in our War of Resistance seems

An Address to the nation on the twenty-seventh anniversary of the Republic of China, October 10, 1938.

more important to us. We are engaged in a life-and-death struggle. We are better prepared today than we were a year ago to prove that the Chinese nation cannot be conquered or destroyed by an alien people. But the purpose of our struggle is not merely to prevent conquest or destruction ; it is also to win for our country a position of independence and equality in the family of nations. For this reason our responsibilities will increase and the struggle will become more intense, more difficult, and more critical. We must be doubly watchful and not tolerate any kind of negligence. Everyone must help and must do his part actively and wholeheartedly. Let us remember that the most difficult moment may be our greatest opportunity for success. Let us all rise as one man to resist the Japanese aggressor and to win freedom for our nation.

A Turning Point in Our Struggle

THE Japanese attack on Hankow was something we had long been expecting. Even prior to the battle in southern Shantung[1] the enemy announced his intention of attacking Wuhan. After his campaign in Honan had ended in failure and his plan to advance in Anhwei had been blocked, he pushed desperately up the Yangtze River with the combined strength of his naval, land, and air forces. Throughout the subsequent five months of sanguinary hostilities, our officers and men have carried on the struggle with great courage, and our people have done their best to help them, making heroic sacrifices and demonstrating a finer spirit than ever before.

As a result, Japanese casualties during this period have exceeded their losses for the whole first year of the war.[2] Now that their plan to annihilate our army has again failed, they have launched an invasion of South China to cover their chagrin. With the sphere of hostilities now further extended, the whole war situation has changed. At this crucial moment I deem it wise to review briefly, for the benefit of my countrymen, our War of Resistance, to explain to them what has already happened and toward what objectives we should henceforth direct our endeavors.

In the first place, I wish you, our people, to have a clear understanding of the latest change in the war situation and of the consequences attendant upon the fall of Wuhan. From the beginning, our plan has been to establish the bases of our resistance, not along the coast or rivers, or at centers of communication, but in the vast interior. In accordance

---

A message to the people of China following the evacuation of Hankow, on October 25, 1938.

[1] Japan's north-south campaign for the possession of Hsuchow, junction of the Lunghai and the Tientsin-Pukow railways, commenced in January, 1938, and ended on May 20, 1938, with the capture of the city only after a heavy reverse at Taierhchwang. The enemy's plan to encircle and then annihilate the Chinese Army failed completely.

[2] For the period between the capture, on June 15, 1938, of Anking, the capital of Anhwei Province, and September 30, 1938, when the Japanese were nearing the Wuhan cities, the enemy's losses in action were estimated at 270,000 with 80,000 additional casualties from diseases contracted during the hard summer campaign.

with the military strategy and policy consistently pursued by our government, our western provinces are the real base of our resistance.

During the past ten months Wuhan has provided a bulwark behind which preparations for reconstruction in the western part of the country could be made, and has also served as a link in the lines of communication between North and South. The principal reasons for defending Wuhan were: to impede and weaken the enemy during his westward advance, to cover the establishment of lines of communication in the rear, and to shield the removal of industrial plants from Southeast and Central China to the Northwest and Southwest.[3] Only through economic development and the completion of a system of communications can these two regions become foundations for armed resistance and reconstruction.

Now that the industrial plants of Central China and much of the manpower have been moved to the western provinces, where the groundwork for economic development and for expansion of transportation facilities has been laid, we are free to concentrate on wide mobile front resistance without having to fight for mere points or lines.

Meanwhile, by determined struggle against great odds, we have succeeded in inflicting heavy losses on the enemy; we have further reinforced our faith in the regeneration of our nation; and we have clearly demonstrated the vigor of our fighting spirit. We have achieved our purpose in defending Wuhan. Moreover, the Japanese invasion of Kwangtung and the cutting of communications between Canton and Hankow have reduced the importance of Wuhan in relation to the whole situation.

Militarily speaking, the value of Wuhan lay not in itself but rather in its being the center of a very wide area. By now, bases of operations have been established in the remoter outskirts of Wuhan; not only in the hilly regions of Hupeh, Honan, Anhwei, and Kinagsi Provinces but also in places behind the enemy lines in Hopei, Shantung, Kiangsu, and Chekiang Provinces. Thus the holding of the Wuhan center had become of secondary importance. In terms of strategy we could not concern ourselves with the defense of Wuhan to the neglect of the

[3] In addition to innumerable small units, the essential parts of 341 large industrial plants, arsenals, etc., totalling more than 130,000 tons, were sent westward from Hankow alone by way of the Yangtze River. When Hankow fell, the western communication network was well advanced. The Burma Road was nearing completion and a highway to supplement the Kunming-Indo-China Railway was under construction. The 345-kilometer railway section between Hengyang and Kweilin had been opened for traffic; work was in progress on other inter-regional railways, highways and waterways.

development of our strength on all fronts. Our strategy is not to lose sight of our major objectives by attending too closely to minor issues; not to desert our long-term policy for the sake of momentary gains or losses.

With the evacuation of civilians and industrial plants, with the transfer of our military forces, and with the completion of new arrangements for operations, we voluntarily evacuated the three cities of Wuhan so that our forces could resist from more advantageous positions.

Even though the enemy has occupied Wuhan temporarily, it has taken him five months and cost him casualties running into hundreds of thousands. What he has acquired is merely scorched earth and empty cities. He has failed in his major objective—the annihilation of our main strength at Wuhan and the winning of a short decisive war.

Henceforth, we shall develop our all-front resistance. The movement of our forces, whether withdrawing or advancing, will be unrestricted and free. The initiative will be with us. On the other hand, the enemy stands to gain nothing. Sunk deep in a morass, his troops will encounter increasing difficulties which will finally spell their doom.

My fellow-countrymen, you must understand that the shifting of our armed forces on this occasion marks a turning point in our struggle; a change in tactics from the defensive to the offensive. It marks also the beginning of a change of tide in the war. It must not be mistakenly viewed as a military reverse or retreat, but as a strategic conservation of our strength which will bring about a victorious conclusion to our War of Resistance.

Secondly, my countrymen, we must keep in mind the consistent program and policy which were resolved upon at the outset of our armed resistance, and thereby fortify our self-confidence. This fixed program consists of three essentials; (1) the war must be prolonged; (2) the war must be fought on many fronts; (3) we must keep the initiative. These are indispensable factors in overcoming our enemy and in attaining victory. For a year now we have adhered to this policy and we shall pursue it to the very end.

Since launching his attack upon Manchuria on September 18, 1931, our enemy has run amuck, with daily mounting greed. Our central authorities realized that great sacrifices would be inevitable when the final crisis came and accordingly laid, in the western provinces, foundations for a prolonged war. We should realize that our present armed resistance is clearing the way for the permanent task of national reconstruction and that without passing through this stage of prolonged warfare we cannot achieve freedom. These phases of our evolution, from unity to resistance and finally to reconstruction, have long been foreseen. I believe that they will be completely realized. If my fellow-countrymen review my utterances and actions in the light of the past sixteen months of war, they will clearly understand the special characteristics of our War of Resistance and the reasons for our determined policy.

In a speech at Lushan, when the Sino-Japanese hostilities first broke out I said, "When we reach the point where the whole nation must take up arms, then we know we shall have to sacrifice to the very end without the slightest hope of avoiding suffering by some sudden turn of fortune." I said also, "Once the battle is joined there can be no distinction between north and south, nor between old and young. Everyone, everywhere, will have to shoulder the responsibility for protecting the country and for resisting the foe. Everyone will have to give everything that he has." Then in my speech for October 10 last year I told my fellow-countrymen with even greater frankness, "This war will not be finished in six months or a year. Only the determination to sacrifice to the very limit will enable us to reach our goal and to secure the survival of our race." I made this statement in case my fellow-countrymen might not have fully realized that this war must last for a long period and extend over a very wide area. I felt that a warning was necessary.

Upon the fall of our capital Nanking, the morale of our people was threatened. Again I informed all my fellow-countrymen, "This war with all its bitter suffering was bound to come sooner or later. Our war is a war of the Three Principles of the People against the brutal forces of imperialism. It is a war against aggression waged by a people whose land has been invaded, a war of survival and independence. It is a very different struggle from the ordinary international war between equally powerful states. Although we knew from the beginning that we were greatly inferior to our enemy in arms, equipment and material resources, yet, because of our revolutionary spirit, we never considered that as a reason for dismay or surrender."

I amplified that statement by saying that the outcome of the war depends on whether one of the parties exercises more initiative than the other. Our way of dealing with the enemy is to prolong the war without surrender; for the deeper the enemy penetrates into our territory, the more he will find himself in a defensive position. These statements were meant to explain the special features of this war and also to show what would be the natural consequences of a long struggle to the end and of our fighting for the initiative.

Since at the very beginning of hostilities we decided upon a long-drawn-out war, no momentary vicissitudes can shake our resolution. We expect to extend the war zones, and no loss of cities can affect the general situation. Furthermore, because our War of Resistance is to be a prolonged and all-inclusive war, we must secure the initiative. There are as many advantages on our side as there are disadvantages on the enemy's. Only by securing and maintaining the initiative shall we be able to defeat the enemy's attempt to win a short decisive war, and to shatter his dream of partitioning our territory.

Ours is a nation of vast size, huge population, and immense resources. The wider the sphere of hostilities extends, the stronger will our initiative become. On the one hand, our aim is to force the enemy, more and more, to stand on the defensive. On the other hand, our own strategy is to be free to take the offensive or to remain on the defensive; to capture or to abandon certain points. Our military preparations in the future will not be like the preparations in Shanghai and Nanking which were largely dictated by topographical and other factors. From now on, no matter how the enemy may attack us or blockade our coast, he cannot in the least affect our initiative and strategy. We are more confident than ever of final victory. I hope that all our armed forces and civilian population will resolve to carry on unfalteringly and to pursue the strategy of an all-front offensive with ever greater courage. The longer the war lasts, the more solid will our strength become. The larger the sphere of hostilities the more scattered will be the strength of the enemy. Regardless of how the international situation may change, the enemy will eventually collapse through exhaustion.

As I have said before, our War of Resistance differs entirely from wars fought for political supremacy. Ours is a war for the very existence of our nation. It is for the completion of our national revolution. Being such, it is beyond considerations of time or space. It cannot be blocked by factors of finance, economics, communications, or by other external obstacles. Neither poison gas, nor high explosives, nor the disparity in armaments, nor the heavy sacrifices we are suffering can deter us from prosecuting the war. Such a war has no time limit; it ends only when the objective is attained. In this war there is no distinction between the front and the rear. Any part of the country may become the battlefield. A revolutionary war is not affected by the apparent difference of strength in the contending forces, by heavy sacrifices, or by shortage of war supplies. Even if we are cut off from every source of arms and from financial assistance, and even if every outlet to the sea is blockaded, the fire of our national consciousness and revolutionary spirit will continue to blaze, and we shall carry on the struggle until we win. Besides, our supplies were assured long ago and there is no immediate danger of the enemy cutting our communication routes in the rear.

History has demonstrated that a long-term revolutionary war is always crowned with ultimate victory. Nations like the United States, France, Russia, and Turkey gained their national independence and freedom after prolonged resistance against their oppressors. The courage of our resistance also has shown that the more aggressive the enemy is the stronger our power of resistance becomes; and that the greater our losses are, the faster we generate new strength. At this crucial moment, when our war of resistance is entering a decisive phase, my fellow-countrymen, we must remember the national policy resolved upon at the outset of the war and also the manifesto issued by the Government upon the removal of its seat to Chungking. We should recognize clearly the true importance of prolonged and all-front resistance, and exert greater efforts to meet the new situation arising from the extension of the sphere of hostilities. Our faith in the cause of armed resistance must not be shaken by temporary change.

From now on, we must be more serious, more firm, and more practical. We must endure greater hardships, and march courageously forward, devoting our entire energy to the all-front war and fortifying our bases of resistance in the rear, thereby assuring final victory. As the proverb has it, "One who sets out on a hundred-*li* journey is only half way when he has covered ninety *li*." In order to win final success we must exert ourselves to the utmost and fight on with the greatest fearlessness. "Rather be a broken jade than a whole tile." Our ultimate freedom depends upon our present determination. The success or failure of our resistance and the fate of our nation hinge upon our resolution today. My fellow-countrymen, let us all strive together in this one great effort.

The Second Stage of War

I REGRET that I am unable to be present at your meetings because of duties at the war front, but I shall be with you in spirit and I wish you every success. I recall vividly the First Session of the Council in Wuhan, when you displayed such a splendid spirit of patriotism and passed a large number of resolutions aiming at the realization of final victory and the fulfilment of our supreme objective—national reconstruction. When the session was over some of you went to Chungking and other places to offer your services to the Government; others went to the front to help in the war; still others of you returned to your homes and did your best to stir up the people. In all this work you have demonstrated real leadership. Your unity and your devotion reveal the true spirit of our nation. Although the Council has had only a short history, its existence has been fully justified.

Now our War of Resistance has spread over a wide front from the Yangtze Valley to the coast of Kwangtung. On the surface it may seem that our difficulties are increasing as the area of conflict is being extended; actually, the invasion of South China only shows that the Japanese are reaching the end of their resources and are becoming desperate. Since June the enemy troops have tried to push their way up the Yangtze River but their advance has been seriously retarded by our gallant troops. Within the short period of five months the Japanese have sent reinforcements five or six times, and the number of their casualties has already exceeded 300,000. Alarmed at the prospect of military exhaustion, the Japanese have tried to divert our attention by invading Kwangtung; they hope that by cutting our lines of communication and by shutting us off from sources of supplies, they may bring the war to a speedier conclusion. But they are grievously mistaken. The change in the military situation simply makes it possible for us to assume a more active role and to turn the tide of war in our own favor.

We have already mapped out a complete new strategy. From the

A message from the war front to the Second Session of the People's Political Council, November 28, 1938.

beginning of the war, in anticipation of the present course of events, we redoubled our efforts to reconstruct Southwest China as a new base for our army as well as a new center for our industries. Here we shall consolidate our new unity and intensify our struggle against the invader, and so ultimately regain our national freedom.

Our policy is unwavering and resolute. For five years we have been trying to awaken our people, soldiers and civilians, to the defense of our country. Now in time of extreme difficulty a new national spirit is emerging and gives us sure promise of ultimate victory. When the enemy tries to move further westward he will meet with such resistance as he has never before encountered.

Since the war started we have foreseen the moves of the Japanese and have been able to offset them with counter-moves. Thanks to the united efforts of the whole nation during the past six months, we have not only improved our military position in the occupied areas but we have also established centers of political activity in these areas. Moreover, we have built an impregnable system of defense west of the Peiping-Hankow and Canton-Hankow Railways. In order to stay the advance of the enemy into the interior, many of our soldiers in the Yangtze and Hwai Valleys have already made the supreme sacrifice. I have nothing but praise for their patriotism and courage.

We have now entered the second stage of the war and we are already gaining the upper hand over the enemy. It is true we shall have to face new difficulties, but that is all the more reason why we should re-dedicate our lives to the great task before us. Keep up your remarkable spirit and be ready to give your best to the nation. While the Council is in session you will offer the Government advice as to what should be done; when the session is over you will no doubt continue to lead our people so that our struggle against the invader may result in victory. Your efforts will encourage those at the front to fight with greater vigor and those in the rear to take more active part in reconstruction enterprises and to prepare themselves for military service. The collapse of the enemy and the triumph of our armies are not far distant. As we fight we are also building a stronger foundation for our nation. So let us firmly resolve to overcome every obstacle and to achieve final success.

Japan's So-Called New Order

COMRADES, we have now entered upon a new stage in our War of Resistance. On several occasions recently I pointed out that the past eighteen months have been the first or preliminary period of the war. The second period has now begun. On both northern and southern war fronts, our soldiers' morale and fighting spirit are stronger than ever before. Our soldiers well know that to the enemy this is a war for the complete subjugation of China, while to us it is a war for national independence; hence their wills are exceptionally firm and their spirits are very high. Our people also realize that the enemy will not pause until he has carried out his aggressive designs and has destroyed China, and that we, unless we brave death to save life, cannot expect to survive. But, difficult as our situation may be, the firm determination of our soldiers and people is equal to it. If those at the front and those in the rear are equally conscious of the national peril and if all the people struggle and sacrifice with one heart for victory, without hesitation or compromise, then I am sure our resistance will succeed.

Aware of our determined purpose and unified will, our enemy has tried many methods of intimidation and deception in addition to his military operations. Following the Japanese government's manifesto on November 3, 1938, the Japanese Prime Minister, the Ministers of War and the Navy, and the Minister for Foreign Affairs have made contradictory and fallacious statements which are intended to mislead their people at home and to deceive the world at large. They vainly hope to poison the minds of our people and to frighten them into submission. Their statements were seconded and echoed throughout Japan by public and private organs of opinion. On December 22, the Japanese Premier announced the readiness of Japan to readjust relations with a "reborn China." This statement is the height of verbal jugglery and shows clearly what Japan's real motives are.

Konoye's announcement is nothing but a wearisome repetition of

A speech addressed to Government leaders at the Central Kuomintang Headquarters on December 26, 1938.

cant phrases. It seems unnecessary for us, in the midst of our War of Resistance, to pay any attention to it, let alone refute it. However, considering it in the light of the enemy's words and deeds the past few months, we perceive that the statement, though outwardly vague and incoherent, has hidden within it a sharp cutting edge. It is a revelation in detail of the enemy's plan to destroy our country and exterminate our race. It is also a complete exposure of Japan's fantastic program to annex China, dominate East Asia, and subdue the world.

Our enemy is especially gifted with the ability to play on words, disguise fallacies, and lay smoke-screens while he brings about the ruin of his victims. For instance, after Konoye's statement the spokesman of the Japanese government declared on December 24 that Premier Konoye had made clear the terms to be required of China and further took it upon himself to say that the Premier's words embodied the views of the moderates in Japan.

My deep anxiety is lest a small number of people in the world may not appreciate what a menace lurks behind the smoke screen and may regard the issue raised as more or less innocuous. Hence I wish to expose the mind of the Japanese so that our own people may be warned and friendly nations may understand to what extent world peace will be jeopardized and humanity imperilled if the Japanese are given full rein. I wish to call the attention of all peoples to the barbarism of the Japanese militarists, to their insanity, to the practice of deceiving themselves and others, and to their gross ignorance. It is of the most urgent importance that everyone should realize what Japan is determined to do. Taking Konoye's statement of December 22 as the pivot of my observations, I shall now recall what Japanese popular sentiment has been championing during the past few months and what slogans have been employed.

First, there is "the creation of a new order in East Asia." In this slogan the Japanese take special pride. According to Foreign Minister Arita's explanation on December 19, "The new order in East Asia means that Japan, 'Manchukuo,' and China shall assist and cooperate with one another closely in politics, economics, and culture, in order to combat the Red Peril, to protect Oriental civilization, to remove economic barriers, and to help China to rise from her semi-colonial status and thus secure peace in the Far East." On December 22, Konoye said, "The ultimate objective of the China Incident is not merely military victory but the rebirth of China and the establishment of a new order in East Asia. This new order will be based on a triangular cooperation between the new China, Japan, and 'Manchukuo.'" Let everyone note that what he means by a reborn China is not an independent China but an enslaved China, a China that would have to take orders from Japan for generations to come. The so-called new order would be based on relations binding enslaved China to Japanese-created "Manchukuo" and to Japan herself.

What is Japan's real aim? Under the guise of opposing the "Red Peril," Japan seeks to control China's military affairs; claiming to uphold Oriental civilization, she seeks to uproot China's racial culture; and urging the elimination of economic barriers, she aspires to exclude American and European influence, and to dominate the Pacific. She intends to use the so-called "economic unity" or "economic bloc" of Japan, "Manchukuo," and China to obtain a strangle-hold on the economy of China. Let us realize how pregnant with evil the words, "creation of a new order in East Asia," are. They mean the overthrow of international order in East Asia and the enslavement of China so that Japan may divide the world and dominate the Pacific.

Secondly, we hear of the so-called "unity of East Asia." "Make a homogeneous body of East Asia" has been a favorite Japanese slogan for the past few months. The application of this slogan is more general than that of the so-called "economic unity" or "economic bloc." Advocating the "indivisibility of Japan, 'Manchukuo,' and China," the Japanese aim to absorb China politically, economically, and culturally into their own country. Japanese periodicals maintain that the structure of the "unity of East Asia" should be vertical, with Japan at the summit, and not in any sense horizontal; the system of relationship should be patriarchal, with Japan as the head of the family and "Manchukuo" and China as children. In other words, Japan is to be the governor and the master, and China the governed and the slave.

What is this but annexation? What does this mean but the total extinction of China? Konoye's recent phrase, "the establishment of *linked* relations of mutual assistance in matters political, economic, and cultural between Japan, 'Manchukuo,' and China," makes us think only of manacles and shackles. His "linked relations" would be chains dragging us down into a pit from which we could never escape.

Thirdly, we hear such slogans as "economic unity" and "economic bloc." This idea has been promoted for many years by the Japanese and has had considerable influence. It is essential to the proposed "homogeneity of East Asia." On the slogan they have rung many changes; now speaking of "economic reciprocity" and again of "economic cooperation." In the manifesto of the Japanese government issued on November 3, "economic union" is used. In the latter part of

November enemy newspapers printed the headline, "Japan, 'Manchukuo,' and China are to form an economic unit and henceforth share a common fate." In his statement of December 19, Arita said, "Japan has decided to convene an economic conference in order to bring about close economic collaboration between Japan, 'Manchukuo,' and China, and to strengthen the idea of economic union."

What is called an "economic bloc" is in reality economic exploitation. Such instruments of economic aggression as the North China Development Company and the Central China Development Company have been set up for some time. Conversations on economic matters have been held more than once by self-styled representatives of "Manchukuo" and China with officials of Japan. Two days after Konoye's statement, what the Japanese call their Planning Board adopted a resolution urging "the expansion of the productive capacity of Japan, 'Manchukuo,' and China." This "economic bloc" is designed to be the means not only of controlling our Customs revenue and finance and of monopolizing our production and trade, but also of gradually limiting the individual freedom of our people even in regard to food and clothing, residence and travel. The Japanese are to have power over life and death, the power of binding and loosening; we are to become their slaves and their chattels. We are to have our substance devoured by tyrants.

Finally, we learn of the "Asia Development Board" set up as a result of agitation for a medium through which Japan could deal with China. The China Affairs Council projected previously has now given way to this. The arrogant inclusiveness of the new name is a flagrant insult to all the peoples of Asia. Japan is bent not simply on ruining and dismembering China; her ambition for conquest now extends to the entire continent of Asia.

On December 15, the day before the official inauguration of this Asia Development Board, Konoye said, "A new executive organ should be constituted for creating a new order in East Asia. This organ in conjunction with other organs will foster close relations between Japan and China. It will become the key to the execution of our China policy, the realization of which is our final objective in the China Affair." The real function of the organ, however, is to carry out a policy of destroying China. It brings together in one organization all the special service branches set up some time ago all over China which have been working all manner of secret villainy. Now, these rascals boldly unmask themselves and are accorded official status. The establishment of this Asia Development Board reveals unmistakably what are the ends and the means of Japanese policy. There is no more concealment.

Let us now examine Konoye's statement of December 22, seeking the true meaning beneath the mists of verbiage. I shall draw attention to a number of important points.

1. The gist of the statement is the so-called collaboration between Japan, "Manchukuo," and China for the "building of a new order in East Asia." Konoye said that his purpose was to make clear the Japanese government's true intentions to China and to other countries. Of course, his real object was to address America, Europe, and the world. Therefore he exercised special care in manipulating his words so as to produce the impression that Japan desired of China neither territory nor war reparations, and was concerned not for her own particular interests but for the good of the Far East. He even ventured to say that Japan desired China to become a completely independent state. Furthermore, he appeared solicitous over the abolition of consular jurisdiction and foreign concessions in China, as if Japan did not intend to take anything from China but actually wanted to give something to China. He assumes that the world is still ignorant of the true meaning behind the phrase "creation of a new order in East Asia," and will be easily fooled by it. But we know that if China is destroyed and if Japan becomes dominant over China, "territory" for Konoye will merely be the area over which Japan has gained control, and "resources" will be what Japan has seized. When these are stowed away as loot, Japan can well dispense with irrelevant demands for territory and reparations. Since Japan lusts for our entire territory and our entire population, Konoye can well afford to declare that Japan has no desire for any particular part of our "territory" or for any special portion of our substance as "reparations."

From China's standpoint, the question of war indemnities depends upon the determination of war responsibility. Where the responsibility in this case of aggression rests is common knowledge to everybody. It is only too obvious that Japan began the war by invading our sovereign territory. As for consular jurisdiction, it will be a mere superfluity if Japan is allowed full control over China. What has been called "the return of the concessions" would simply mean the turning over of all of them to Japan. Popular sentiment in Japan has indeed agitated not only for the taking over of the foreign concessions but also for their being made into one large Japanese concession. If China should recognize the so-called "new order in East Asia" and the "collaboration of Japan with 'Manchukuo' and China," Japan could easily transform our entire territory into a huge Japanese concession. Even if China should not actually become a slave state yet she would certainly descend

61

to the status of a protectorate; and such a fate would be equivalent to annexation by Japan. When Konoye speaks of making China a truly independent state, who will not recall the status of Korea as defined by the Treaty of Shimonoseki?

Before Konoye made his statement a section of the world entertained the hope that Japan might repent. But since the statement appeared, I am sure that no one in China with any sense of right and wrong and any understanding of current events will again entertain the hope of making peace by compromise.

2. Konoye speaks of "economic cooperation" and "joint defense against Communism." I have dealt with the nature of "economic cooperation" in connection with the so-called "economic bloc," and need not say more on this point. By "joint defense against Communism" Konoye means the participation of China in the anti-Comintern bloc, the stationing of Japanese troops on Chinese territory, and the setting aside of Inner Mongolia as a special area for combating Communism. It is useless for us to discuss such a plan while we are engaged in putting the Three Principles of the People into practice. The phrase, "joint defense against Communism," is simply a cloak under which Japan plots to control our military affairs and then to manage our political, cultural, and even our diplomatic life. Japan was vainly striving to achieve this in the years before the beginning of our resistance on July 7, 1937. Because we did not fall into Japan's trap and chose rather to endure suffering and to resist we still exist as a nation today.

Certain sections of world opinion entertain the view that Japan's policy is directed against Soviet Russia. The truth is that Japan entered the Anti-Comintern Pact and planned the "joint defense against Communism" neither to combat Communism nor Soviet Russia, but as a pretext for destroying China. If Japan's purpose was only national defense against Soviet Russia, then why, during the Changkufeng Affair in July and August of 1938, did Shigemitsu, the Japanese Ambassador at Moscow, retreat and finally yield so ingloriously before the Soviet Foreign Minister? The Japanese anti-Communist arguments are designed to mislead public opinion abroad and at home, and are also a trick to obtain from China the right to station troops in China and completely control Inner Mongolia.

Clearly, if we could consent to Japanese troops being stationed in China and to Inner Mongolia being set aside as a special area, we should not have begun to resist. If we could be overawed by Japan, we should not have fought our way to Peiping when our Revolutionary Army was blocked by Tanaka's forces in Tsinan in the seventeenth year of the Republic.[1] We should have politely offered Japan North China and Inner Mongolia. But when our Revolutionary force had gathered momentum and the Three Principles of the People had evolved, no hardship could prevent us from attaining our goal. Konoye's demands betray a sad lack in his understanding of present-day China. He does not know his own country, much less China; nor does he recognize current trends. No power can stop us now.

3. The latter section of Konoye's statement demands that China accord Japan special facilities in developing North China and Inner Mongolia. This is again making capital of the term "joint defense against Communism" in order to monopolize China's national economy and repress her economic freedom. The statement also demands that Japanese subjects be granted rights to reside and trade in the interior of China. Superficially, this demand appears quite harmless. Unfortunately, Konoye does not seem to be aware of the deep marks that the evil-doing of Japanese subjects everywhere have left upon the minds of our people. The very mention of the word Japan reminds our people of Japanese special organs, Japanese ronins,[2] smuggling of opium, peddling of morphine, manufacture of white-powder, sale of heroin, operating of gambling dens and houses of ill repute, smuggling of arms, conspiracies with bandits, bribing of traitors, and a hundred other Japanese devices for disturbing and debauching our people.

After the jurisdictional rights of China are completely restored, the freedom of other nationals to reside and trade here may be considered. But such freedom for Japanese nationals now would mean that we must endure their poisonous disturbances, forfeit our own right to maintain peace and order, allow them to destroy our good customs and traditions, and let them suck at our economic veins. The Japanese are forgetful! Is not this demand for the right to reside in the interior and freedom to trade similar in essence to that Japanese demand years ago for concession agreements in China's Northeast? In the eighteenth year of the Republic [1929] we refused because we would rather see our Northeast occupied by the Japanese army than willingly enter into unequal treaties which would imperil our country and impair our sovereign rights. Why? Because wherever the Japanese

[1] On May 3, 1928, the Nationalist Army forces, commanded by Generalissimo Chiang Kai-shek, driving toward Peking on their triumphant Northern Expedition against the warlords, were blocked at Tsinan, the capital of Shantung Province, by Japanese troops illegally stationed there. The resultant clash, known as the Tsinan Incident, marked the beginning of Japan's open hostility toward a unified China.

[2] A Japanese term, literally "lawless men."

went, China's policing and economic rights were being destroyed. If Japanese nationals were given rights to reside and trade in certain areas, our people in those areas would lose their freedom, or even be forced to evacuate.

At that time, although the issue was limited to the Northeast, we refused; and now, when Konoye broadens the issue to include our entire sovereign territory, and does so under the slogan of a "new order in East Asia" should our people hesitate even a moment before saying no?

4. Konoye speaks of the "amalgamation of our two races." Friendly relations on the basis of equality and mutual respect are the road we seek. But Japan's idea of amalgamating, judged by many statements, is simply absorption of the Chinese by the Japanese and the destruction of our race. Japan's idea of cooperation is that we should be slaves, and give everything Japan demands from us. We cannot assent to such a policy of "amalgamation" and "cooperation."

These are the principal points in Konoye's statement. Konoye described them as "Japan's minimum demands." If these are the minimum demands I should like to know what more will be asked. They are many times more comprehensive and dangerous than Hirota's "three principles."[3] Our enemy hopes vainly that we may be inveigled into accepting them. But if we should not accept Hirota's "three principles" at the commencement of hostilities, how can we now accept these degrading terms?

Konoye's statement has completely bared the pernicious nature of Japan's designs for the destruction of her neighbor. Furthermore, the "Meiji Doctrine" and the contents of the "Tanaka Memorial," both of which the Japanese have tried vainly to deny, have all received confirmation. Tanaka said, "In order to conquer the world, we must first conquer China." If Japanese aggression is not defeated, it will

[3] Koki Hirota, Japanese Foreign Minister, advanced in January, 1936, the following "Three Principles" as those upon which Japan was determined to govern her relations with China: "(1) China must definitely abandon her policy of playing off one foreign nation against another, and must not attempt to check the influence of Japan by cooperation with Europe and America. Friendship with Japan should be exclusive of that with European and American Powers. (2) China must show her 'sincerity' toward Japan by a formal recognition of 'Manchukuo,' but as a preliminary step, she must at any rate respect its *de facto* existence. (3) China and Japan must agree upon one effective plan for anti-communist purposes. Inasmuch as the communist movement derives its origin from a 'certain' Power, it is absolutely necessary for China to come to an arrangement with Japan to prevent the spread of communism in China's northern frontier regions."

cease only when China is destroyed. Let all friendly nations take warning.

Japan's continental policy has now broadened into an oceanic policy. Besides advancing northward, Japan is now moving southward. She is pursuing simultaneously a policy of continental and maritime aggression. While attempting to annex China, Japan is also seeking to overthrow international order, dominate East Asia, and banish European and American influence. When that has been achieved, what Japan will do next is all too plain.

Japan has revealed the secret ambitions and designs which she labored hard to conceal during the last few decades. When we referred before to Japan's intentions, what we said was regarded by some people as a provocative exaggeration, for they thought that Japan could not entertain such wild plans. I now make bold to say that from now on neither China nor the world at large will be deceived regarding Japan's real intentions.

Judging by Konoye's statement, we are convinced that Japan's real desire is to annex our country and destroy, once and for all, our nation. Japan is not really interested in such things as the so-called "Sino-Japanese cooperation" or "economic collaboration." Compared with Japan's more comprehensive designs, cession of territory and payment of indemnities are of minor importance. By means of the so-called "economic bloc," Japan aims to absorb our resources and manage our finances, which would effectively take the place of "reparations." Japan demands the right to station Japanese troops in China and Inner Mongolia, and freedom to reside and trade in any part of China, because she prefers ruling over China's entire territory, oppressing and enslaving our people, to "cession of territory."

We well remember that before Korea was annexed by Japan, Korean nationals were treated with such hypnotic slogans as "Japan and Korea are one," and "Japan and Korea must not be separated." Today, Japan cries, "Japan, 'Manchukuo' and China must not be divided," and "East Asia must be a cooperating unit," which simply means the annexation of China. All the talk about a so-called "creation of a new order in East Asia" is a mere smoke-screen. It is truly a new invention of Imperial Japan for the destruction of another country and the extermination of its people.

Japan has made ready her plans and her methods to ruin China, and her aggressive intentions can no longer be concealed. What Japan lacks is a readiness on our part to be deceived or a willingness to fall into her trap. When the issues are so clear, we should be insane if we still sought safety under the jaws of the tiger, or looked for independence and equality by means of peaceful compromise. Once our spirit surrenders, we are forever doomed; and once we are chained, we shall never find release. I may also add that though Japan's malevolent intentions have only now been completely exposed, they have been brewing for generations in the minds of the Japanese militarists.

During the past decade, Japan's political leaders have passed away one after another, leaving not a single statesman who comprehends the high principles governing the rise and fall of nations. In consequence, Japanese militarists have without restraint violated laws and discipline and have taken things into their own hands. The greater Japan's national danger becomes, the more desperate and ambitious they become.

Fortunately, in July, 1937, our countrymen rose up to offer resistance, and thus frustrated Japan's hope that we might yield without a struggle. Furthermore, we forced the Japanese to reveal their real intentions until now the world sees clearly just what they are trying to do. If we had failed to resist and had allowed the enemy to nibble at our territory, our nation would, like a patient suffering from a malignant and incurable disease, gradually have worn away, have lost its senses, and have perished within three to five years. Look at Korea. While Japan pretended to maintain Korean independence, she yet used every direct and indirect device to dismember Korean territory. Unconsciously, Korea finally became a Japanese possession.

Through eighteen months of fighting, the national consciousness of our people has been heightened. Our unyielding stand and the gallant sacrifices made by more than a million of our men at the front and by millions of our people in the rear have compelled the enemy to take off their mask and reveal their vicious features. As a result China has escaped the peril of being annexed and destroyed, and at the same time the world has been forewarned that this insatiable nation, if allowed free rein, would endanger the peace of the whole world. It is true that we have made immense sacrifices, but in waging this war we have saved our nation from the brink of destruction and we are eliminating a future menace to the world. Our bitter sacrifices bear a profound significance. Our unwavering and unyielding spirit has already erected a strong bulwark for our national existence. Let us see this clearly and press on to complete fulfillment of our responsibilities.

The enemy desires to control our military affairs in the name of "joint defense against Communism;" he wishes to reduce our resources through the device of an "economic bloc," and he plans to direct our policies and our culture by "cooperation." To him the "unity of East Asia" means the ultimate extinction of our nation.

Speaking of culture, what independent culture is there in East Asia except that of China? The center of gravity of East Asia is in China. Speaking of economics, if China should lose her independence, what would be left of the present economic structure in East Asia? Speaking of politics, has not the traditional political thought of China, founded on neighborliness, loyalty, humanity, peacefulness and sincerity, been the central support of East Asia? Today the Three Principles of the People as bequeathed by our late Tsungli are the fundamental principles of equality, liberty, independence, and of corporate existence. They are also the safeguard of enduring peace.

For us, the year and a half of war has laid a solid foundation for national regeneration. We fear no difficulties, nor are we concerned over impending dangers. We merely lament the fate of Japan, whose present condition has come about in spite of the effort and sacrifices of her earlier reformist patriots. Today, her people are without power, her throne without authority, and her politicians without knowledge or integrity. A few hot-headed young militarists can do as they please. They are sapping Japan's national strength, shaking her national foundations, and advancing savagely on the road of self-seeking at the expense of others. In the eyes of these young militarists, China and the other countries of the world do not exist. They do as they please, guided by their own greed. If such conduct be allowed to continue, the future of Japan is indeed full of peril. Although we are sworn enemies of the Japanese militarists, we are still neighbors to the Japanese people, who share with us a language of common origin. Reviewing Japan's history and looking forward to her future, we see only danger in her path and are sad for her.

We should realize that the Japanese militarists are now heading blindly into a maze. They have forgotten their own history and their own position in the world. They neither see the world outside nor the crisis within. They do not recognize their neighbor, a revolutionary China. There are but two aspects to their thought. On the one hand, they are so blind to facts as to hope that China will accept their outrageous terms, and on the other hand they rely on their cunning to hoodwink the world. Because they themselves are stupid, they believe the people of the world can be fooled. Because they themselves are violent, they believe that force can dominate the world.

Konoye shows by his statement that he wants to close China's Open Door and scrap the Nine-Power Treaty by "establishing a new order in East Asia," to expel European and American influence from China by creating an "economic bloc" and the so-called "unity of East Asia," and to revive the Twenty-one Demands presented to Yuan Shih-kai [4] by "stationing troops in China" and "setting aside Inner Mongolia as a special area." Moreover, Japan intends to force China herself to close the Open Door and break the League Covenant and the Nine-Power Treaty. She wants us to follow in her footsteps and, by breaking faith and despising loyalty, to hasten her control of East Asia, after which she may realize her dream of world domination. Throughout five thousand years, China has always been guided by good faith and sincerity in her statecraft. Why should the threats of Japan make us abandon this stand?

China as a state is founded on the principle of not oppressing the defenseless and not fearing the aggressor. Here particularly, she is not willing to violate pacts, or, by breaking faith, to destroy the principles governing the relations of mankind. I remember the meeting of Tanaka and our late Tsungli in Shanghai in the third year of the Republic, at the time of the outbreak of the Great War in Europe. At that time Tanaka proposed that East Asiatic nations should denounce all treaty relations with foreign countries and "erect a new order in East Asia." Dr. Sun asked, "Would this not involve the breaking of international treaties?" To which Tanaka replied, "Would not the denunciation of international treaties and termination of unequal obligations be advantageous to China?" "Unequal treaties should be terminated by straightforward and legitimate procedure," solemnly declared Dr. Sun. "China is not prepared to become a party to illegal, though advantageous, denunciation of treaties." Comrades, this is China's spirit. It is also the spirit of the Three Principles of the People. We have depended on this spirit to resist invasion. Moreover, by this spirit we shall be sustained so that we may restore order in East Asia as our contribution towards enduring world peace.

To conclude, this war on the part of Japan is violent banditry brought about by the total collapse of morals and sound principles in that country. As far as China is concerned, we have courageously taken upon our shoulders the world responsibility of fighting for justice and righteousness. Of late, the Japanese militarists have lost their senses and are rapidly wrecking civilization and destroying the happiness of

[4] In 1915, taking advantage of the European War, Japan occupied parts of Shantung Province and, on May 7, 1915, presented to President Yuan Shih-kai the infamous Twenty-one Demands designed for effective and thoroughgoing encroachment on China's territorial and administrative integrity.

mankind. Nations of the world bound by treaty obligations should have acted promptly to maintain the sanctity of treaties and to apply punitive measures against the aggressor. But the nations looked on and hesitated. Unmindful of sacrifice, China took upon herself the immense responsibility of defending righteousness and justice.

Internally, our object in prosecuting this War of Resistance is to complete the task of national reconstruction and secure for China independence, liberty, and equality. Internationally, our object is to restore the prestige of treaties and to re-establish peace and order. This is a war between good and evil, between right and wrong. It is a war between justice and force, between a breaker of the law and a keeper of the law.

A Chinese proverb says, "Virtue never lacks company; it will ever find support." The force of world justice will rise, and men of goodwill will ultimately cooperate with one another. We should fix our eyes steadfastly on our goal and be firm in our determination. Our firmness should increase with our difficulties, and the longer our resistance the greater should be our courage. Let the entire nation carry on with a brave heart. I urge our comrades, our army, and our people to redouble their efforts in order that the final victory may be ours.

China Cannot Be Conquered

THIS assembly meets as we enter upon the second stage in our War of Resistance. It is, therefore, an especially significant session and lays heavy responsibilities upon us. As I have repeatedly pointed out, our war may be divided into two periods. During the first period, which ended with the fall of Canton and Wuhan, we tried to wear down the enemy's strength and, at the same time, to protect our rear so that solid foundations might be laid for the second period of protracted resistance. We had to prepare for the military strategy and political policy of the present stage.

Our present task is to build upon the accomplishments of the first stage, to carry out the plans we have formed for the second stage, and to concentrate our efforts upon victory and reconstruction. We are now turning defense into attack, and defeat into victory. What we now do will determine the survival or the ruin, the rise or the fall, of our nation. Our business at this momentous session is, therefore, to review the past and, facing the realities of the present, to fix our future course with courage and determination.

The morale of our army and of our people is higher than at any previous time. The situation within and without the country is increasingly favorable. Our fellow-countrymen believe that the nation has passed its most serious crisis. They are full of optimism and confident of victory. This means that our Party is charged with greater responsibilities and a more urgent mission than ever before. We must concern ourselves more earnestly with the nation's future, and seek out the very best courses to follow. All our actions must be measured by their revolutionary spirit. If we are filled with a revolutionary determination to resist, then ways and means can be found. Our revolution, advancing along the road of the Three Principles of the People, has proved that simplicity can overcome subtlety and that the ill-provided can defeat the well-supplied.

If we can fight on with the same spirit of sacrifice which we showed

A speech delivered on January 26, 1939, at the opening of the Fifth Plenary Session of the Central Executive Committee of the Kuomintang, held in Chungking.

in the first period of resistance and if we can bring our minds to bear upon the situation with even greater discernment, then there can be no doubt as to the issue of the struggle. Otherwise—if our actions fail to keep pace with our knowledge, if we exert ourselves but half-heartedly and fall by the way when but half the task is done, if we are concerned more with superficial forms than inner realities, if our hopes are not accompanied by definite plans, or if when we make plans we lack the courage to carry them out, if we constantly pass by good opportunities for action—no subsequent good fortune can possibly atone for our failures. Whether our cause succeeds or fails depends upon our revolutionary spirit, upon our resoluteness and our faith. Only with an inflexible purpose can we make effective plans and execute them in the face of seemingly insuperable obstacles and dangers. Therefore, the first thing I ask of you, my comrades, is an unshakable faith and an indomitable purpose. Such determination and faith are born only out of a sound knowledge and clear understanding of the aims of our resistance and of the whole war situation. Knowledge and understanding will give us a rationally informed, not merely impulsive, enthusiasm and will establish our faith upon a sure foundation.

We are fighting this war for our own national existence and for freedom to follow the course of national revolution laid down for us in the Three Principles of the People. We are fighting an enemy who would deny us not only our freedom but our very life, an enemy with whom we cannot compromise without bringing utter ruin upon our nation. Only resistance can preserve us from national slavery. Only resistance can save the world from the collapse of international morality and breakdown of all guarantees of peace. Dr. Sun Yat-sen devoted his life to the movement for the salvation of his country and at the same time of the world. All that he planned and achieved our enemy would throw to the winds. Since the Japanese Government and Premier Konoye issued their statement [in December, 1938] the world has clearly perceived Japan's ambition to monopolize the Pacific from the vantage point of a conquered China and eventually to dominate the world. But let me assure you, our enemy is even now defeated and will in the end be involved in absolute ruin. We have only to fight on and victory will certainly be ours. To the enemy, eighteen months of war have meant the loss on all battlefields of over 700,000 men and military expenditures of nine billion yen. His country is being impoverished, his agriculture and industrial development is being retarded, his social life is becoming corrupt, and his political stability is threatened by unrest. Since he launched his attack upon us, his military and political strategy, his ideas and calculations regarding us, his understanding of contemporary events have all been based on fundamentally false assumptions and consequently he has sunk deeper and deeper into error.

As we face the road leading to victory or defeat, national survival or death, I feel it my duty to put before the assembly a detailed statement, illustrated by facts, of the reasons why our enemy will surely be defeated. In the first place, as you all know, his present campaign of aggression is an attempt to carry out his long-cherished continental policy. According to this policy, he would gradually occupy all of China from the north southwards, and then from China as a base he would dominate the Orient and extend his control over the entire world. But his precipitate and premature invasion of China Proper ran directly counter to the prepared strategy of the Continental Plan. It not only placed him in a dilemma regarding future moves but has also forced him to show his hand in Central and South China. He came to a point where he could not advance further without arousing the enmity of other Powers. To military embarrassment was added diplomatic anxiety.

Secondly, his scheme for defeating us depended primarily upon our yielding without resistance. He did not expect us to fight as we have fought. As he pushed his way step by step inland his hopes of a short war and quick victory vanished and he sought instead an immediate peace.

Before we withdrew from Wuhan the enemy's press echoed loudly the wish of the Japanese Government to bring an end to hostilities or to bring about a truce. Meanwhile, the enemy tried all sorts of tricks to lure us into the trap and to deceive the world, and finally resorted to such ill-conceived schemes as the establishment of a so-called "Asia Development Bureau" and the promotion of so-called "collaboration in East Asia." But today not only our own people but the people of the whole world are fully aware of Japan's true motives. Herein lies Japan's second failure.

In the third place, Japan's military strategy has failed. Japan has not only gone contrary to three fundamental military principles but has also made three serious military blunders. (1) Without accurate appraisal of their own strength or of their opponent's strength, the Japanese did not dream that we could resist for eighteen months and still gain in strength. Nor did they calculate that after a certain stage Japan would have to forfeit five soldiers to China's one. (2) They have relied too much on good fortune to win, and have disregarded the fundamental principle that victory is achieved by swift and agile movement of troops. Internal political upheavals, the growth of anti-war feeling, and the collapse of

Konoye's boasted war cabinet prove the truth of Sun Tzu's famous saying, "A prolonged military campaign is disadvantageous to the state." [1] (3) The old caution against "massing a big force in the enemy's interior" was originally intended as advice to the stronger party, and yet the Japanese troops have advanced recklessly some hundreds of miles into China's hinterland. The occupied areas have become fields of activity for our regular and guerrilla forces. Subjected to repeated thrusts and harassing assaults, the Japanese forces find themselves in a position where advance and retreat are equally dangerous. They have become, in the words of Sun Tzu, "an army with fighting edge dulled by failing strength and exhaustion of supplies." They are face to face with the critical moment when, as the same writer puts it, "opponents are awaiting their collapse to attack them." The enemy is now "suspended in mid air," out of touch with both earth and sky. He has reached the point where "having failed to win he can hardly return." This state of affairs shows most clearly the failure of the Japanese military strategy.

Fourthly, Japan has failed politically. The Japanese have been able to utilize as puppets only rascals, outlaws, and other undesirable elements of the Chinese population. By so doing they simply corrupt their own army and expose their knavery and stupidity to the ridicule of the world. Not sensing their weakness they vainly seek to absorb China's ancient and independent civilization into their hodge-podge of a civilization. They have tried to possess themselves of our economic resources by military force and political aggression. The result, however, has been directly contrary to their expectations. They have failed to achieve their objective and have intensified rebellious sentiment at home.

Japan, while aiming to ease her diplomatic relations with Soviet Russia, has merely betrayed her own fears. Seeking to establish cordial understanding with the United States, she has succeeded only in arousing resentment. Aspiring to break the British, American, and French front, she has only contributed to its solidarity. Miscarriage of plans and inconsistency of action everywhere! If a course of action is wrong in its fundamental beginnings, what follows cannot but be wrong.

Fifthly, Japan has failed to realize the mighty power of our national resistance, the irresistible growth of our national spirit, and the true significance of our national history. The Japanese blindly hold that China can be tricked and subdued as she was by the Khitans and the Chin at the time of the Sung Dynasty, by the Mongols of the Yuan Dynasty,

[1] Sun Tzu, who lived during the stirring times of the Seven Warring Kingdoms (*circa* 350 B.C.), has ever since been regarded as China's master strategist. His book, *Military Strategy,* is studied in China's present-day military academies.

and by the Manchus of the Ch'ing Dynasty.[2] They do not understand the reasons for China's subjection in those times. They do not realize that it was the weakness of a few officials which brought about the submission of the government, a thing that should not be confused with the surrender of a whole nation. Today the Japanese cry, "Build a new order in East Asia," and expect in a short time to rule over all China. They forget that it has taken them more than forty years, a huge army, and vast expenditures to get even a tenuous hold upon our Northeastern Provinces. They refuse to take warning from past experiences, and now foolishly overstretch themselves to conquer the whole of China. Again they will fail.

Japan fails because she does not understand the characteristics of our race, the force of the Three Principles enunciated by Dr. Sun Yat-sen, the temper of our Government, the signs of the times, and China's revolutionary military strategy and tactics. When Napoleon was attacking Imperial Russia, the strategy of all-front and even prolonged resistance was not known. But even with his remarkable military genius and huge armies Napoleon was not able to avert defeat. How can Japan possibly succeed against republican China with its new and fervent national spirit? United against a common enemy and under the guidance of the National Government, our people have been able to carry out modern revolutionary military tactics, and no armed force can subdue us. Sun Tzu, in his treatise on topography, outlines the three military principles of knowing "where the enemy cannot be attacked, where one's own troops cannot attack, and upon what ground a battle cannot be fought." I would state Sun Tzu's principles thus, "Know where the enemy can be attacked, know where one's forces can attack, and know upon what ground a battle can be fought," and add, "Unless one knows the right time to attack it is useless to expect victory." Our enemy does not know whom he is attacking and he also does not know when to attack. For all these reasons Japan will unquestionably fail to conquer China.

In the first period of the war, when battles were being fought in areas with good communications, the Japanese were able to make full use of their land, sea, and air forces, and mechanized units. And yet after eighteen months our enemy has utterly failed to subdue us while we have gained in experience and strength. From now on, in the second period of resistance, when the war is carried into difficult terrain, the enemy is bound to face increasing military hardships in maintaining communications and in securing food supplies.

[2] Sung (960-1276), known as Southern Sung from 1127 onward, with North China under foreign rule; Yuan (1277-1367); Ch'ing (1644-1911).

74

Furthermore, it is well-known that Japan has already sent to China eighty-five per cent of her total army strength. Originally, Japan intended to use thirty per cent of her army against China and keep the other seventy per cent in reserve in case of war against Soviet Russia. Not only has Japan used more than twice the force originally set aside against China, but the casualties sustained by her invading forces have exceeded thirty per cent of her total military strength. Comparing our position from now on with that of the enemy, I may say that, in view of the experience we have gained in the past eighteen months, Japan will need to use at least three men in the field to our one, and spend at least three rounds of ammunition to our one. Therefore, if we do not provide the enemy with an opportunity whereby he may take advantage of us, our final victory is assured.

How would we give the enemy an opportunity? By allowing our spirit to be cowed, by letting our resolution be shaken, by yielding of our own will, or by seeking a hurried compromise. The enemy hopes desperately that we will do these things and give him a chance to escape from an otherwise inextricable position. Hence, if we prolong our resistance we are bound to win; but if we weaken and compromise, then the enemy is certain to take full advantage of our position and impose upon us the most humiliating terms. If we should reach that stage our nation would, under the "new order in East Asia," simply cease to exist and we should all become slaves.

From what I have said you can clearly see how Japan has worked her own ruin and has sealed her own doom. If Japan should emerge victorious in the present hostilities, then all existing military theories and principles of military strategy would be disproved. I will go further and say that all scientific theories and fundamental principles of cause and effect would be proven wrong. Knowing that the enemy will try every possible method to coerce and allure us into submission, we must be more strongly fixed than ever in our determination to resist. We must allow the enemy neither to overawe our spirit nor to deceive us by his cunning. We must fight to the end not only to upset the enemy's plan of a quick victory but also to prevent him from gaining a premature peace. This is now our only strategy; and it is the key to our victory and to Japan's defeat.

Comrades, after eighteen months as the responsible Commander-in-Chief of our fighting forces, I have reached the following solemn conclusion. I commend it to your special consideration. You should instruct our people to take lessons from the annals of the Sung and Ming Dynasties. The fall of these two dynasties was not caused by outside enemies with a superior force, but by a dispirited and cowardly minority in the governing class and the society of the time. Today the morale of our people is excellent; the foundation of our revolution is deep and strong; and the Three Principles of the People give us a charter of liberty in harmony with the spirit of the modern age. If we do not destroy ourselves, no outside force can destroy us.

The situation that faces us is plain. Our enemy is bound to marshal all his offensive resources in another desperate attempt at victory. Our policy is simple and clear. Since the beginning of the second period of resistance we have been using revolutionary strategy and tactics to weaken the morale of the enemy and exhaust his strength and so to hasten his final collapse.

I wish to add another word of warning. To seek compromise and peace now is equivalent to entering a trap or committing suicide. We should realize that what ex-Premier Konoye proposed on December 22, under the guise of adjusting international relations in the Far East, was not terms for discussing an equitable peace but merely a piece of verbal trickery designed to bring about our submission. To discuss peace on those terms is tantamount to surrender. We have fought for more than a year and a half; but although sacrifices have been immense, our strength increases with the progress of the war. We can take only one road now: to be worthy of our ancestors and parents, to be worthy of our heroes and martyrs in this war, to be worthy of our descendants, to be worthy of ourselves, we must set our faces resolutely against any form of surrender. We must fight on until we reach our goal. To submit is to court death while we live. To fight is to find life even though we die.

It is certain that our enemy will fail. It is just as certain that we shall succeed. Sun Tzu says, "In the beginning make it impossible for the enemy to win and then await the time for the enemy to be defeated." To keep the enemy from winning we must, of course, shed our blood and exert ourselves to the utmost. Judging from our history, geography, civilization, economics, and national spirit, as well as the facts of the recent past, I dare to declare that our enemy has no way of overcoming us. If we combine strenuous human effort with our national advantages there is no doubt that we can defeat the invaders.

Speaking of history, I have already said that the downfall of the Sung and Ming Dynasties was that of the ruling families and not the extinction of the entire Chinese race. In more than five thousand years our race has never been really conquered and has most certainly never been exterminated. Furthermore, the dynastic downfalls were due to the cowardice, ignorance, lack of integrity, and selfishness of a small number of corrupt officials. The happiness and welfare of the common people did not concern them. During those despotic regimes a great gap existed between the government authorities and the common people. There were no ways by which the authorities could mobilize the power of resistance residing in the people. Yet, as a matter of fact, the spirit of the nation as a whole did not suffer from outside oppression and the people steadily opposed aggression. After an interval of two or three hundred years, the aggressors would be driven out and the nation's territory would be recovered.

Our present Government, which is republican in form and revolutionary in spirit and which fights for the welfare of the nation and the people, has a far greater chance of expelling the invader. Our Government is fully aware of its responsibilities and intends to complete the revolution and carry out the Three Principles of the People. It has no fear of bullying aggressors. Our resistance is a united effort of Government and people. Sun Tzu says, "A virtuous government has the support of the people; it can command life or death from the people without exciting fear or complaint." Concord between Government and people is the first essential to victory.

In our present struggle against Japan we have been able to live up to this high principle. The hearts of our people are absolutely united. Under the guidance of the Government even the old and the weak, the women and children, are conscious of the necessity of defending themselves against the enemy and of obeying implicitly the orders of the High Command. Indeed, their spirit is such that they are willing to lay down their lives without a murmur. No one will barter his national birthright for slavery to Japan. The barbarism of the Japanese has everywhere aroused the spirit voiced in our ancient saying, "Prefer death to disgrace." Judging from the history of the past and the national consciousness and strong morale of our people today, China cannot be conquered.

From the geographical point of view, our country possesses natural advantages for defense. Our ancestors, two thousand years ago, took advantage of the mountainous terrain in constructing the Great Wall. From east to west our country extends through more than sixty-five degrees of longitude. From north to south it includes the climates of the frigid, temperate, and torrid zones. In any discussion of military success or failure we have always considered topography and climate of great importance. Rivers, mountains, and deserts abound in our interior and in the west; arctic cold alternates with tropical heat. Invaders in the past have succeeded only in holding a part of our country for a limited time.

They have never permanently controlled the whole of our country for a long time. Even in the Yuan and Ch'ing Dynasties, when the strongest forces attempted to conquer us, they were able to occupy only certain strategic points and the spirit of resistance among the people was not crushed. Today a nation of only 70,000,000 people thinks it can absorb a nation with six times its population and with a far older history and civilization. What a mad dream! Topography and climate are again combining against China's invaders. No weapon in the world will be effective against this combination, reinforced by the firm determination and mighty strength of our people. Geographically, our country cannot be conquered.

China is the only nation in the Far East with an independent cultural achievement. This is borne out by history. Chinese civilization has been adopted by other peoples, but no alien civilization has ever succeeded in replacing China's own. China's civilization is imbued with a peculiar spirit. I need not amplify this point. It is only necessary to recall the heroic behavior of our people in face of the enemy to realize the deep roots of our civilization. Japan is now trying with her mongrel civilization of neither the East nor the West, to destroy our racial spirit. But she has met with repeated failures in the occupied areas. If we are united at heart, and if we struggle with determination, the spirit of our people will be further strengthened. This resistance will infuse into our civilization a new splendor and power. Our civilization and our racial spirit can never be conquered or destroyed.

Economically we have the advantage. Modern wars usually arise out of economic conflicts and the outcome is determined by the economic strength and resources of the belligerents. China is essentially an agricultural country. Aggression descended upon us while we were in the period of national reconstruction. At first this seemed a major crisis, yet during the eighteen months of hostilities our financial structure has not been seriously injured, our currency has remained steady, and the livelihood of the people in the rear has been little affected. Owing to the excellent harvests in several provinces last year and the campaign of thrift, there are signs of plenty among our people. This is possible because we are an agricultural nation and strong in endurance, whereas industrial nations suffer more quickly from the consequences of war.

I am confident that our wartime economy will encounter no serious difficulty in this second period of our resistance. In the Southwest and Northwest, bases of our resistance, we are rapidly introducing national defense industries and light industries, and are developing our mineral and lumber resources. We are mobilizing the nation's technical skill and capital, and are laying a sound and permanent foundation for our national economic life. Neither our military forces nor our people will be in want. Our enemy has not reckoned with our endurance as an agricultural nation, which will be a prime factor contributing to his defeat. Economically, China is capable of protracted resistance and cannot be conquered.

In prosecuting a modern war, it is essential not only to have a thorough knowledge of the enemy and of oneself, but also to understand the trend of international developments. Our enemy has failed to realize not only his own weakness and China's strength but also the current international situation.

The international situation during the past year has been fraught with grave dangers, but the main undercurrent has been in the direction of maintaining international obligations and world peace. Although the influential democratic states of Europe and America have been exceedingly cautious in dealing with the changing situation, their peoples have become steadily bolder in denouncing aggression and advocating justice. Their statesmen are doing all within their power to ease the international situation, while at the same time they are strengthening their national defenses. From all angles we can see that they are resolved to check aggression and maintain world peace. Signs of such a policy are even more apparent of late.

Since the invasion of Manchuria in 1931 we have seen clearly that the only road upon which all mankind can march together is the road of justice and righteousness. A nation that aspires to become strong and independent cannot allow itself to be checked by temporary hardships and sacrifices. In the course of time it is bound to earn the sympathy and cooperation of other just nations. The international developments of the past seven years have fully borne out our judgment. We claim no prescience; we have only maintained the position held by our revolutionary leader, Dr. Sun Yat-sen: to save our country is also to save the world. Our judgment has been guided by principle.

Dr. Sun often said that after China had recovered her independent national status she would have a large responsibility to the world. In his addresses on Nationalism and on other occasions, Dr. Sun frequently declared, "China is the pillar of the Far East and the largest country in Asia; when China is strong, her four neighbors will be safe and on cordial terms with each other, and the surrounding races can retain their independence and share peace and happiness." Dr. Sun pointed out also that "China has never attempted by economic weapons to oppress other races . . . China's aspirations for peace were fully evolved even at

79

the time of the Han Dynasty." [3] We do not oppress the weak and we do not bow before tyranny. We favor mutual assistance and we seek to strengthen ourselves. Dr. Sun further observed, "China had been strong for several thousand years without affecting the existence of Korea; but Korea was annexed after Japan had been strong for only twenty years." China's traditional policy has been to aid the weak and to support the falling, to live and to let live. Our national revolution is reinforcing our own historic love of justice and peace and is hastening the advent of enduring security and happiness for all mankind.

At the conclusion of the World War Dr. Sun Yat-sen wrote his *Program of National Reconstruction* with a view to modernizing China's productive enterprises. He had in view also the provision of a good outlet for the world's capital, machinery, and technical skill so that mankind might not degenerate into another bitter strife over raw materials and markets. Alas, this noble plan of helping ourselves and the world could not be carried out. Taking advantage of tension in Europe, Japan intensified her aggression on China. After the Manchurian crisis we were patient because we desired peace, but the enemy persisted in aggression. He did not know that we were coming into a day of self-determination and self-government for all peoples. Smaller peoples and weaker races were seeking independence and the Great Powers were beginning to change their attitudes and policies. Yet Japan continued to think that she could conquer China. After the Tangku Truce our national life was already at low ebb, but Japan kept on striking. She created incidents and finally occupied Peiping and Tientsin. Not allowed to preserve even the minimum requirements of national life, we saw that it was futile to seek existence under conditions which would mean death and extinction. There was no choice for us but to fight for life.

It was said of old that when two armies meet, the army more gravely concerned will win. When our resistance was launched there was no other alternative before us. Our people as well as our soldiers were inspired by anguish and indignation. Never before in the world's history has an army been made up of such indignant and determined soldiers. Our armed resistance was launched not only to safeguard our own national existence, but also to maintain world peace and international good faith. Our war is in every sense a "righteous war," while the aggressive campaign of our enemy is nothing but a "war of outrage."

We saw clearly when we began our resistance that our sacrifices and hardships might be even tenfold or a hundredfold greater than what we

[3] 206 B.C.-A.D. 219.

had yet undergone. But now that we have taken this sacred duty upon our shoulders, we must, no matter what the cost, complete our task of national revolution, check the evil forces of aggression, and restore the efficacy of international commitments. To strengthen the cause of justice and righteousness in the world we must demonstrate that brute force and violence do not avail: By our resistance we can help to change the war mind of mankind and to ensure permanent peace for the world of tomorrow.

Comrades, you must know that before our resistance began our country was regarded by the world as weaker than a third-rate Power. Nevertheless, we have succeeded in holding Japan, a first-class Power, for more than a year and a half without being overcome. We must be ready to encounter more difficulties but we need no longer be frightened by our brutal enemy. Having entered this second period of resistance we believe that the military operations will daily turn in our favor. The only question is whether we have the strength of will to continue resistance, and whether our unity and determination will increase with every day of the struggle.

Comrades, from what I have said you will realize our own power. You will recognize the enemy's military strategy and political policy. You will understand the other factors at work in the changing situation. You will appreciate the reasons that determine success or failure. Courage is born of wisdom. If we see clearly the meaning and purpose of our struggle we will have a faith and courage that cannot be vanquished.

The war has now entered its second phase. There is no use denying the fact that we have lost much territory and most of our communication lines. We have sacrificed heavily the lives and wealth of our fellow-countrymen, and have abandoned vast material properties and resources. But we should realize that any revolutionary work must begin from the ground up. From now on we should base our calculations on the land, the man-power, the military strength, and the financial spirit that stirred our revolutionary forbears to combat alien rule with little more than their bare hands. Let us learn to plan from small, lowly and hard beginnings and, having made our plans, to carry them out in full, giving to the task our whole time and strength and our very life blood.

Our enemy is now saying that the present conflict may become another Hundred Years' War. We maintain that resistance and national reconstruction have no time limit. If we do not succeed in five years, we shall go on for ten years, or even a hundred years. We shall not stop until our objective is achieved.

We must now direct our efforts in line with our understanding of the

81

enemy's situation. Our enemy today is in the state of approaching collapse described by Sun Tzu "when the people disregard the anger of their authorities, when soldiers fight among themselves in front of their foes, and when all are losing confidence in their own strength." Knowing this we should reinforce our own unity and concentrate our own efforts to take advantage of the enemy's confusion. We know that during the hostilities many of Japan's industries have been rendered inactive and that the weaknesses in Japan's economic structure have daily become more apparent. We should call upon our peculiar strength as an agricultural country and, by our own thrift, industry, and ability to endure hardship, aggravate Japan's weakness.

As an industrial nation, we are aware too that Japan's main object is to destroy our national economic foundation. Hence, we should strengthen our constructive wartime enterprises, building up our own strength for long-term resistance and hastening the break-up of Japan's social order. The people of Japan, who have been driven by their rulers to war, are also experiencing other trials. Since last year Japan has been afflicted by many kinds of natural disasters, such as storms and earthquakes. Let us make the best use of all the natural advantages of soil and climate that have been given to us, let us increase our own agricultural production, and let us not bring upon our people any unnecessary hardships such as the people of Japan are forced to bear. The Japanese people are suffering more and more and anti-war feeling is rising rapidly. Let us earnestly endeavor to carry out the Three Principles of the People and in this way show our superiority to the enemy country which disregards the sufferings of its own people as well as of other peoples. With spiritual force we can overcome material forces; with industry we can remedy our lack of supplies; with redoubled efforts we can make up for our past mistakes; with firm determination and confidence in victory we can offset our shortage of modern armaments.

These are heavy responsibilities to the nation and towards the Revolution which we, members of the Kuomintang, must recognize and assume. It has not been an easy thing for us to gather here in the tense atmosphere of war. We should therefore make the very best use of our time. We should formulate and define the policy and program for the second period of resistance. Before the picture here of our revolutionary leader, Dr. Sun Yat-sen, let us make a solemn pledge that we will do our duty, fight to the end, abide by the Party's decisions, observe Party discipline, strengthen the Party's foundations, and carry out the Party's mission. Let us not worry about the difficulties of resistance, but let us examine ourselves again and again to see whether or not we are fully discharging our responsibilities.

Never has an independent and strong revolutionary party failed to accomplish its object. Never have a people with a long history, great territory, large population, and advanced culture failed to achieve independence, equality, and freedom.

Remember, "To know is difficult, but when we know, to act is easy." Remember that we can save our nation only by our own efforts. If we can act, and act quickly, bravely, forcefully, and effectively, then nothing can prevent our final success. Today, I earnestly and sincerely wish this assembly a successful session and the accomplishment of our great revolutionary task of resistance and national reconstruction.

China's March Toward Democracy

THE Third Session of the People's Political Council and its proceedings have attracted wide attention both in China and abroad. During these ten days we have deliberated together with eager enthusiasm on important policies of the State. I am grateful for the approval you have given to the hopes which I expressed at the opening meeting. My own faith in our ultimate victory and in the future of our nation has been greatly strengthened by the remarkable spirit of unity and cooperation manifested in these meetings.

During this session responsible officials of the Central Government have won our confidence by their frank and full reports on the work and problems of administration. In our debates upon various resolutions and recommendations, we have given special attention to the pressing needs of the hour and we have concentrated our thoughts and energies upon a number of concrete and constructive wartime measures. The resolutions passed, while not numerous, are to the point and useful. The reports by many members of the Council upon their actual war experiences, describing their joys as well as their hardships, and offering various sound and practical suggestions, will undoubtedly be of great help to the Government in carrying out its program. With the Government and the people constantly exchanging their views and sharing difficulties, we may be confident of success in our heavy task of war and reconstruction.

Though the Council will soon be in recess, its members will not for a moment cease their patriotic activities. I am sure that if the Council continues to display its spirit of positive action and of mutual help, not only will the Government be benefited but the people also will be inspired to give everything to the struggle. Our power to conquer the enemy and to secure final victory will be enlarged and a strong foundation for post-war reconstruction will be laid.

This Council will occupy, in the future history of Chinese political institutions, an illustrious place. As I said at the First Session the mis-

An address to the Third Session of the People's Political Council held in Chungking on its closing day, February 21, 1939.

sion of the Council is to pave the way for a constitutional form of government, and to lay the foundations for a genuine democracy. When Dr. Sun Yat-sen advocated the *San Min Chu I* he made democracy the final aim of his *Min Chuan Chu I* [Principle of the People's Sovereignty]. If a people cannot look after their own interests, manage their own public affairs, and take an active part in the government, they cannot build up a strong nation. The most powerful and at the same time most stable nations in the world are founded on the will of the people, and the interests and policies of the government are identical with those of the people. The object of Dr. Sun's Principle of the People's Sovereignty is to create a nation in which the government is "of the people, by the people, and for the people."

We are now prosecuting the war and at the same time carrying on reconstruction. To be successful in both, we cannot rely on military strength alone. We must mobilize the spirit of the whole nation and organize the spiritual forces that are awakened. We must transform the will of our people into a powerful weapon for our men at the front, and into a dynamic force for the development of our great hinterland. Besides strengthening our military forces, we must mobilize the spirit of our people and unify their will.

The Kuomintang convoked the People's Council last year with the hope that the Council would facilitate the expression of genuine public opinion and give the Government guidance in its policy by making known to it the sufferings and aspirations of the people. There was also the hope that the members of the Council would truly represent the people and would contribute their abilities and their experience to the service of the Government. If this is done, the Government will be able to satisfy the people and the words and actions of the people will strengthen the Government. Government and people will share the glory that comes with success or the humiliation that comes with failure. When the Government and the people become one in spirit and purpose, new strength will be added to our resistance and greater achievement will reward our efforts at reconstruction.

True, it is our duty as members of the Council to fight for national independence and freedom, but upon us also depends whether China can, during this difficult time of war, complete the pattern of a genuine democracy and lay a foundation for lasting peace and order. How are we to discharge our responsibility in this connection? As a member of this Council, I wish to consider with you the nature of the genuine democracy which we desire for China, and the steps we must take to achieve it.

Dr. Sun Yat-sen was well acquainted with both Chinese and Western scholarship. He had a thorough knowledge of world movements and of conditions in China. Out of his forty years' experience as a revolutionary leader he formulated the Three Principles of the People, believing that the application of these principles would make a prosperous, powerful, peaceful, and happy country. Dr. Sun's hope was to bring about a democracy which would be more thoroughgoing and more practical than other democracies. In his lectures on the Principle of the People's Sovereignty, he criticized the theory of natural rights and started a revolutionary school of thought concerning people's rights. Furthermore, he wanted the Chinese people to exercise fully the direct political rights of election, recall, initiative, and referendum. But he was more than an idealist; he was also a practical revolutionist. The higher his ideals soared, the surer became his steps. He maintained that the people must practise revolutionary principles and fulfill their revolutionary responsibilities before they could be given elementary political rights. He also held the view that the people must be trained before they could exercise the more advanced rights of election, recall, initiative, and referendum.

Dr. Sun wished to establish a true democracy without any make-believe or artificiality. Unfortunately the Chinese people had inherited all kinds of evil practices from many dynasties of rule, and were at a low ebb of intelligence and vitality. The people were habitually disorganized and selfish. Serious obstacles to internal progress existed. To bridge the chasm between such a historical background and the ideal of democracy meant strenuous toil in the face of great difficulties. Certainly the goal could not be reached at a single stride. Consequently, Dr. Sun declared that China's revolution must pass through the stages of military rule, political tutelage, and constitutional government before it would be complete.

Accordingly, the National Government proceeded first to unify the country. Then followed the period of political tutelage. It was originally hoped that this would hasten the realization of constitutional government and the completion of the national revolution. Unfortunately, soon after internal unity had been achieved, new difficulties arose. For five or six years the Government had to devote a large part of the manpower and financial resources of the nation to operations which should have fallen within the period of military rule. Scarcely had we gained our second wind before Japan began her long-premeditated attack upon us, every day striking deeper into the heart of our country. To protect our sovereign rights and to preserve our national existence we were forced to resist. For nineteen months now we have engaged in bitter war. Our losses in territory occupied by the enemy and in lives and property sacrificed by our people cannot possibly be measured by numbers alone.

Judging by present conditions, not only has our program for the period of political tutelage received a serious setback, but much of the work of the period of military rule has to be done all over again. We must first of all crush the aggressor's military force, destroy all traitors and puppets, and eradicate all influences harmful to our nation and antagonistic to our revolutionary cause. We must recover our lost territories and clear up our internal situation before we can really talk about political tutelage and constitutional government. Strictly speaking, we are still in the period of military government. According to Article Six in the *Outlines of National Reconstruction,* the main tasks of this period are as follows: "All organizations must be under military control. The Government should on the one hand employ military force to clear the country of all internal obstacles, and on the other it should propagate its principles (i.e., The Three Principles of the People) for the enlightenment of the masses."

As I have frequently said, the most urgent task before us now is the defense and rebuilding of our nation. We must unify the thinking of the people and call forth all their powers for the completion of this twofold task. During the war we should strengthen the people's sense of responsibility toward the State and their understanding of the Three Principles. Although we are in another period of military government when obstacles to our national independence are being removed, yet political tutelage should still be carried on.

The training of the people in government is essential to the early completion of our national task; only we must not let it interfere with our military activities during the war. On the contrary, we should use the program of political training as an aid in prosecuting the war. Until the war is over military affairs must receive first consideration and military victory must be our primary objective. Political training is important but secondary. For the present, the winning of the war must be central in all our thinking and planning. Since we aim to build a strong and genuine democracy, we must not neglect the procedures and steps necessary for its realization. Before the coming of real democracy our people, who for thousands of years have been accustomed to autocracy, must be given the right psychological preparation and must be thoroughly trained in the process of self-government.

Besides dividing the process of revolution into three stages, Dr. Sun

Yat-sen also gave us this grave warning, "Within a few months after the outbreak of the Revolution of 1911 there came about the downfall of an autocratic form of government more than four thousand years old, and simultaneously the overthrow of the Manchus who had been the rulers of China for over two hundred and sixty years. No one can deny the tremendous destructive power of the revolution. Yet up to the present the realization of the *San Min Chu I* has been as uncertain and remote as ever. Why? Because after the destruction we failed to rebuild in accordance with the program that previously had been decided upon."

At that time people made the mistake of neglecting the steps necessary for achieving democracy; instead, they simply vied with one another in talking about democracy. That is why the provisional constitution then adopted degenerated into a mere scrap of paper. Disorders and disasters followed one another in a vicious circle. The supreme laws of the State were manipulated by the politicians and warlords so as to cover up their own evil doings. In the name of democracy numerous barriers to democracy were set up and untold sins against democracy were committed. The resulting situation could best be described in the famous words of Mme. Roland during the French Revolution, "O Liberty! Liberty! how many crimes are committed in thy name!"

In order not to repeat this mistake, we must start from the very beginning, and seek genuine liberty for our nation and people. Since the formation of this Council, its members have willingly sacrificed their individual freedom and personal preferences in order to lay a foundation for democratic government. This is the most gratifying thing that has happened during the war and, for that matter, since China became a republic in 1911. I feel confident that in the future we shall follow more closely the teachings which Dr. Sun Yat-sen bequeathed to us and shall earnestly promote the program of political training. We must set an example for the people by displaying a high sense of responsibility and by actual accomplishments, and avoid the pitfall of irresponsible and unrealistic thinking and behavior. We must make it clear to our people that democracy is not a synonym for lack of law, nor order a synonym for anarchy.

Democracy must be based on a sound and collective public opinion which truly represents the will of the majority. The freedom with which democracy endows the people must not be in conflict with public welfare, nor must it go beyond the limits marked by the laws of the State. With our nation facing the most severe crisis in its history, we must teach the people to respect the power and authority of the State. The State is the enforcer of laws, and the guardian of the nation's welfare. In order to protect the interests of the people and the welfare of the nation, the State must punish those who violate its laws and destroy its political institutions. Sanctions applied in accordance with the law should not be mistaken for oppression. In all democratic countries there are governments, political institutions, and laws. The latter two especially must be respected by the people and their destruction by a few must never be tolerated.

In order to lay a foundation for democracy during this war we must inform the people of the real meaning of democracy. We members of the Council are the leaders of the people. It is our duty to train the people and to protect their interests. We must fully exercise the authority of just public opinion against all those who in the name of freedom or democracy violate the laws and institutions of the State and weaken our power of resistance. Hypocrites and obstructionists have no place among us. Our people must realize that military government is essential to the prosecution of our war and that political tutelage is a prerequisite to national rebuilding. A lasting foundation for genuine democracy can be laid only if we follow the plan outlined for us by our late leader, Dr. Sun Yat-sen.

The entire aim of Dr. Sun's life and struggle was to carry out the Three Principles and to restore the government to the people. But a people without training in government cannot govern. Therefore Dr. Sun called upon the intellectuals of the nation and his comrades of the revolution to become guardians of the people, and as public servants to teach and guide the people. This is the road we must take in rebuilding our nation.

In Chinese history there are two good examples of political tutelage: Premier Yi Yin and King Tai Chia of the Shang Dynasty, and Duke Chou and King Cheng of the Chou Dynasty.[1] King Tai Chia was a minor when he came to the throne; so Premier Yi Yin took upon himself the task of teaching and guiding the youthful monarch. His counsels were later compiled in an essay named after himself. It happened that King Tai Chia at first did not heed his advice but became addicted to evil habits. Premier Yi Yin thereupon sent the King to the Tung Palace and had him kept there. In spite of suspicion and slander Premier Yi Yin ruled the Kingdom as regent and at the same time used all possible means to teach and guide the wayward monarch. The three

[1] Shang (1783-1123 B.C.) ; Chou (1122-222 B.C.).

89

chapters about Yi Yin in the History of the Shang Dynasty form a lasting testimony to his love for the nation and his loyalty to the throne. Later, when King Tai Chia repented of his wrongdoings and learned the meaning of responsibility and acquired the necessary abilities for administration, Premier Yi Yin turned over to him the reins of government and himself retired from political life. When he left he presented the King with an essay embodying his views on public administration.

In the other case, Duke Chou was entrusted by Emperor Wu with the responsibility of helping the Crown Prince. At the time of his father's death, King Cheng was young and his power of moral judgment was still undeveloped. Duke Chou had to take measures against Wu Keng's revolt and at the same time bear with the mischievous rumors circulated against him by Kuan and Tsai, two uncles of King Cheng. Duke Chou's position was extremely difficult, but he carried on in spite of untold hardships and humiliations. Not a moment did he shirk his heavy responsibility for establishing peace and order in the Kingdom and for helping and teaching King Cheng until he himself could rule. The four verses in the *Book of Odes* [2] which describe in metaphorical language Duke Chou's love for the nation and his loyalty to the King still inspire all who read them:

> Owl, O owl, hear my request,
> And do not, owl, destroy my nest,
>   You have taken my young,
>   Though I over them hung,
> With the nursing of love and of care.
> Pity me, pity me! Hear my prayer.
>
> Ere the clouds the sky had obscured,
> The mulberry roots I secured.
>   Door and window around,
>   Them so firmly I bound,
> That I said, casting downward my eyes,
> "Dare any of you my house despise?"

[2] The *She King*, Part I, Bk. XV, Ode V, translated by James Legge. Duke Chou describes himself as a bird whose young ones have been destroyed by an owl. He justifies the severe measures taken against the rebels among whom were his own brothers. In spite of revolts against the throne and rumors accusing him of disloyalty to the young king, his nephew, Duke Chou did not falter. He defended the dynasty at the risk of his own life and has been honored ever since in history and song.

I tugged with my claws and I tore,
And my mouth and my claws were sore.
　　So the rushes I sought
　　And all other things brought;
For to perfect the house I was bent,
And I grudged no toil with this intent.

My wings are deplorably torn,
And my tail is much injured and worn.
　　Tossed about by the wind
　　While the rain beats unkind,
Oh! my house is in peril of harm,
And this note I scream out in alarm.

Later, when all uprisings in the Kingdom had been quelled and when King Cheng had come of age, Duke Chou like Premier Yi Yin restored to his master the reins of government. Then, as if still not fully satisfied, Duke Chou recorded his precepts in an essay entitled *No Leisure,* to remind King Cheng of the hardships which his ancestors had experienced in founding the Kingdom and of the need for constant vigilance in the performance of duty.

We are passing through an unprecedented national crisis. We are far from completing our task of national reconstruction. How can we fail to share the deep feelings which moved Duke Chou?

Dr. Sun Yat-sen, the great pioneer of our national revolution, often likened himself to Premier Yi Yin and Duke Chou. He advocated the division of our revolution into three periods—military rule, political tutelage, and constitutional government—because he wanted to train the people before giving them the right of self-government. In the light of history how great was our late Leader's wisdom and sense of responsibility!

In an essay, *Singleness of Virtues,* Premier Yi Yin said, "It is not that Heaven has any particular love for the Shang Dynasty, but Heaven treasures the singleness of the virtues Shang stands for; it is not that the Shang Government seeks the support of the people, but the people are won to Shang by its singleness of virtues." Since the overthrow of autocratic rule the Republic of China has also had "singleness of virtues" to guide the nation. This is none other than the Three Principles of the People. Our responsibility today is to carry on the work left to us by our revolutionary leader, Dr. Sun Yat-sen, as well as to emulate the spirit of Premier Yi Yin and Duke Chou. We must put the *San Min Chu I* into actual practice so that the entire nation may be influenced by it. This and the building of a solid foundation for democracy are heavy responsibilities which the members of this Council must assume. We are leaders of society and of the people and we must set a good example.

It is our duty to educate the people and to help them understand what their responsibility is and how they can fulfill it. We are the Premier Yi Yins and the Duke Chous of today and the people are the King Tai Chias and the King Chengs. We must look upon the people as our masters, and teach, train and protect them until they are mature and governing powers can be returned to them. When the people are ready to assume full responsibility, then democratic government will be established.

To carry out our mission we members of the Council must bear ourselves in an exemplary manner both inside and out of the conference room. We must obey laws and orders, observe strict discipline, and perform all our duties faithfully. The ancients said, "If a man is upright he will be obeyed without orders." And again, "One who teaches others by his own example has many followers." If we are to be examples to the people, we must practice what we preach, and observe strict discipline. We must be responsible to the nation and the people in all we say, and all of our actions must conform to law and order. Then the people will naturally accept our guidance, and with training and inspiration will be prepared to build up a real democracy.

Whether democracy can be established in China depends entirely upon us in this Council. The ultimate aim of the *San Min Chu I*—universal brotherhood and the ideal world described in the *Book of Rites*—cannot be achieved without earnest and united effort.

The three things which the Fifth Plenary Session of the Central Executive Committee of the Kuomintang asked of the nation—the strengthening of our national unity, the intensification of our struggle against Japan, and the speeding up of our reconstruction program—have been crystallized in the resolutions adopted by this session. Now the members of the Council should publicize these resolutions and lead the way in putting them into effect.

This Council is not an ordinary peacetime legislative assembly but a body of men and women who have struggled and suffered together and who have gathered for conference here under extraordinary circumstances to give guidance to the nation. This Council is not only a place where public opinion can be expressed but also a place where the power of public opinion can be centralized.

After returning to our various places of work let us all, in accordance with the resolutions of this session, help to raise the national morale and to revive the traditional virtues of our people. Let each one work hard at his post and help to put into execution the resolutions adopted by this session: the revision of the conscription system, the enforcement of spiritual mobilization, the expediting of economic reconstruction, and the reform of the *pao chia* system.

If we strive hard we cannot fail to have results, and our Government, our nation, and our people will all be richly benefited.

As this session comes to a close and I think of the arduous labors that lie ahead of you, I am still full of hope and confidence. You are like people in the same boat in time of storm. I believe you will not fail to bring the ship safely to port.

Spiritual Mobilization and Victory

BEGINNING from May 1, the entire nation is to observe in full the Outline for National Spiritual Mobilization and the Measures for its Enforcement promulgated by the Supreme National Defense Council on March 12.

The very existence of our state and the fate of our nation depend upon this mobilization of our spiritual resources. I urge all citizens and especially all public leaders to promote this movement with all their strength and spirit.

Why must we strive to bring about a National Spiritual Mobilization? First, because spiritual strength is more powerful than material and armed force; and second, because we must make up for our spiritual deficiencies in the past.

Dr. Sun Yat-sen has told us that the spiritual and material are complementary, not mutually exclusive. A person without spiritual life is not a complete or free person. A nation that loses its soul does not deserve to be free and independent. Spiritual force determines in the end the success or failure of any struggle. Visible material or military power does not completely determine victory or defeat. As Dr. Sun Yat-sen said, true strength must be nine-tenths strength of spirit.

That spirit is more important than material force has been amply demonstrated in many instances where a handful of Chinese soldiers have succeeded in routing many times their number of opposing troops, and where Chinese women have successfully defended themselves against the cruelties of the enemy. Our success in resisting the invader and in reconstructing our nation in the hinterland has been due largely to the strength of spirit and high morale of all our citizens. The closer we approach victory, the more difficult and dangerous will our task become, and the more necessary it will be to mobilize all the spiritual forces of the nation in order to achieve final success.

As for our spiritual deficiencies, we recall that a few months after the outbreak of the war opinion abroad constantly declared that China

A radio message to the people of China, broadcast from Chungking on April 17, 1939.

was not strong enough from either a military or spiritual point of view to resist a foreign foe. This criticism challenged us to searching self-examination.

It is true that the Chinese people have displayed great heroism in the course of this war, yet we must realize that hostilities are not yet finished, the enemy has not yet been repulsed, and the final victory has not yet been won. We should constantly ask ourselves, "Have we done all we should do?"

Has the morale of our citizens become stronger with the duration of the war? Have our past defects been remedied? Have those in responsible positions fulfilled their responsibilities? Has everyone worked to the limit of his ability and strength? Has cooperation between the front and the rear become complete and efficient? Have military necessity and military victory come first in our thoughts? Have we in speech and action placed the state and the nation above all else? Can we resist to the end and keep firm, unselfish, and honest no matter what happens? Can we give every citizen complete confidence in the final success of our Resistance and Reconstruction program? Can we make the enemy, the puppets, and the traitors realize that our national spirit is a force to be reckoned with? Have we changed our ways of living to meet the demands of wartime? If we face these questions conscientiously we shall find there is much more that we can and should do.

If a nation is deficient in material things and the efficiency cannot be remedied immediately, this cannot be considered a national disgrace. Material production requires manpower, resources, and time, and the replenishment of material deficiencies is a slow process. But it is different when we are deficient in spiritual things. When the spirit fails, the possession of weapons and material resources is of no use. If a country is invaded by an enemy and lacks the will to resist, it does not merely suffer humiliation; it commits a great sin.

Remember that if we emerge victorious from this war and succeed in our program of national reconstruction, our history as a race will be unbroken and we may look forward to the establishment of a new China based on the Three Principles of the People. On the other hand, if we do not possess the iron will to resist, our independence will be lost, and historians will hold us up to shame for a hundred generations to come. Now is the time when the country needs every citizen and when every citizen should give his best to the country.

The Citizen's Pact is an instrument for resisting the enemy. We swear not to render service to the enemy or to traitors. If we are coerced at gun-point, we should prefer death to the breaking of our oath. We promise not to violate the Three Principles and not to do anything against the interests of the nation. No pressure of any kind or even threat of death should be able to make us break this solemn promise.

We must be ready to die for our country. We must be ready to dedicate every bit of strength we possess, and every drop of sweat and blood in our bodies to the defense of our native land and to the glorious future of our nation. If we do not fear to die, our enemy will fail and our nation will live. If our spirit is unconquerable, we cannot be conquered and the ultimate victory will be ours.

The Citizen's Pact

TODAY marks the inauguration throughout the nation of the Spiritual Mobilization Movement and the promulgation of the Citizen's Pact. The opening ceremonies of the People's Monthly Political Meetings are being held today. It is also Labor Day. On such a significant occasion, I wish to share with you some of my hopes, and also to send a word of encouragement to our comrades suffering under Japanese military rule.

Our nation faces a turning point in its history. We have come to a crucial hour in our War of Resistance. During the past twenty-two months we have paved the way for China's final victory, but the enemy is intensifying his efforts to conquer us; we dare not relax our vigilance. Only the most resolute determination will bring us victory. From today on, we must radically examine ourselves to search out any moral and spiritual weakness. We must be willing to root out all corrupt habits and make a new beginning in our thinking and living.

At the opening ceremony of the Spiritual Mobilization Movement, we swear before our ancestors and before the Father of our nation that we will carry out in full the Citizen's Pact, that we will forego all undue love of ease, and that we will complete the task bequeathed to us by the patriots and martyrs who have died for our country. From today on, let us redouble our efforts to avenge the wrongs done to our country, and wipe away the stains of humiliation upon our national history.

Most of China's "humiliation days" come in May, each one reminding us of some shameful experience at the hand of Japan. Let every descendant of Hwang Ti, let every citizen of the New China, resolve that we shall turn these days of humiliation into days of glory for our nation.

Here let me express my profound sympathy for all our compatriots in the "occupied" areas, especially for those in North China and Manchuria and along the Hangchow-Shanghai-Nanking, Tientsin-Pukow,

An address at the formal inauguration of the Spiritual Mobilization Movement, Chungking, May 1, 1939. The speech was broadcast to the nation.

Peiping-Hankow and other railways, and all who are under alien rule. I am particularly moved at the thought of the aged—our fathers and elders—in these areas. Although I cannot see you face to face, yet I do not for a moment forget your sufferings. I know that you are eagerly longing for the day when we shall recover our lost territories, and that you are keeping alive the spirit of patriotism and resistance. Whenever I hear of your killing one enemy soldier, or destroying one pile of enemy goods, I am moved more deeply than by reports of military successes at the front. To kill one Japanese soldier in the Japanese rear is more important than killing one hundred on the battlefield. To offer moral resistance to the enemy and to refuse cooperation with him in the rear is just as important as fighting him at the front. All of our officers and soldiers remember you in your trials and are grateful to you for your unwavering loyalty to our country. We shall do all we can to measure up to your expectations of us and to free you from oppression.

We are from one ancestral stock. The same blood flows in our veins. War may separate us physically for a time but it cannot divide our love of country and our spiritual unity. If any today are not awake to the nation's peril, if any still indulge in loose and careless living or pursue selfish ends, if any still quarrel and loaf and temporize, they are not worthy citizens of the Republic of China; they are not true descendants of our great ancestor Hwang Ti!

I call upon all Chinese living in the foreign concessions of Tientsin, Shanghai, Hankow, and in cities like Hongkong, especially young men and women, not to forget their nation's distress and humiliation. Be strong and self-reliant; preserve integrity of character; be faithful to duty; distinguish between right and wrong. I say this because of distressing reports that have come to me of young men and women in the foreign concessions who still spend their time in profligate pleasures with little thought of the dire need of their country. Let us not give the enemy reason to despise us; let us not give friendly nations occasion to criticize us. If they see that our youth are honest, brave, hardworking, patriotic, and self-sacrificing, they will have unbounded hope in our nation and respect for the character of our people. The time has come for all of us solemnly to subscribe to the Citizen's Pact and promise that:

1. We will not act contrary to the *San Min Chu I* [Three Principles of the People].
2. We will not disobey the laws and orders of the Government.
3. We will not betray the interests of the state.

4. We will not become traitors to our country or subjects of the enemy.
5. We will not participate in traitorous organizations.
6. We will not become officers or private soldiers in the enemy or puppet armies.
7. We will not serve as guides for the enemy or for traitors.
8. We will not spy on behalf of the enemy or traitors.
9. We will not work for the enemy or traitors.
10. We will not accept banknotes of the enemy or puppet banks.
11. We will not purchase enemy goods.
12. We will not sell foodstuffs or other articles to the enemy or to traitors.

If we thus arm ourselves with moral strength and resist the temptations of the enemy, soon he will become afraid of us and give up the attempt to conquer us. Let us all, whether in free or "occupied" territory, take active part in the spiritual mobilization of our country, and resolve that from today on we will keep the Citizen's Pact and be strong, fearless citizens of China.

"Five minutes' enthusiasm" is not enough to make the Spiritual Mobilization Movement a success. We need unflagging determination and unfailing perseverance. The aim of the Movement is not only to arouse the moral energies of every citizen, but also to forge, out of this long and fiery trial, a new life for our people. Not once but again and again, not one day but every day, must we renew our determination to fight on, until the power of the aggressor is broken and China realizes her national ideals.

Spiritual Mobilization and the Citizen's Pact are invisible weapons stronger than airplanes and bombs; they are invincible means of resistance. The People's Monthly Meetings will be our spiritual fortresses, more effective than reinforced concrete, if we give up our careless old ways, and discipline ourselves to genuine hard work. The People's Monthly Meetings should also be like a drum-call to vigorous action, like a tocsin to warn us of the shameful servitude into which we will fall if we let the enemy conquer us. We should constantly remind ourselves: our country has been invaded, our fellow-countrymen have been murdered, our homes have been destroyed, our parents and brothers have been killed, our sisters have been raped. If we keep these things and the humiliations that our nation has suffered in the past fifty years always before us, there will be no danger of our relapsing into the old apathy. We will be stirred to superhuman efforts to wipe out our national disgrace and to regain our national liberty.

Let those who can lead lead, and set a good example to the people. Let the people encourage one another. Remember that one unworthy citizen is a disgrace to all. We are responsible for others' actions as well as for our own.

Let us learn from the history of our nation. Dynasties were overcome by alien races only when they became corrupt and decadent. When the government was good, when the nation was united, when the national spirit was strong, no outside power was able to subdue China. Our trials today are the result of misrule and corruption in the past. We must overcome the past, and build a new future. If we all are loyal and faithful, if we put the state and the nation above everything else and give first place to the war and all its demands upon us, if we keep our eyes fixed upon the final goal of victory and independence, then we will be unconquerable and our nation will come into a new and glorious day.

Bombing of Civilians and Open Towns

SINCE the beginning of this month, enemy planes have bombed residential districts throughout the country on more than fifty occasions. Civilian casualties in Chungking alone are counted by the thousands. Other cities subjected to ruthless and wanton bombings have been Foochow, Sian, Loyang, Hsiangyang, and Fancheng in Hupeh besides many cities and towns near the front lines. In addition, the following unfortified towns containing no military establishments whatsoever have been bombed, their streets covered with blood, their skies lit up with conflagrations: Chuanchow, Changting, Lunghai, and Tungan in Fukien; Kiungchow, Shiukwan, and Swatow in Kwangtung; Ningpo and Kinghwa in Chekiang; Hengyang, Chikiang, and Yuanling in Hunan; and Hangchung (Nancheng) in Shensi. The enemy has often said that he bombs military objectives only. But the falseness of this statement is apparent to everyone in China and abroad.

The enemy has three objectives in his widespread and cruel bombings of our towns and civilian populations. First, by incessant air raids he hopes to strike terror into the hearts of our people, forcing them into submission and surrender. Second, by fierce intensive air raids he hopes to hinder or destroy productive enterprises, destroying the livelihood of the masses. Third, by concentrated air raids he hopes to create disorder in the rear, weakening our powers of resistance.

The enemy well realizes that the people constitute the strongest bulwark against aggression, the real foundation of our revived nation. That is why he seeks to destroy our people, raining death on peaceful non-combatants in crowded centers. Even more terrible attacks from the air may be expected. We must, therefore, devise better ways of protecting ourselves. We must also strive to avenge the death of our innocent fellow-citizens. There are three things we must consider.

1. In nearly two years during which we have been resisting invasion, the unprecedented high morale and unity of purpose shown by our soldiers and civilians have won the genuine admiration of the whole

A telegraphic message to the nation on May 16, 1939, following the severe air raids on Chungking and other cities.

world. Seeing this, the enemy has decided that only extreme ruthlessness will save his aggressive designs from failure and his military
situation from immediate collapse; within the past half month he has
indulged more and more in savage, unscrupulous bombings, the like of
which the world has never seen. For nearly two years our people have
borne their sufferings with patience, courage, and fortitude. Since the
recent massacres from the air at Chungking they have gone about their
work as usual and have shown the same calm and steady courage. Such
sterling qualities of character will render futile the nefarious schemes
of the enemy. In addition, all branches of the Government have been
working night and day to devise efficient and permanent measures for
safeguarding the people against the danger from the air. These measures are better and better each day, so that when raids occur in the
future they will cost the enemy dearly without accomplishing his main
objective of terrorizing our people.

We must realize that in the coming months the enemy will not con-
fine his aerial bombing to one town or to one city. Since he is aiming
at the whole Chinese race he will drop bombs everywhere. Past experience shows that although seats of government and military establishments have been bombed frequently, the damage has been com-
paratively slight, because our anti-aircraft guns have forced the enemy
planes to keep a high altitude. But places with no military objectives
and with little air defense are also being bombed, incessantly and indis-
criminately. It is clear that unless we strengthen our military defenses
and carry on this War of Resistance to the bitter end, our nation will be
disarmed, our people will be killed, and not only our own generation
but generations to come will suffer the humiliation and misery of alien
domination. We must fight on, and wrest life from death.

I am sure that the suffering of the air-raid victims is deeply graven
upon the hearts of our people everywhere. They will not forget the
brutality of the enemy until the death of our unfortunate brethren is
avenged and the invaders are driven from our shores.

2. Before giving orders to city dwellers to evacuate, the Government makes all necessary preparations. The rural villages, with fertile
fields where the people can plow and reap, and simple, plain cottages
where they can work and rest, are the foundation of our national life.
Such villages around our cities and towns are numbered by the thousands. If each rural family takes in one city person, there will be more
than enough room to accommodate the whole of our city population.
However, all those making their way into the countryside must obey
the regulations laid down by our Government. In return for the hos-

pitable welcome of their rural brethren, those who have technical abilities should help in rural development, and those who have received an education should help to teach the children of the farmers. In such an atmosphere of mutual assistance and good will our city people will be able to settle down in safety, and our country folk will become more progressive.

This movement to the countryside is not merely a temporary means of accommodating our refugees; it is a permanent highway to national reconstruction. To strengthen the villages and to increase rural production is to reinforce the foundations of our nation. Not only is the second objective of the enemy being frustrated, but our immense work of national rehabilitation will actually be accomplished that much sooner. Even though the enemy exhausts his aerial resources in attacking us, yet the area that he can damage in proportion to the extent of our territory and the number of our villages, will be like "a kernel of corn in a huge granary." When our city brethren are scattered into the villages, the enemy will be at his wit's end.

3. All government workers must intensify efforts to secure the safety of those who are obliged to remain in the city, by opening fire lanes, preparing sandbags, storing water, and by other precautionary methods. They must be faithful in the performance of their duties, and every citizen must obey orders. Then let the enemy bomb as he pleases; even if every missile hits its mark, it will destroy only an empty house. This will be more of a loss than a gain to the enemy. With more fire lanes opened there will never again be a great conflagration of closely connected houses, such as occurred on May 3 and 4. Other cities should follow the example of Chungking which, under strict government control, has a specified dugout for every inhabitant, an assigned position for every worker, and every detail organized. Thus the risk to those remaining in cities will daily decrease, and life for those out in the country will become settled. With peace of mind thus secured, all will work in harmony, each in his own place, and each with a definite task. It is certain that the enemy will come again and again to attack us, but if everyone follows the prescribed regulations we shall be able to live through this extraordinary time with everyday calmness and order, thereby avoiding unnecessary sacrifices. Let all branches of the Government, all police officers and men, and all ranks of officials and civic leaders help in the general mobilization, and in the maintenance of discipline and order. Thus the enemy's third aim will also be frustrated.

Regarding military developments: despite twenty-two months of effort on the part of the enemy forces, our soldiers are still heroically resisting the invaders around Lukouchiao, Peiping, and Tientsin; in the region northeast of Chahar and Suiyuan; and along the Kiaochi [Tsingtao-Tsinan], Shanghai-Nanking, and Shanghai-Hangchow railways. They are actively attacking and recovering important cities and towns on the southern front. Although Anking and Kaifeng, former provincial capitals of Anhwei and Honan, fell into enemy hands a year ago, they are not only subjected to constant Chinese raids but are frequently occupied by our forces.

Henceforth, the attack, defense, occupation, or abandonment of important cities and towns in the "occupied" areas will rest in our hands. Never before in history has such a thing been witnessed in a war of national liberation. The enemy, sucked into deepening mire, is not only under constant counter-attacks but is even being encircled. The danger facing him is far more serious than is yet realized by the world, a new thing in the history of warfare. If one leaves out of consideration the resolute determination of our people and the economic stability of our country, and judges merely from military developments and the comparative advantages and disadvantages of both sides, there is ample evidence to show that the final victory will be ours.

The enemy has boasted to the world about his well trained army, but its record since it has met our resistance is known to all. The effective strength of the enemy's air force is not more than two thousand planes. Even if these two thousand planes could be used to the fullest extent, they might bomb our two thousand county seats, but they could never destroy our 70 million farm homes. They might kill a number who had no time to reach safety, but they could not shake the determination of 450 million people to resist.

Our indomitable national spirit has been manifested again and again in our long history and most vividly during alien invasions. Shining examples of loyalty and patriotism might be cited, when men faced death calmly and heroically, "as if it were but a going home." The massacres of our people by the Manchus at Yangchow and Kiating, and in recent years by the Japanese at Tsinan and Nanking, have but added to the glory of our national spirit. The enemy's reckless bombings cannot shake our will to resist. They will only refine our national character, strengthen our national unity, and make more solid the foundations of our national life.

Furthermore, this ruthlessness of the enemy has become a boomerang, producing disastrous effects among his own people. Were not the explosions of army depots and chemical works near Tokyo, Osaka,

Fukuoka, Fukuji, and other places caused by war-weary and anti-war elements?

The recent bombings of our cities have been cruel and hateful enough, and yet the enemy, in his desperation, has not confined his atrocities to aerial massacre. Our fellow-countrymen in the "occupied" areas are suffering more than we who live merely under the threat of bombings. Men are being enslaved, women maltreated. Many are being forced to take poisonous injections and narcotic drugs. The enemy would not only murder us from the air, but also make us eat poison and destroy ourselves. Unless we unite and drive out this terrible enemy we cannot hope to avenge the wrongs inflicted upon us, or save our nation from ruin.

Let all provincial, municipal, and local governments guide the masses, in accordance with the orders of the Central Government. Let all our armed forces and civilians work together with one heart and one soul to wipe out our national humiliation, to win our War of Resistance, to accomplish our national reconstruction, and to lay the foundations for a free and independent China.

Prepare for Victory

TODAY is the second anniversary of our War of Resistance. Compared with a year ago the battle fronts are longer and fighting is more intense. The determination of our armed forces and civilians to sacrifice for the national good is much stronger, and the weaknesses of the enemy militarists are more apparent. The enemy is becoming more desperate and ruthless and his intrigues increase in number and malevolence.

We are fighting for our national independence and for international justice. In a war which is revolutionary in nature, the time factor counts but little. Let us struggle on until we reach our goal of national reconstruction. Let us overcome every obstacle on the way to ultimate victory. Let us not forget the supreme sacrifices made by our fallen heroes, the gallantry of our soldiers at the front, and the untold sufferings of our war-stricken fellow-countrymen.

While we sorrow for the dead, let us not forget the responsibilities of the living. Let everyone do his utmost to wipe out our nation's disgrace and to fulfill the mission upon which our nation is now engaged. On the occasion of this sad but grand anniversary, I wish to send a special message to our military forces and to all our compatriots at home and overseas.

On July 7 of last year I outlined the general military situation and forecast future developments, pointing out our duties and responsibilities. I shall not repeat what I have said but I ask that you read again that message and compare what I then said with the situation as it is today. You will find that my predictions have come true.

First, let us speak of ourselves. Although we have experienced severe trials and difficulties during the past twelve months, yet the longer we fight the stronger and more determined grows the will of our people. The spirit, purpose and activities of our people have been further unified under the guiding principles of the *San Min Chu I,* and everyone is now ready to die for his country and for the realization of the Three

A message to the Chinese armed forces and civilians on the second anniversary of the war, July 7, 1939.

106

Principles. With loyalty, courage and hope we shall fight on to the end. Comparing our present achievements with those of the first year of hostilities we see that the battle lines have been extended, warfare behind the enemy lines has become more intense, and reconstruction in the hinterland is increasingly effective. Furthermore, the masses have a deeper understanding of the issues at stake in the war.

The enemy's fighting strength, on the other hand, is steadily weakening, and therefore he resorts to indiscriminate bombing of our cities and towns and slaughter of our innocent civilians. With what result? He merely adds fuel to the fires of hatred, and makes us more determined than ever to fight to the end. As the leader of our military forces I am happy to tell you that we have overcome most of our past shortcomings and that both our soldiers and our civilians have shown great improvement during the past year.

We have made gains in our international relations. Article 16 of the League Covenant, which last year was reluctantly considered by the Powers, has this year been invoked against Japan. The League has definitely named Japan as the aggressor. Public and private bodies in friendly nations throughout the world have denounced Japan's aggression and have helped us by boycotting Japanese goods, by refusing to sell to Japan and by sending money and medical supplies. Our sympathizers have increased a hundredfold and are giving active expression to their sympathies. Our relations with friendly powers have been improved; they are helping us more openly and in more concrete ways. They manifest growing friendship for us and growing antipathy toward our enemy. We are deeply grateful for all these expressions of goodwill, but even more do we rejoice in the greater support for justice and righteousness in international relations.

From the Marco Polo Bridge Incident to the first anniversary of the war a year ago today, the enemy advanced 1,800 kilometers, while from July 7 of last year to the same date this year, the advance was only 510 kilometers. Although the hostile forces were reinforced many times during this period, yet their successes were much reduced. This decline means that our victory is drawing nearer.

According to the enemy's own reports, his casualties up to March of this year totalled over one million, and the number is now much greater. Notwithstanding his reckless sacrifice of men during the past three months, our enemy has accomplished nothing. The so-called "mopping-up" campaigns have met with severe counter mopping-up operations. As for the enemy's boasted successes in his April and May campaigns, everyone can see how insignificant they are.

107

Early this spring Konoye's cabinet, called in Japan the "only cabinet," collapsed. The enemy is becoming desperately poor, unemployment is increasing, prices are soaring, gold reserves are already being exhausted, and rural economy is on the verge of collapse. Anti-war feeling is becoming more widespread. Thousands of professors and other intellectuals have either been put to death or imprisoned. Japanese soldiers in China have become infected with the same anti-war sentiments. On the diplomatic side there is every possibility that Japan will find herself one day in complete isolation. The proposed alliance with Germany and Italy, by which she hoped to bolster up her morale, was coldly frowned upon by these countries because of Japan's declining military strength and increasing poverty. Thereupon Japan, seeking to deceive the democratic nations into believing that she was still on their side, pretended that she did not want to join the Fascist bloc!

When this scheme failed, the Tientsin Incident was created and all sorts of illegal demands were made on England. We may predict that as Japan draws nearer to the end of her tether she will create more such incidents, but we can be certain that she will fail in the future as she has failed in the past. As Japan becomes more desperate she will take greater risks until at last she collapses, just as a man, mad with thirst, takes a drink of poison for temporary relief only to fall dead later. Our enemy has brought upon himself not only the condemnation but also the punishment of the civilized world. During the past two years we have played the active role in military and diplomatic affairs, while the enemy has followed step by step in the road we have marked out for him and is now entangled in a snare from which there is no escape. The longer our enemy struggles, the more he involves himself in difficulties; while the longer we struggle the stronger and more determined we become.

One of the most important statements made during the past year was that by Prince Konoye on December 22, 1938. Since the beginning of our second year of resistance the enemy has longed for a speedy victory. But he has not shown any realization of the wrongs he has committed, nor any evidence that he intends to relinquish his policy of aggression. Since he has failed to conquer us by armed force, he is now attempting all kinds of peace intrigues. The peace he proposes would be worse than that made by Japan with Korea, for he would want to swallow the whole of China. At the time I made a complete refutation of Konoye's statement, and I am sure that our soldiers and civilians have a clear understanding of the situation. The failure of the enemy intrigues and my full exposure of them have been a severe blow to the enemy and clearly presage the enemy's downfall. However, Japan has not abandoned her vain hopes. She cannot withdraw the slogan of a "New Order in East Asia." Though the so-called "Unity of East Asia," "Asia Development Bureau," and such phrases are empty of reality, yet Japan clings to them.

It is hardly necessary to assert that we shall fight on with the same resolution that has marked our resistance in the past. The sad thing is that there have actually been some men shameless enough to respond to a statement that would spell China's doom and to turn openly against the Party, the nation and the people. These men have already been denounced by public opinion and condemned by state law. But we have to admit that their treachery forms the darkest chapter in the history of the last twelve months, and is a disgrace which keeps our fallen heroes from sleeping in peace. Frankly speaking, the traitors' peace movement is nothing but a movement for the destruction of our nation. The day the "New Order in East Asia" is established, that day China becomes a vassal state. Since the announcement of the "New Order in East Asia," Japan has clearly shown that she wants to destroy our nation and to enslave our people. There is therefore no ground for talk of peace. We have no choice but to fight on until we achieve complete victory and attain fully the goal of our War of Resistance. There is no other road for us to take. Surrender half-way will mean only a traitors' peace, a slaves' peace, the peace of death. No one but those who want to sell their country would deny this.

Since the beginning of the second phase of the war at the end of 1938, both our internal and external affairs have taken a more favorable turn. Final victory is now in sight. Just at this critical time the traitors plan to break our fighting strength by lying propaganda. They hope to deceive the masses, shake our faith in the war, impair the morale of our blood-stained and heroic defenders, and bring to naught the labor and sacrifice of those who have died for their country. They would drag their own country in the mire to save an enemy country. Never before in all history has there been such heartless and shameful behavior.

We know that the Japanese militarists are digging graves for themselves and for all traitors who sell out to them. And yet these traitors seem willing to drag the whole Chinese race, with its glorious history of five thousand years, to death with them. What heartlessness, what utter insanity! Our soldiers and civilians, tried by this experience, show that they can clearly distinguish between right and wrong and that they are not at all shaken in their devotion to the nation. This is one of the greatest achievements of the past twelve months.

From now on there will be no serious dangers to fear if only we push steadfastly on to the goal of victory. We have already covered the most difficult nine-tenths of the way. Let us redouble our efforts and shatter the morale of our enemy and of all traitors. Let us give our very flesh and blood in exchange for victory; let us wash out the disgraceful stains which the traitors have brought upon our racial character. "We will not stand under the same sun with traitors." He who does not understand this declaration is not a true Chinese. He who is not determined to defend his country is not a true son of Hwang Ti.

Soldiers, and civilians, the most important thing at the present time is an inflexible will to victory and a confident faith in final victory!

The longer any war lasts the more difficult it becomes for all engaged in it. The nearer we approach the end of the war the more we will need to possess courage and endurance. I do not for a moment deny the hardships and sufferings of all our soldiers and citizens, but our determination to endure and to sacrifice must be further strengthened. As the war is prolonged our fighting powers must be further increased. Our sufferings and sacrifices will not be in vain! They already possess the highest value and the most sacred meaning. By them the glorious heritage of our ancestors is being preserved and the happiness of our posterity is being assured. If we of this generation do not begrudge hardship and do not fear danger, if we do not yield but hold out to the end, our sufferings of the moment will secure the well-being of our children and our children's children for a hundred generations. But if we shirk difficulty and shrink from danger, if we become lax and easy-going, and simply hope that by some good chance our nation will escape destruction, our moments of ease will bring upon our descendants long years of humiliating slavery and generations of untold suffering. The enemy is trying every possible scheme against us. We are not afraid of difficulties or dangers; they cannot be avoided but they can be overcome by our united efforts. Aggression is not stopped by surrender or compromise. It can only be overcome by armed opposition. To be undaunted by superior military might is to demonstrate the traditional spirit and the moral integrity of our nation and of our army.

The road before us becomes brighter each day. At the same time our responsibilities become heavier. We must persevere the more, we must be the more on our guard, and we must ask ourselves the more earnestly whether we are striving to the limit of our strength.

Today is the beginning of the third year of war. Everyone of our compatriots should resolve to do his best wherever he is serving. Two especially important duties are laid upon us. The first is a moral and spiritual duty. We must understand clearly the principles of the Spiritual Mobilization Movement and know how to express them in action. We must consolidate our unity, strengthen our patriotism, and increase our self-confidence. We must believe that the enemy fears us, not we the enemy. We must be diligent and hardworking, get rid of all bad habits of laziness, carelessness and inefficiency, learn to be quick and accurate, and strive hard to finish our tasks. We must recognize that the first requirement of a citizen today is absolute support of the authority and laws of the State, especially wartime laws which are as strict as military orders. Nobody should try to stand outside the law. All our soldiers and civilians who understand the profound importance of the law and of the national policy, should give united and unfailing support to them. Then they will be a credit to the Chinese nation and deserve the name of sons of Hwang Ti.

Our most urgent military duties are: to improve the political training of officers and soldiers; to strengthen our military organization; to increase our fighting strength; and to elevate the morale of the army. Those at the front must redouble their efforts to drive out the enemy. They must take to heart all the lessons we have learned in blood; they must map out more careful plans; they must frustrate the enemy's advance more effectively and hasten his total collapse. In the war zones there must be closer cooperation between the various mobile units, and between these units and the people. Their duty is to keep the enemy in check and to attack him constantly in the rear. All citizens must be willing to enlist, undergo military training, enter the army and dedicate themselves to the nation. All government agencies, military and political, must faithfully perform their duties. All officers and men must maintain the high standards and reputation which the Chinese soldier has earned in this war. All the people of the nation must demonstrate their loyal, brave and militant spirit and be ever ready to sacrifice themselves in the cause of righteousness.

Officers, soldiers and citizens! Your repeated sacrifices and your sustained resistance have shattered the enemy's malicious designs and have laid the foundations of our final victory. Although the situation has turned in our favor, yet this is a most critical moment. Let us now make a supreme effort and press toward our goal. Let us push the enemy into the pit which he has himself dug. Let every man do his full duty and stake everything he possesses on the salvation of our nation. We know that life without honor is not life but death. A slaves' peace would bring doom upon our race. On the other hand, death in the battle for freedom is not death but life. Victory in our War of Resistance will bring happiness and blessing to our posterity for ten thousand generations.

Whether it is to be renaissance or annihilation, freedom or slavery, glory or dishonor, victory or defeat—only we by our own efforts can decide. Let all our officers, soldiers and civilians, with sorrow and anger but also with fiery determination and Herculean strength, throw themselves into this life-and-death struggle, drive out the alien invaders, efface all humiliations from our annals, bring about the rebirth of our national life, and prepare for the glorious day of victory and freedom.

A Common Front Against Aggression

TODAY China stands on the threshold of the third year of her War of Resistance against Japanese aggression. On behalf of the Chinese people, I take this occasion to convey our sentiments and hopes to the governments and peoples of all friendly Powers.

Japan's policy as formulated by her militarists is that of world conquest. To realize her inordinate ambitions, Japan must first subjugate China.

Prior to the outbreak of the Sino-Japanese hostilities, the world did not fully realize the significance of Japan's policy. The developments of the last two years, however, have revealed only too clearly the sinister outlines of that policy. No one can deny that the present chaos in international affairs, which undermines the very foundations of law and order, is directly traceable to Japan's military occupation of our Northeastern Provinces in 1931.

Japan's policy of the so-called "New Order in East Asia" was publicly announced by Prince Konoye last December. Since then, events in the Far East have shown beyond doubt that the aim of the Japanese militarists is to make Japan mistress of the Pacific by dominating China on the one hand, and by eliminating European and American interests from Asia on the other. Our people have continued to make untold sacrifices of life and property in order to defend their own freedom and independence, to check the infamous designs of Japan, and to restore peace and order in this part of the world.

Since the Great War, there have been three great declarations of solemn international obligations: the Covenant of the League of Nations, the Kellogg Peace Pact, and the Nine-Power Treaty. The object of these treaties is the pacific settlement of disputes between nations, and the maintenance of world peace and order. I should like, with your permission, to call attention to the Nine-Power Treaty, which was sponsored by the United States of America, and to which both China

A message to friendly Powers on the second anniversary of the war, July 7, 1939. A translation of the speech was broadcast to the United States by Madame Chiang Kai-shek.

and Japan are parties. The underlying principle of this Treaty is, in the words of the preamble, "to stabilize conditions in the Far East, to safeguard the rights and interests of China, to promote intercourse between China and the other Powers upon the basis of equality of opportunity."

The Japanese are now trying to substitute for this sound and just principle what they choose to call the "New Order in East Asia." By the establishment of this "New Order" Japan is destroying the validity of all treaties. We are glad, however, to note that the friendly Powers who are parties to these international agreements have not only consistently respected them, but have also repeatedly condemned the violation of them by Japan.

In order to further their schemes, the Japanese militarists have recently brought pressure to bear upon certain countries in the hope of forcing them to act in accordance with Japanese dictates. They plan to break up the united front of the Powers by dealing with them one at a time. Foreign nationals in China have been subjected to inhuman and disgraceful treatment at the hands of the Japanese. They have been robbed of their property, and deprived of their freedom of movement. Even their religious, cultural, and commercial establishments have been destroyed by indiscriminate bombing. All this is meant to be a challenge to the West. However, our resistance during the past two years has so exhausted the enemy that his threats will not, I believe, have any effect upon the determination of the democratic Powers to uphold international justice and treaty obligations.

I wish to remind the world that we Chinese have been a peace-loving people for over five thousand years, and I firmly believe that our 450,-000,000 people still have something substantial to contribute toward human progress. True, China is weak from a military point of view, but such is our faith in the ultimate triumph of right over injustice that we are not afraid of brute force. But we do expect from the signatories of the various treaties the honorable discharge of their responsibilities and the fulfilment of their obligations.

In this complex world, peace is indivisible. Those countries which are eager to preserve peace must now unite in a common front against aggression. Those countries which are reluctant to face realities by adopting an attitude of indifference or a policy of appeasement will only encourage aggression. After six years of futile efforts at conciliation, China finally had to resist. We found that no amount of reasonable concession on our part could satisfy an aggressor who aims at holding one-fourth of the earth's population in bondage. I hope that the world will take warning and watch Japan carefully.

If the signatories of the League Covenant and the Nine-Power Treaty had acted firmly against the peace-breaking State, I am confident that we would not be facing the present unstable condition of world affairs. It is not too late for the friendly Powers with rights and interests in the Far East to apply economic sanctions against Japan. If this opportunity is lost, no words can adequately describe the international calamity that will take place. It will be difficult for the friendly Powers to escape the just judgment of posterity for their inaction at a time of great crisis.

We gratefully remember all the sympathy and assistance given by the governments and peoples of various countries to China. Since we have been fighting not merely for our own existence, but also in the common interests of other nations, we feel justified in appealing to the Powers to apply economic sanctions without delay. You are no doubt aware that the sale to Japan of war supplies, such as petroleum, iron and steel, makes it possible for her to continue her cold-blooded mass murder of innocent Chinese civilians and to menace foreign lives and property in China. Should effective economic sanctions be immediately applied against Japan, the time required for checking aggression on this continent would be considerably shortened.

Japan's invasion of China now enters its third year and becomes more vicious every day. It now assumes the added form of an anti-foreign movement calculated to drive all occidental rights and interests from Asia. The Powers, if only in defense of their own rights, should take more positive action. China is determined to carry on her resistance indefinitely. She will not disappoint her many friends who have given her so generously both moral and material assistance.

The nations of the world are now so inter-dependent that China cannot get along without the cooperation of the West, and the West cannot get along without China. China is fulfilling her obligations in the cause of international justice. She expects that every peace-loving nation will contribute an equal share toward that end.

In a word, we must do everything possible to frustrate the Japanese plan of establishing a "New Order in East Asia," which, in its final analysis, means Japanese domination of Asia and the closing of the "Open Door" to the West. Only if Japanese aggression is checked can we look forward to a day when the nations of the Pacific will live in peace and harmony, and each do its part toward the advancement of civilization.

Resistance in the Enemy's Rear

TODAY is the second anniversary of our War of Resistance, and the first day in the third year of war. How to continue this difficult, glorious struggle, how to strengthen our resistance, recover our lost territory, drive out the invaders and how to construct a new China of, by, and for the people—these problems face us all, but the burden rests most heavily upon our compatriots in "occupied territory."

Fellow-countrymen, who suffer such terrible oppression and cruelty and who live constantly in the dark valley of the shadow of death, do not think that I forget you even for a moment. Daily and hourly I consider how we may free you from your sorrow and suffering. But you must also help yourselves. You too must rise and struggle with us for your freedom.

Fellow-countrymen in the war areas! The stories of your perseverance and courage in resisting the enemy have been reported to me and have given me unbounded hope for our nation. Your loyalty and bravery are the guarantee of our victory. No matter what cruelties and torments you suffer, resolve that you will die rather than surrender. You have preserved the great heritage of the Chinese nation and have manifested the noble virtues of the Chinese race. Your struggles have reinforced China's all-front resistance. Guerrilla bases are daily increasing in numbers and strength and the plan to turn the enemy's rear into our front is being fully realized. During the past year, the disposition and activities of our troops behind the enemy's lines have been closely coordinated with our all-front resistance. In many places throughout the extensive war areas we have already succeeded in encircling the enemy and can launch attacks on all sides at once. When he fights on one front we attack on another. Hence, he has not only failed to advance but has suffered heavy casualties. Our countrymen in the occupied areas have brought about this situation. If resistance in the enemy's rear is kept up and further intensified he will receive a mortal blow. All occupied areas, large and small, will become so many bombs which will explode inside the enemy's lines and cause his destruction.

A message broadcast to the Chinese people in the war zones and the occupied areas on the second anniversary of the war, July 7, 1939.

As a result of the past two years of war, the enemy has become weaker and weaker while we have become stronger and stronger. In military matters, in transport and communication, in political and financial affairs, the enemy is floundering in a sea of difficulties from which he is making a last desperate effort to escape. He hopes to extract himself by political and cultural intrigue, and also by the exploitation through military and economic means of Chinese resources and manpower in the occupied areas. These malicious designs are the final resource of the enemy in the hour of his approaching downfall, and their frustration means victory for us.

Let me speak first of the enemy's political intrigues. I exposed these in detail at the end of last year when I assailed Konoye's so-called "New Order in East Asia." However, there are some shameless traitors who are willing to become tools of the enemy. Although condemned by the people of the whole nation, yet they have not stopped their treasonable activities. At the same time, the enemy is attempting to carry out his new policy of "winning over the Chinese" and is intensifying his lying propaganda. We must endeavor to lay bare all these poisonous schemes.

Frankly speaking, by his proclamation of the so-called "New Order in East Asia," the enemy has clearly shown the utter impossibility of any real peace negotiations. We know that the so-called "New Order" means nothing but the destruction of the whole Chinese nation and the enslavement of all the Chinese people. There is absolutely no other way to secure true peace but to fight on to victory. If we were all as much afraid of hardship and death as the traitors are, and were willing to surrender even halfway, submitting to what they call "peace," we would only be shamefully "opening the door and inviting in the pirates." "Peace" with such a meaning cannot be found in the dictionary. The "peace" of the traitors means slavery and death. I cannot but call it "traitors' peace." We Chinese, descendants of Hwang Ti, possessing moral integrity and a courageous spirit, must in this time of lying propaganda by the enemy and traitors, strengthen our determination, maintain our personal character, and display our fighting spirit.

The enemy maliciously plans to strengthen his position in the occupied areas by exploiting Chinese resources and manpower. He wants to use our people simply as cannon fodder. Recently, he has been employing the larger portion of his forces in so-called "mopping-up campaigns." In economics, he has changed his former policy of blockade, destruction and plunder to one of "development" and "rehabilitation." In order to frustrate these venomous designs we must emphasize "counter mopping-up" campaigns, and also counter development and counter rehabilitation so that the enemy's attempt to save himself by sucking our blood may fail.

I wish to stress the following points as guiding principles for the struggles of our fellow-countrymen in the occupied areas.

First, we must carry out counter mopping-up operations, incessantly checking, encircling, attacking and exhausting the enemy, disrupting his communications and destroying his reconstruction projects. We will so wear him out that the occupied areas will daily be reduced in size, and our guerrilla bases will constantly increase in numbers and strength. We must employ guerrilla warfare on a large scale in order to engage the largest possible number of enemy troops.

Secondly, we must destroy all reconstruction and development projects of the enemy and persuade the masses not to pay taxes or supply labor to him, not to use his military or bogus notes, not to buy his goods, and not to give him foodstuffs. At the same time, our people must be frugal and industrious and spend their energies in production. They must conserve their strength for a prolonged war, work hand in hand with the political departments of our armies, make constant surprise raids on enemy property and prevent him from obtaining even the slightest benefit from our natural resources.

Thirdly, we must carry out the mobilization of our moral and spiritual forces and eradicate all traitors. On the one hand, we must enforce the Citizen's Pact, and increase the national consciousness of the people and their understanding of the war; on the other hand, we must put an end to all treasonable activities. Let us be proud that we are citizens of the Republic of China and descendants of Hwang Ti! Let us be faithful followers of our late Leader, Sun Yat-sen! Let us not misinterpret in any way his principles and teachings. Anyone today who distorts these teachings, spreading false principles of surrender and submission, should be regarded as a traitor, and be severely punished.

Fourthly, we must hasten the dissolution of the enemy forces, and spread defection among the puppet troops. We must resist the "Pacification Policy" of the enemy and of the puppets. Our people in the war zones should try by all possible means to make the enemy soldiers who have been deceived by their militarists and forced to come to China, understand that aggression is the way to self-destruction and death while opposition to war is the way to salvation and life. As for the puppet soldiers we should urge them more strongly to show their courage, turn their guns on the enemy and come over to our side to defend our common fatherland. Our people in the war areas should admonish and inspire, encourage and love one another, and unite to break up the enemy's intrigues. Anything advantageous to the enemy is harmful to us; therefore we should refuse to do what he wants us to do, and do what he opposes us in doing. What he says is good will be bad, and what he says is bad will be good; therefore every word and action of his must be refuted and checked.

Fellow-countrymen in the war areas! Our two years' War of Resistance has laid a solid foundation for our final victory. If the whole nation, at the front and in the rear, is bound closely together, then the longer we fight, the stronger and braver we will become. The day of liberty, equality and independence for the Chinese nation will without doubt soon dawn, and you will certainly be liberated from your iron yoke. For the present, we must endure pain, we must sacrifice and struggle to the end. The little suffering that we now bear will mean the happiness of future generations and will be rewarded tenfold. The sacrifice of our individual life will preserve the eternal life of the whole nation. Let us all redouble our efforts to save ourselves and the nation, fulfill our responsibilities as a great people and gain for ourselves and our descendants a glorious and final victory.

No Far Eastern Munich

WE ARE entering upon the third year of the war with a greater national solidarity and a stronger will to resist than ever before. The intrigues of the enemy and his puppets only fan our revolutionary spirit and make us more determined to fight on. The more difficulties we meet, the more vigorously will we press the struggles and the more quickly will we achieve victory.

Our military situation has vastly improved since the fall of Hankow. From now on we will only advance, never retreat. We have gained in unity within the Party and Government by the departure of Wang Ching-wei, and are now of one mind and purpose in the prosecution of the war. I believe that we are now ready to surmount all obstacles on the way to freedom. Difficulties will only spur us on to more intense effort. This has been true in all revolutions. Think of what severe privations Turkey and Russia endured in the course of their revolutionary struggles. I have said on several occasions, "Our present trials are nothing compared with what we must yet endure. We will have to suffer far more in the future. But it is in the midst of difficulty and danger that we discipline ourselves to fight, and it is out of strain and suffering that we will win our final triumph." The present War of Resistance is the culmination of our revolutionary struggle. The course of our revolution is not affected by changing currents in the world situation. Our enemy is trying to demoralize us by instigating treachery against us and to isolate us from the nations friendly to us. But we are not afraid of such tricks. They merely make us more united and determined. We cannot possibly be isolated as long as the majority of the common people in the world support justice and fair play and sympathize with our cause. Our revolution has not depended merely upon material support. Before 1926 we fought our way with bare fists. Our enemy shows little understanding of the spirit that inspires us today if he thinks he can make us submit by threats against the nations friendly to us or by inciting traitors to undermine our economy.

Part of an address to Government officials on July 24, 1939, at the Monday Morning Assembly of the National Government.

According to some foreign opinions, Japan expects to bring about a "Far Eastern Munich." But this is simply a guess on the part of certain newspapers as to the motives and aims of the Japanese militarists. In reality there cannot possibly be a "Far Eastern Munich" because nations on friendly terms with us are too well-informed on world conditions and too conscientious to abandon their obligations as well as their legal position in the Far East. They will certainly not overlook their own vital interests. It is true that the British Government is at present carrying on conversations with the Japanese Government regarding China. But China cannot in any way be compared with Czechoslovakia, for our new nation was created by our own revolutionary efforts while Czechoslovakia was born out of the European War and the treaty following it. After two years of war only a few shameless traitors have left our camp. Our country is more united than ever and the determination of our soldiers and people to resist is absolutely unshakable. We will not surrender under any circumstances nor give up our inalienable right to defend our country. The world knows this.

If a nation when attacked does not exert itself and resist the attack bravely, it cannot hope that other countries will make unavailing sacrifices on its behalf. This explains the tragedy of Czechoslovakia. From the vantage point of our own two years of struggle we can see that the forces making for justice in the world are gathering momentum and when the right time comes they will make themselves powerfully felt. We firmly believe that "Heaven helps those who help themselves" and that in all phases of our struggle—military, economic, and diplomatic— we must rely chiefly upon our own efforts. If any nation wants to help us, we welcome the help; if no nation helps us, we must struggle all the more resolutely to the very end. No friends will abandon or betray us if we ourselves are strong and upright. If we remain true no friendly nation will be frightened by the enemy into changing its fundamental policy toward us.

The crooked thinking and propaganda of the enemy are really beneath our contempt. Putting aside all legal and moral considerations and speaking only in terms of self-interest, we cannot conceive of Britain really compromising with Japan. Great Britain knows Japan even better than we do; she well knows that Japan is no longer her Far Eastern watch-dog of twenty years ago but rather a mad dog turning against its former benefactor. How can Britain possibly give up her own rights and interests and yield to Japan? As much as Britain desires a peaceful solution, she can make only such concessions as will not conflict with China's rights and with the provisions of the Nine-Power

Pact. Otherwise she will be supporting Japanese aggression and helping Japan to destroy the Pact. This would be equivalent to attacking China, and if Britain turns against China she will make enemies of all the other signatories of the Pact. It is unthinkable that Britain should sacrifice her long-established relationship with China and cast aside her partner America for the sake of placating a faithless and unprincipled aggressor nation. We refuse to pay attention to wild Japanese propaganda about a change in British policy; we place our confidence in the governments of friendly nations and in the influence exerted by public opinion in these nations on the side of justice and right.

Moreover, any understanding with regard to China arrived at by two Powers, such as the rumored Anglo-Japanese agreement, would have no validity whatever and could not be put into effect without the approval of the National Government of China.

I am confident that the international situation will rapidly change in our favor. And yet in the end our own courage and determination will be the decisive factors. We should not rely upon others. Wishful thinking and a dependent attitude are incompatible with the spirit of our revolutionary struggle.

In closing let me repeat: We must rely upon nothing but our own exertions. The aid of friendly nations will be forthcoming if we can show that we are able to help ourselves. Meanwhile let us strive to win by our own revolutionary spirit. Only by unflinching tenacity of purpose can we overcome the material obstacles in our way. Our greatest dangers, I believe, are behind us; having borne up during the past two years, we now find the ground firmer beneath our feet. Difficulties are to be expected and we must face them. Everywhere now—with our armies at the front, among our people in the rear, in our relations with other Powers—we find much to encourage us. Let us then fight on, fight on until we destroy the evil of Japanese militarism, fight on until we achieve the revolutionary goal of China's national independence.

An Appeal to Britain

THE best course for Britain is to cease negotiating with Japan. This is my frank opinion.

After reading the formula for the negotiations on Tientsin agreed upon by Britain and Japan, I expressed the opinion that concessions to Japan at China's expense will conflict with the Nine-Power Treaty and will help the Japanese to undermine the treaty. I still maintain that opinion with regard to the present negotiations in Tokyo.

How can there be a rapprochement or compromise between Japan and Britain? Japanese militarists are so obsessed with the idea of their divine mission to rule Asia that any temporary arrangements for the protection of British interests in China are only like feeding raw meat to a tiger. Even if Britain should surrender to Japan all her rights and interests in China patiently acquired during the past century, this certainly would not stop the aggressive activities of the Japanese militarists. The complete abandonment of Britain's position in the Far East —the relinquishing of India, Australia, and New Zealand, in fact Britain's whole position and influence east of the Red Sea—might possibly bring about a rapprochement for ten or twenty years between the two countries. But even this would not, I venture to prophesy, completely satisfy the ambitions of the Japanese expansionists.

Moreover, the so-called "formula," vague and elusive in itself, cannot make one believe in the possibility of a genuine Anglo-Japanese understanding. The world is perplexed as to whether Great Britain has fallen into Japan's trap, or Japan into Britain's trap.

For my part, I deeply regret that China, singlehanded up till now, has not been able to score a decisive victory over Japan and has thus forced our friend, Great Britain, to assume such an attitude and to enter into preliminary arrangements, of doubtful value, with Japan.

I firmly believe that the British Government and people will not treat an aggrieved nation in the same manner as an aggressor nation, that they will remain faithful to their promise to respect international

An exclusive statement for the *News Chronicle,* London, during the Anglo-Japanese discussions in Tokyo, and published on July 29, 1939.

treaties, and that they will not help an aggressor nation against the people of China, who are fighting to defend themselves and to uphold justice in the world.

I am confident that the British Government will fulfil their treaty obligations and keep the faith of the 450,000,000 people of China, and all other right-minded peoples in the world.

Mission of the People of Shanghai

ON THE occasion of the second anniversary of the outbreak of war on August 13, every one of us at the front and in the rear is thinking of Shanghai and of our fellow-countrymen who remain in that city. I wish today to send a special message to the people of Shanghai.

The development of Shanghai during the past hundred years has been closely associated with the modernization of China. Your city has had a particularly intimate connection with the National Revolution. Since September 18, 1931, all our national efforts have been directed towards the achieving of national independence and the building up of our national strength. A great contribution to the cause has been made by the people of Shanghai especially in economic, journalistic, cultural, and industrial fields.

Because of the important position Shanghai occupies in our revolution and reconstruction, our enemy and his puppets always launch their offensives there and make Shanghai a base of operation for all their poisonous intrigues. They want to extinguish the fires of nationalism and patriotism lit by the people of Shanghai. Past events, however, tell us that the more our enemies carry on their nefarious activities, the more intensely do the people of Shanghai hate them, and the more determined are the people of Shanghai to continue the struggle against them. Our compatriots in Shanghai have resolved to carry out their historical mission in our fight for an independent China.

We recall that two years ago today in Shanghai the heroic struggle began. The enemy attacked us fiercely with warships and airplanes; his officers and soldiers committed unparalleled atrocities. We suffered heavy losses in life, property, and industry; our universities and cultural institutions were bombed and destroyed; our commercial districts and industrial areas which we had built up by great effort are now waste lands. Many of our laborers and industrial workers lost their livelihood; yet they are supporting our War of Resistance more firmly than ever. During the fighting in Shanghai, the people of Shanghai enthusiastically contributed money and materials for the soldiers at the front and were

A message sent on the second anniversary of the beginning of hostilities in the Shanghai area, August 13, 1939.

125

ready to endure any sacrifice. You have written many glorious pages of our national history. You have broken the Japanese dream of conquering China in weeks and have changed the international opinion about China. Now the Japanese know that China is a nation not easily beaten, and the future of our resistance is bright. The struggle and sacrifice of our people in Shanghai illuminated the first stage of our resistance and assured us that the final victory would be ours. Although two whole years have gone by, yet all of us remember well all that you have done.

Because of changed conditions due to war, we moved our factories from Shanghai and its neighborhood to the interior. Many skilled technicians and laborers have travelled thousands of miles inland to play a new part in our program of national reconstruction. Most cultural institutions have moved to the hinterland and to the southwestern provinces. But a majority of the patriotic people of Shanghai still remain, and with undaunted spirit and firm determination, are opposing the enemy. Many civic leaders from various towns now under Japanese military occupation have come to Shanghai for refuge. All these are manifesting the spirit—"To die from starvation is a small thing, but to lose one's virtue is a very serious thing." During the past year and a half, Shanghai has been a place in which the new vitality of the Chinese nation has been most clearly demonstrated. In spite of the vile intrigues of the enemy and his puppets, our people in Shanghai continue to defend the morale of the nation. Consequently, the enemy and his puppets do not dare to come out in broad daylight. This unshakable determination which the people of Shanghai are showing to the world encourages us immensely. Though you have compared your present position to that of a "desert island," yet the spirit you have shown is like the bright beams of a lighthouse.

More than a thousand miles separate us, yet spiritually we are in constant communication. The stout resistance you put up in the first half year of war and your persistent purpose during the year and a half since then have won the admiration of our entire nation and also of the world. What I want to tell you as we enter the third year of our War of Resistance is this: Just as your situation has become even more complicated and difficult, so your responsibility toward the nation has become even greater. Now that there are signs, from the military, diplomatic, and economic standpoints, of a turn for the better in our War of Resistance and of the rapid approach of final victory, our enemy has to resort to all kinds of intrigues in order to intensify his political and economic offensives. Although far away from you, I can clearly see the difficult situation in which you now find yourselves and I can understand the trials and sufferings you have been enduring. In the first place, there are now enemy puppets who make Shanghai a base of operations for all their intrigues. They support our enemy's "New Order in East Asia" so as to sell out our nation and enslave our people. They have resorted to all kinds of deception to get our people to work for them, and having failed in this objective, they now employ terrorism and inflict bodily harm on those who stand in their way. Our compatriots in Shanghai are indeed faced with a very difficult situation. Secondly, Shanghai is a city in which are located important international markets. The city has long been a financial center. For the past few months, because of enemy manipulation and speculation in the black market our national currency, *fapi,* has suffered fluctuations in foreign exchange. Utilizing this opportunity, our enemy has fabricated all kinds of wild rumors with a view to shaking our determination. All of these intrigues show that our enemy is in a hopeless position and is fast approaching exhaustion. Meanwhile, I can see that the trials which our compatriots in Shanghai are suffering will become even more severe as time goes on, and therefore the responsibilities falling on them will be heavier and heavier.

The message I wish to send to the people of Shanghai is this : I believe that you will not be misled by any tempting offers our enemy and his puppets may try to make, and that your determination to resist will not be shaken. I know that all of you have confidence in the National Government and in our final victory. So I wish to review all that I have said since the outbreak of war. Since we have determined to resist against Japanese aggression, we cannot avoid difficulties and hardships. As a matter of fact, we have actually experienced fewer difficulties and hardships than we had expected. If only our spirit is not shaken our resistance will be firm and strong. The more difficulties and hardships we encounter, the sooner will final victory come. Today loyalty and disloyalty cannot exist side by side. There are only two roads before us : One, which the enemy and his puppets want us to take, leads us to surrender and enslavement; the other is the road of continued struggle. If we are firm in our determination to face any difficulty and hardship, we can win final victory and achieve national regeneration. All true patriots, knowing full well the responsibility which their ancestors of five thousand years bequeathed to them, will choose the latter road. Our compatriots in Shanghai have a strong national consciousness. All our fighting forces and civilian population feel gratified that the difficult struggle which we have been carrying on for the past two years has raised our international status. Now that the military situation is being stabilized and the international situation has turned in our favor, we must exert greater effort to win the final victory. If we relax a little now we shall lose everything we have gained. And so I urge all our compatriots in Shanghai to keep up their spirit. maintain their integrity, and continue the struggle to its bitter end. In order to let you know where your responsibilities lie, I shall enlarge on a few points.

First, I wish all cultural workers and journalists in Shanghai to build up strong spiritual fortresses. Shanghai has been a news center and cultural center. As such, it has assumed a position of international importance. Since the puppets extended their traitorous activities, they have freely employed bribery, intrigue, and even terrorist methods, but up to this day our press has maintained its integrity. This is the best expression of our national spirit. I hope all our cultural workers and journalists will preserve this spirit, and carry on their share of the struggle by reporting authentic news and denouncing editorially the views expressed by enemy puppets. By so doing, they will frustrate the designs of the enemy to fool our people and will expose his shamelessness.

Secondly, I want the bankers and financiers in Shanghai to continue their confidence in our currency. You know well that the fluctuation of our national currency in the foreign exchange market has been caused by enemy manipulation and speculation. The actual value of our currency has not fluctuated. Our currency system was created in response to the needs of our national economy. The relation between national currency and foreign exchange exists only in foreign trade. Since our basic economic needs can be fully met, the fluctuation of our national currency in foreign exchange will not affect our national economy as a whole, nor the value of the national currency itself. Further, the reserve of our national currency lies in our total national resources, and since there are unlimited resources at our disposal, we also have unlimited reserves for our national currency. Compatriots in Shanghai, as you have faith in our final victory and in the bright future of our nation, you must not let monetary fluctuations shake your faith in our national currency. The Central Government is now considering effective measures to put our wartime finance on a normal footing and to defeat enemy manipulations. Finance is a life artery of our resistance. The Government will naturally take measures to safeguard our national interest so that the livelihood of our fighting forces and civilian population will not be affected. Our people should know that to support the national currency is an expression of their support of the nation, and that the flight of capital is tantamount to selling our nation to the enemy. In the meantime, direct all your efforts to the strengthening of our wartime finances; the Government will never allow individuals to suffer the slightest loss. We have good harvests this year; so there will be no trouble in supplying our nation and our army. The basis of economy in the interior has been strengthened and is firmer than it was last year. The value of our national currency should, therefore, increase. I wish our bankers and financiers in Shanghai to defend our economic fortresses by faith in, and support of, our national currency. If you can do this, then you may be said to have fulfilled your greatest responsibility.

Thirdly, I hope that the youth of Shanghai will bravely face all difficulties and hardships, which may be even more severe in the future than at present and that they will make a clear distinction between what is shameful and what is honorable. Youth is another important artery of our national life. Whether there will be an honorable future for our nation depends upon whether our youth today act with honor. Our nation being in so difficult a position, we should devote our best and our united efforts to national defense and reconstruction. Hence, none of our youth should indulge in excessive pleasure-seeking; if they do, it means not only personal degradation, but national degradation as well. We have to think of our soldiers at the front who have been fighting so heroically and of those who have been driven out from the war areas and are enduring all kinds of hardships. We have a saying, "When there is a funeral on the street, we do not sing." So, if we have any conscience, we should pay our respects to those who have suffered during the war. You Shanghai youth may not have the opportunity of joining the army, yet you must maintain your personal integrity and distinguish between what is virtuous and what is sinful, between what is honorable and what is disgraceful. You must concentrate all your efforts on uplifting activities, and be prepared to stand every hardship. You should remember that because of its better communications with the interior, Shanghai has more facilities for research than any other city. You should utilize these advantages to strengthen all kinds of research organizations, and to study all subjects that may have a bearing on our resistance and reconstruction. Thus prepared, you can contribute your share to the nation when you are called upon to do so. Above all, youth must know that discipline and the strict observance of rules of conduct are essential to our national spirit in wartime.

Fourthly, I wish all our laborers in Shanghai to stand united in support of our resistance. I believe that Shanghai working men understand clearly what is our national interest. As your spirit is the most revolutionary, so your faith in the ideology of resistance must be firmer and firmer as time goes on. I recall that in the beginning of our war in Shanghai, all of you gave enthusiastic support to the factories moved to the interior, you too faced many risks in assisting the successful evacuation of our industrial plants from the Shanghai area. Thus you helped our efforts at national reconstruction, and your spirit has set a good example to all workers in our country. You must maintain this glorious tradition. My fellow-countrymen in Shanghai, you must realize that your strength is just as great as that of our soldiers at the front. You are our most powerful and greatest reserve at the rear of the Japanese lines. If only you would strengthen your organizations and help each other in carrying on the bitter struggle, then you could strike a death-blow to the enemy. Those of you who work on the wharves could refuse to handle enemy goods, and then the enemy would not be able to move his goods. Those of you who work in factories, if only you would refuse to work, then our enemy would not be able to make any profits. Others who work in transport service, in postal and telegraphic offices, in the selling of newspapers, and in machine shops can all do the same thing. Workers in Shanghai, there is great strength in you and you can determine whether our enemy live or die. Especially at a time like this, when our enemy and enemy puppets want to sell you out by boring into your organizations, you must take double precaution. Tighten up your organizations, encourage yourselves mutually, and know what is right and what is not, who is your friend and who is your enemy. You must endure every hardship and defeat all intrigues for surrender. Do not let the enemy puppets injure your good name. Maintain your integrity; demonstrate your national spirit.

Fifthly, I wish all our compatriots in Shanghai to help each other. Our War of Resistance is going to be a long one. The longer we resist, the more difficulties we shall face in our national livelihood. Such a tendency is inevitable for any country at war. You have only to see the conditions now existing in our enemy country. There, they have issued domestic bonds amounting to more than 200,000,000 yen. You can see the effects. The depreciation of the yen and the rapid increase in prices have led the Japanese nation into a very sad state of affairs. Everything is controlled by the State and there is not the slightest freedom. The Japanese people live a much more difficult life than ours. As a result of the increase in population, the rise in prices and the curtailment of employment, I can see that our compatriots in Shanghai are having a much more difficult time now than two years ago. But, since we are now struggling for our very existence, all kinds of hardships must be expected. We are primarily an agricultural people, and we have the traditional virtue of being able to meet hardships. Sufferings that might prove unbearable to an industrial or trading people, can still be borne by us. Now that we all are in a difficult state, we must encourage mutual assistance. This can be done by persons coming from the same district, by persons belonging to the same trade or guild. Those from the interior who have come to Shanghai for refuge are worthy men. You must regard them as honorable fellow-citizens and render them every assistance. In case they want to return to their native places, you must help them financially. You must also extend financial help to those who do not want to return. You must know the difference between disgrace and honor and between right and wrong. If all of us could observe strictly the spirit of the Citizen's Pledge by not surrendering to our enemy, by not becoming "obedient subjects," by not accepting "bogus notes," and by not using enemy goods, then we would have no regrets before our nation and our ancestors. If only we could achieve this, then, although we may be poorly clothed and inadequately fed, we will be happy and find life sweet. Then we can continue our resistance and win our final victory. Then we can crush all enemy intrigues.

The above points may not cover all that you want to know. But I can say this to you: politically, diplomatically, and economically, we are prepared for every eventuality. We can stand every hardship and difficulty, and we are confident that the final victory will be ours. Our former difficulties have largely disappeared. The difficulties we now face are those inevitable for any country at war. Our enemies are having a much more difficult time than we. The success of the Revolution depends on successful resistance. Whatever sacrifices we may have suffered have always been a glorious price for freedom. Let all of our compatriots who remain in the "desert island" show the spirit of the "five hundred heroes of Tien Hung" [1] and emulate their deeds. We all honor you for what you have done. Like strong grass in the storm and like true gold in the fire, you have stood the test at this trying time and we are confident that you will continue to enhance the glory of our nation.

[1] Tien Hung lived in the third century B.C. Uncompromising, he withdrew to an island with his last five hundred followers. Their loyalty and sacrifice made them famous in Chinese history.

China and the European War

DURING the half year since the adjournment of the Third Session of this Council, not only has immense progress been made in national resistance and reconstruction but at the same time the crisis in international affairs has been generally favorable to our national cause. At the opening of this Session, however, we find ourselves confronted with a second European War. Naturally we are deeply concerned how best to deal with this new world situation and also continue our policy of prolonged resistance. I shall therefore state the most important problems which should be considered at this meeting of the Council.

I believe that in view of the European conflict we should reinforce our fighting spirit and reaffirm our faith in China's ultimate victory; in this way we may make a still greater contribution toward the new world order. We must have a clear understanding of the international crisis and be ever on our guard. At the same time we must concentrate upon our goal so as to win our war against Japan in the shortest time possible and with the least possible expense. The most urgent tasks before us today are: (1) Concentration of personnel upon reconstruction work in the rear; (2) Strengthening the army in order to achieve military victory; (3) A careful watch upon international events and the active furthering of our wartime diplomacy.

1. *Concentration of Personnel.* In order to achieve the objectives of our War of Resistance we must strengthen our base in the rear and carry through our various economic, industrial, political, cultural and local-government projects. We must lay solid foundations for our resistance and reconstruction, irrespective of international changes. This is our fundamental, unchangeable policy; only by following this policy can we hope to frustrate our enemy's wicked designs. In our reconstruction program we must pay special attention to the northwestern and southwestern provinces, with Szechwan and Sikang as our base of operations. At the last session of this Council, we decided to organize

An address at the opening of the Fourth Session of the People's Political Council, Chungking, September 9, 1939.

a Szechwan-Sikang Reconstruction Planning Commission and a Szechwan-Sikang Survey Commission. You will be glad to know that during the last few months members of the Commissions have travelled over these two provinces, promoting closer relations between the people and the Central Government, and collecting valuable information as a basis for planning reconstruction projects. How to utilize the important data which these commissions have obtained is one of the important questions for this Council to consider. I am sure the Government will welcome any recommendations which this Council may wish to make with regard to reconstruction work in the border area.

It is of prime importance that we secure the proper personnel. The People's Political Council is formed to mobilize the nation's best talents for reconstruction, and with your cooperation I trust that we shall obtain the personnel we need to push our various reconstruction enterprises. China is now engaged in a life-and-death struggle, and every Chinese citizen should make his contribution towards the nation's rebuilding. I hope that you will not only make recommendations during this session regarding national reconstruction, but will after the session closes help to mobilize the abilities of all our citizens so that our program of resistance and reconstruction may be carried through to a successful conclusion.

2. *Strengthening the National Army.* Detailed reports about military developments since the last session of this Council are being given at another time on the program. Briefly, during the last six months the Japanese have not only failed to achieve any military success except the capture of Nanchang (which the Chinese forces gave up only after inflicting heavy losses on the enemy), but they have been compelled also to evacuate many areas previously taken from the Chinese forces. For example, the Japanese have employed no less than eight divisions to attack our army in the Taihang and Chungtiao mountain regions of Shansi, but our recapture of Tsingcheng has brought their plans to naught. In northern Hupeh, the Japanese have been attacking Nanyang, Hsiangyang, and Fangchen, hoping to annihilate our troops in that sector. The result is that they have suffered heavy losses, and have been forced by our men to retreat towards the Sinyang-Hankow section of the Peiping-Hankow Railway, without any strength to re-attack our forces. South of the Yangtze River, they tried to take Changsha from the direction of Nanchang; they not only failed to reach their objective but also lost the strategic city of Kaoan in northern Kiangsi. In other places such as Canton, Tsungfa, Sunwai and Chaochow the Japanese have met with repeated reverses and have

wasted a lot of men and materials. On all the fronts, north, south and east, there are evidences that the Japanese troops are gradually weakening. Our army, on the contrary, has been greatly strengthened and improved since the fall of Hankow. Last year I said that our chances of victory would be increased when the war area extended west of the Peiping-Hankow and Canton-Hankow Railways. Events during the last half year have justified that statement. I can assure you now that we have not only recovered our pre-war military strength but have actually doubled it. Our ammunition supplies have also been greatly replenished. But this is not saying that we shall have no more problems or difficulties in our War of Resistance. Actually our future is fraught with all kinds of dangers. We should lose no opportunity, therefore, to strengthen our army, to improve its training and discipline, to bring about closer cooperation between the army and the people, and to promote self-government in all provinces. Members of this Council can contribute information regarding their respective districts, make recommendations as to future courses of action, and help the Government to further its program of mass organization and training.

3. *Wartime Diplomacy.* Finally, in regard to our foreign relations the vital issue today is how to carry on our war of protracted resistance in the face of the new situation in Europe. We all know that the Sino-Japanese conflict is not only a world issue but also the most important world issue. The present confusion in the world is chiefly due to Japan's invasion of Chinese territory and violation of sacred international treaties. We are fighting to protect our sovereignty and safeguard our own national existence, and also to check the rise of international gangsterism, of which Japan is the leader. World peace can never be attained if the Japanese are not driven out of China. In short, the Sino-Japanese War was the starting point of a general conflict, and is the real center of the present world-wide struggle. Since China represents one-fourth of the world's population, she must bear an especially heavy responsibility for building the foundations of world peace.

Since September 18, 1931, our national policy has been based upon the following principles: (1) Resisting Japanese aggression in order to protect our sovereign rights and territorial integrity; (2) Upholding the sanctity of treaties, particularly the League of Nations Covenant, the Nine-Power Treaty, and the Peace Pact; (3) Refusing to join the anti-Comintern Pact; (4) Conducting our diplomatic affairs on the basis of our own right of self-determination and our own national interests in such a way as to achieve equality and freedom for China, and to strengthen the foundations of world peace. During the last eight years, the National Government of China has consistently upheld these principles.

Now that the European War has broken out, we should redouble our efforts to carry out this policy, irrespective of changes in the international situation. Our enemy has declared a policy of neutrality and non-intervention in European affairs. In other words, Japan now intends to concentrate all her energies upon ending the war in China, and she will reject any mediation on the part of Third Powers, so that she can establish her own supremacy in Asia. As I have said before, Japan seems to want a world of her own, without any relation to the world of interdependent nations in which we live. In spite of all that has taken place during the last two years she still dreams about creating a New Order in East Asia. Now she reveals her opportunist tactics in the face of the new developments in Europe. But our national policy has already been decided and will remain unchanged; we long ago foresaw the difficulties and dangers we would be called upon to face, and under no circumstances will we deviate from our determined course of action. If the enemy concentrates all his energies on solving the so-called China Incident, we will concentrate all our energies on resisting him. At this late hour Japan still boasts about liquidating the China problem, forgetting how her efforts of two years have failed. Japan is at the end of her tether; she is beginning to lose confidence in herself; her troops are becoming war weary; her domestic situation is rapidly deteriorating. Since she has failed in her military campaign, she is now employing political and economic weapons to extend her power and to build up what she calls the "New Reformed Government in China," but what is really a slave government.

However, within the last half year the puppets and traitors have by their own actions exposed their ulterior motives and criminal intentions. They are not only despised by their fellow-countrymen at home but are condemned throughout the world. Despite their high-sounding names the puppet governments in China are simply creations of the Japanese military regime and tools of the Japanese China Affairs Board and China Coordination Committee. They are servants of the Japanese militarists and are in no sense Chinese. Hence, no matter how many puppet governments Japan may establish in China, or how many treaties she may sign with so-called "reformed governments," our determination to resist Japanese aggression will not be in the slightest degree affected; our fighting spirit will only be augmented. Our chief problem today is not the strength or weakness of our enemy, who is in fact already suffering defeat; our chief problem is how to mobilize all our efforts and concentrate all our resources to carry out our reconstruction program and lay a solid foundation for victory.

Let us not forget that China is engaged in a struggle for her very life. The international situation is capable of sudden and manifold changes, but our policy is fixed and upon it depends the success of our War of Resistance. If we stand firm, we shall not only achieve military victory but also reach all our other goals. I hope, therefore, that you will deliberate with care, realizing that your words and actions may determine the future of our country for a hundred years to come. Let what you do be based upon our unshakable national policy and point the way to future progress.

Rights and Obligations of the
Chinese People

THE Fourth Plenary Session of the People's Political Council opened in the wartime capital, Chungking, on the day of the anniversary of the Canton Uprising[1] led by Dr. Sun Yat-sen, and has continued for ten days. One hundred and forty-one members have attended. Having heard reports of all the measures undertaken and contemplated by the Government and having examined the resolutions adopted in previous sessions, members of the Council feel gratified that the Government has resolutely carried out our national policy of resistance and that our fighting forces and civilian population have stood up courageously against every hardship and difficulty.

This session was convened after the outbreak of war in Europe. Members of the Council now feel that our enemy is fast approaching exhaustion and that our final victory is near. We should promote our political, military, economic, and diplomatic activities with more intense effort so as to adjust ourselves to the new world situation. With this in view, members of the Council have carefully examined various government reports and have proposed 89 resolutions, 82 of which have been passed by the Council. The most important measures adopted are: a request that the Central Government convoke the People's Assembly and adopt the Constitution; non-recognition of the puppet regimes and the issuing of a circular telegram denouncing our public enemy, Wang Ching-wei; a program of reconstruction for the provinces of Szechwan and Sikang; organization of a commission to inspect and comfort the soldiers at the front; proposals regarding stabilization of finance, the relief of the wounded and the care of civilian refugees. After the conclusion of business, the Council will take recess.

This closing session is held on the eighth anniversary of the Mukden Incident. Moved by the sorrowful recollections of this day, we should

An address at the close of the Fourth Plenary Session of the People's Political Council, September 18, 1939.
[1] The first abortive attempt of the revolutionists to overthrow the Manchu rule took place in Canton on September 9, 1895.

resolve to go on with a firmer resolution and with increased courage. Representing the unanimous opinion of the members of the Council, and in full accord with our predetermined national policy, the People's Political Council wishes now to issue the following message to China and to the world:

(1) At the beginning of our resistance against Japanese aggression, we decided on certain absolutely essential objectives. Not until these objectives are achieved shall we cease our struggle. In the Manifesto issued by the First Plenary Session of this Council, we declared: "The sovereignty and administrative integrity of China must be restored, for this is the minimum requirement of any independent State. The people of China are resolved to achieve that end and nothing can stand in their way. For self-defense and for the sake of decency in international relations, the Chinese nation has resolutely mobilized all its resources to combat that most criminal aggressor nation, Japan. We will not relax our efforts until the day of final victory comes." This is our aim in waging the war, an aim that has been constantly in the minds of all our fighting forces and civilian population. Japan, that lawless neighbor of ours, has been relying for two years now upon her material forces to conquer our nation and to enslave our people. But because of our heroic resistance all her attempts have proved futile. The present fighting strength of China not only exceeds that of last year, but is actually superior to that at the beginning of the War of Resistance two years ago. Those of our members who have been to the front and in the rear all agree that our fighting forces and civilian population are still in high spirits. Particularly since last winter, progress in all lines has been marked. Extremely gratified with what they have seen, members of the Council wish all the fighting officers and soldiers, all the workers in different lines, and all the people in different parts of the country to know how the situation has changed between our nation and the enemy, and to know that final victory is fast approaching. Because we have moral authority behind us, the longer we fight the stronger we become; while our enemies, since they have committed a crime of aggression, are becoming weaker and weaker. All of our fighting forces and civilian population should appreciate this important trend and understand its deep significance. The fighting forces at the fronts in the North and in the South and in the various guerrilla areas must combat the enemy with renewed vigor, while those at the rear must intensify their mobilization of material resources and manpower. Members of the Council, knowing that it is their duty not to expose military secrets, cannot speak freely about recent strategical

developments; but I wish our compatriots to know that China will surely win the final victory. That final victory, however, can only be won through a long period of difficult struggle, and during that long period we must stand united with one will, and fight with fortitude and endurance.

(2) Knowing that it is impossible to conquer China by military force, Japan now turns to political and economic methods of attack. We hate her cunning designs and laugh at her foolishness. The Republic of China is an independent State with sacred sovereign rights that are not to be violated. We are an independent nation with a long and rich history of culture and thought. We can maintain our existence only by the sweat and blood and united spirit of our four hundred and fifty million people. The heroic resistance of our soldiers and civilians during these past two years proves that China can remain free. Having failed to crush us by armed force the aggressor now thinks that he can steal our country by means of intrigue and deception. The Manifesto of the First Session of the People's Political Council has already declared: "The puppet organizations in the North and in the South are prisoners of the enemy militarists and renegades of our nation. Although they call themselves governments, they do not possess any real power. They are simply the tools of the enemy militarists and their position is even worse than that of a protectorate." The Manifesto also said: "Since inviolable and sacred rights of government have been vested in the National Government by the will of the people, it follows that those who do not recognize the National Government are, in effect, repudiating the existence of the Chinese nation." Japan has recently been trying to get Wang Ching-wei to organize a new puppet regime in order to carry out her sinister purpose of destroying China's independence. This shows how desperate Japan has become. Although Wang Ching-wei once held important posts in the National Government, since his desertion he is nothing but a criminal guilty of high treason. To Wang Ching-wei, surrender is cooperation and national enslavement is peace. Having his loyalty to the enemy, he now attacks his own fatherland in order to court the favor of the enemy militarists. Our compatriots at home and overseas have sent out repeated circular telegrams denouncing the traitor, and this Council has just passed a definite resolution of condemnation. The Council now expresses the hope that all our fellow-countrymen will cherish the inviolability of our national sovereignty and will resolve that loyal patriots and traitorous puppets shall not exist side by side. We must repudiate the puppets' conduct, smash their intrigues, and answer their devilish designs with

positive action. Meanwhile, members of the Council request that the National Government carry out their recommendations and warn all friendly Powers not to fall into the trap set by our enemy. We have confidence that world opinion will see the facts clearly.

(3) The outbreak of war in Europe is a great misfortune for mankind. But we can see clearly the cause of it. Eight years ago Japan tore international treaties to pieces and began her aggression in China. Our national life is based on the *San Min Chu I* and our traditional foreign policy is respect for treaties; we keep our obligations; we oppose aggression; we love peace. We pay special attention to the obligations stipulated in the Covenant of the League of Nations, the Nine-Power Treaty, and the Anti-War Pact. It is unfortunate that since September 18, 1931, foreign Powers have not enforced effective measures, as agreed upon in these international commitments, to check Japanese aggression. As a result of their failure to do this, Europe too has been at the mercy of aggressor states, and the spirit of aggression and violence has spread like wildfire. Having carefully studied the diplomatic situation, members of the Council feel that our foreign policy in the past has been satisfactory. Our nation stands upon the foundation of morality, and the *San Min Chu I* is the expression of our highest moral virtues. The *Min Tsu Chu I* (Principle of Nationalism) seeks for China liberty and equality, and, at the same time, respects the liberty and equality of all other nations. That is why we are against all wars of aggression and support all attempts at maintaining world peace. Since the outbreak of the War of Resistance, we have won worldwide sympathy. In the Manifesto of the First Plenary Session of the Council we have already expressed our gratitude to the friendly nations. The chief signatories of the Nine-Power Treaty declared their stand last winter, while member states of the League of Nations have also pledged themselves to support our cause. Although war has broken out in Europe, the situation remains unchanged. Vis-à-vis Europe, we shall abide by our obligations as a member of the League. Our chief responsibility is to intensify our resistance against all kinds of intrigues and atrocities on the part of the aggressor state in East Asia. Not only will we frustrate its plan of conquest in China, but we will also obstruct its efforts to bring pressure upon the Powers, and all its other international manipulations. You should know that our international status has been raised as a result of our two years of heroic resistance. China, having one-fourth of the world's population, is undoubtedly the main pillar of world peace. The future of East Asia depends on China. We hope that Great Britain, the United States,

France, and the Soviet Union will apprehend clearly that the Sino-Japanese problem is the crux of the world problem. The Chinese nation believes that the successful completion of resistance and reconstruction in China is the most important factor in world peace and progress. Whatever changes take place in the international situation, the Republic of China will never absolve itself from the moral obligations which it has assured. This we can tell the world.

(4) Although Japanese militarism is fast approaching defeat, it still has many designs of one kind or another. Because of the changing international situation, Japan is becoming more opportunistic and ambitious. As for us, we must mobilize the entire nation and intensify all the measures for prolonged resistance so that we may successfully achieve the absolutely necessary objects in this war. In the Fifth Plenary Congress of the Kuomintang, it was resolved that a date be fixed for the convocation of the National Assembly and the adoption of the Constitution. This, however, was postponed because of the war. After two years of war, during which the fighting forces and civilian population have supported the *San Min Chu I* whole-heartedly and have done their part splendidly in all kinds of war work, the nation has achieved a unity and a solidarity that has won the admiration of the world. We cannot be satisfied with what we have achieved, for the enemy is still trying to attack us by every conceivable method. We must utilize all of our resources and mend all our weaknesses. After careful deliberation, the Council has come to the conclusion that the enlarging of the people's rights and the strengthening of the national life are the most urgent needs of the moment, and therefore has resolved to request the Government to carry out the resolution passed by the Kuomintang Congress to fix a date for the convocation of the National Assembly and the adoption of the Constitution. We hope that all those who have supported the Government's policy of resistance will just as strongly and unitedly support the Constitution as the realization of Dr. Sun Yat-sen's Three Principles of the People, and will fulfill their obligations to it. The foundation of the nation will then be firmly established and internal peace will be permanently maintained. Members of the Council believe that this is the most important contribution they have made in this Session.

Members of the Council also feel gratified that the Government has paid special attention to reconstruction in the rear. The resolution on the reconstruction program in the provinces of Szechwan and Sikang passed by this Session is one of the first steps toward the carrying out of this policy.

In conclusion, the main work of resistance from now on will be to strengthen all the spiritual and material resources for resistance. The day when we become strong is the day for our enemy to collapse. All the resolutions passed by this Session have but one object: to augment all the material and spiritual resources available for defense and reconstruction. We not only expect our Government to carry out this policy to the fullest extent; we also urge the whole-hearted support of the entire nation.

Members of the Council, we have compared the situation of the enemy and the situation at home and we have considered the road which lies before the enemy and the road before our own nation. Let all our compatriots pay homage to those soldiers who have sacrificed their lives for the nation, and to all who have been loyal to the cause of resistance in other lines of work. For two years now, every drop of blood and every bead of sweat shed in this struggle, both in the front and in the rear, has gained its highest reward. A strong, armed Power like Japan, which has sent all its best troops to China, has proven powerless to shake our determination and our spirit. No other way left, she now resorts to the old trick of dealing with traitors. This is another proof that our enemy is near exhaustion and that victory will be ours. Compatriots, you should bear this in mind: China today is more powerful than at any other period in her history. Although we have not yet driven our enemy from our soil, our material and human resources are more powerful every day, while the enemy's strength is steadily diminishing. In this time of crisis let every compatriot exert himself to the utmost in order to hasten the revival of our nation; a slight relaxation may mean national enslavement. Life or death is in our own hands. On the occasion of this closing session, members of the Council express the earnest hope that our fellow-countrymen will clearly perceive the way to victory and will move unitedly in that direction. Then we shall not only achieve the restoration of our territorial sovereignty and administrative integrity and free ourselves permanently from external aggression, but we shall also free the Japanese nation from its domination by militarists. Only thus can real peace be established in East Asia.

The People's War

ON THE twenty-eighth anniversary of the founding of the Chinese Republic, I wish to say a few words to the Chinese people in general and to our brothers and sisters in the Japanese-occupied areas in particular. China has already been engaged in war for two years and on this day of days we are bound to be reminded of the difficulties which the heroes of the Revolution experienced in the early days of the Republic. China has a bright future. I am confident that the Chinese people will do their best to drive out the enemy and to sweep away the traitors so that we may lay the foundations for a free and independent nation. During the past six months, Japan has tried to tighten her grip on China and the traitors have been intensifying their activities. Our recent victory in northern Hunan[1] has brought great comfort and encouragement to us all. Our task is by no means finished, and I wish, therefore, on this glorious day of China's history to put forward for your consideration some of the things that have been uppermost in my mind.

First of all, we must realize that China is in a revolutionary stage, and our War of Resistance is really aimed at the fulfillment of the *San Min Chu I* and the completion of the Nationalist Revolution. Revolutions in the past have succeeded only after surmounting many obstacles; there is no short cut. However, once the forces of revolution are set into motion, they do not stop until they reach their goal. Once the national consciousness is awakened, no external force can suppress it. Considered from every angle, the Chinese Revolution is destined to succeed. We were much less favorably situated on the eve of the Revolution twenty-eight years ago than we are today. Yet in spite of all difficulties, under the leadership of our late Leader, Dr. Sun Yat-sen, we overthrew the Manchu Dynasty and established a republican form of government. From this it is clear that the success of any revolutionary attempt is entirely dependent upon conformity

A message to the Chinese people on the twenty-eighth anniversary of the founding of the Republic, October 10, 1939.
[1] The First Battle of Changsha, October 2-16, 1939.

with the will of Heaven and the wishes of the people, and the spirit of the nation as a whole; and is not dependent upon material factors. We need not make light of the difficulties we are facing in this War of Resistance; in fact, it is beginning to look as if we shall meet with greater difficulties in the future. But when we observe the turn of international events in our favor and the improvement of our economic and military defenses, we can say that we have made a good start. We need now to strengthen our spirit of sacrifice and determination to fight to the end, in order that we may be worthy of the sacred trust which the heroes and fathers of our Revolution have put into our hands in order that China may enjoy liberty and equality in the family of nations.

Secondly, we should all realize that the success or failure of the war will also be dependent upon our will to fight. Militarily, we are confident that final victory will be ours, and this confidence is shared by all our soldiers at the front, who are doing their best to defend the country. From now on, besides our military operations, we must do our best to counteract the Japanese political and economic offensives. Above all, we must stir up the people and set them against the traitors in order to frustrate the enemy's political designs. Especially in the occupied areas, the Chinese people should firmly resolve not to co-operate with the Japanese but to put into practice the articles of the Citizen's Pledge, to develop guerrilla warfare, and to destroy all Japanese enterprises such as mines, factories, commercial organizations, granaries and munition depots. They should work hand in hand with the Chinese soldiers in the surrounding war areas to destroy Japanese-controlled railways, highways, telegraph and telephone lines, transportation facilities, and storehouses. In this way, the Japanese and their puppets will not enjoy any peace politically, and their economic enterprises will not succeed. This kind of work, of course, cannot be done entirely by the soldiers at the front. It must also be done by the Chinese masses in the occupied areas and areas adjacent thereto. This kind of work does not require much special training or any particular kind of weapons; it can be done by every one of us, and yet its results will be so great that it will become a death-blow to the enemy.

In the third place, in order to succeed in this war we must exterminate all the traitors who have become instruments of Japanese aggression. The Japanese have now resorted to the method of making the Chinese fight against China; they have put many Chinese under arms and have forced them to fight against their own people. All this shows that the aim of the Japanese warlords is not only to overthrow our Government but also to destroy our race. They can do this, of course, only as they are helped by traitors, big and small. As a Chinese saying goes, "Nothing is sadder than the death of the heart." Chinese traitors have tried to sell not only themselves but also their families and country. Their hearts are dead and no punishment would be too severe for them. We must get rid of them all, and we must realize that to be a traitor is the most disgraceful thing on earth. We must determine to fight all traitors, though they may be our immediate relatives, for according to the Chinese tradition, we must sacrifice even our relatives in the interest of righteousness.

In conclusion, may I remind you of what I said two years ago today. I said then that the present war will be a long one and will not be finished in one or two years. I realized at that time, as I am fully aware now, that the outbreak of the war was merely the beginning of a long and difficult struggle. The war will not end until we have fulfilled our task of national revolution and reconstruction. For this reason, we must not be impatient, neither must we lose heart. We must be prepared to meet whatever difficulties may come in our way, and we must not vainly hope for an early cessation of hostilities or for any immediate change of heart on the part of Japanese militarists. We must realize too that unless China achieves final victory, there can be no lasting peace in the Orient, and not until we have driven the enemy from our soil will the Japanese people have a real awakening. If all the people of China, at the front and in the rear, soldiers and civilians, men and women, should assert their united will, bravely contribute their full share toward winning the war, and make whatever sacrifices they were called upon to make, then the final victory would be only a matter of time. We must neither accept the defeatist psychology of the traitors nor cherish any false hopes of early peace. As the saying goes, "It is easier to defeat the bandits in the mountains than to destroy the bandits in our hearts." The "bandits in our hearts" against which we must fight today are unwillingness to suffer hardships, desire for ease, and a spirit of defeatism before the struggle is won. Such bandits must be destroyed. Although the way of revolution is fraught with difficulties, yet we must keep marching forward. When we are defeated, we must not feel downhearted; when we are victorious, we must not become over-confident. Only thus can we hope to achieve final victory in our War of Resistance and success in our program of national reconstruction.

III
China Fights and Builds
(1940-1941)

New Life in Wartime

TODAY is the sixth anniversary of the inauguration of the New Life Movement. It finds us in the fourth year of resistance and in a critical period of the struggle. When, six years ago, I first promoted the movement, my aims were to get everybody to realize the crisis in national affairs, to effect the revival of our established moral traditions, and to make the life of the nation accord with the needs of wartime, to the end that the stain upon our honor will be washed away and a future of prosperity and independence assured our people. After thirty-two months of sacrifice and effort, the foundation for final victory has been firmly laid. We are growing stronger as the war proceeds. However, more than a million enemy soldiers are still trampling the soil of our land and inflicting cruelties upon our fellow-countrymen. The weight of our responsibility for national reconstruction increases as time goes on; we must therefore be ever putting forth greater efforts in the struggle to fulfill the vast mission of resistance and rehabilitation. To commemorate this anniversary, let all of you reflect searchingly upon the past and advance along the road that lies ahead with bolder and more determined steps.

On the occasion of the fifth anniversary of the movement I said in the broadcast address I then gave: "1939 must be a year of progress for the New Life Movement; everybody must order his or her life as the needs of wartime dictate, for the increase of the strength behind resistance and for the creation of a new future life for the nation." At the same time I went a little deeper than on any previous occasion into the significance of the movement's four moral criteria, propriety, justice, integrity and conscientiousness. "Propriety," I said, "must be conceived as implying rigid discipline; justice, magnanimous sacrifice; integrity, thoroughgoing frugality; conscientiousness, resounding struggle." Since then, a year has rapidly passed by and in reviewing the record of what we have done we have to ask the question whether our citizens have or have not made progress in their ways of thought

A broadcast address to the nation on February 18, 1940, on the occasion of the sixth anniversary of the inauguration of the New Life Movement.

and life, whether our fellow-countrymen have thoroughly realized the requirements of wartime living. I am prepared frankly to state that people generally, and in particular public servants, have really not done their best to meet wartime responsibilities. Our lives are still insufficiently self-denying, our minds are too little aware of the urgency of the situation, our behavior too little orderly and restrained, our work lacking a high enough standard of accuracy and speed. Despite the fervent enthusiasm for the national cause to be found in all sections of society, there is still too wide a gap between actual living habits and the difficulties of wartime. Apart from a very small minority, our homes, government departments, schools and public institutions are rarely free from some loose, unclean or irresponsible doings. Unless these faults are eradicated, we shall continue to be unworthy of the men at the front and of all those who have given their lives for the country. Such unworthiness, in my view, is a great disgrace to the nation, and it means that the New Life Movement has not gained any sure effect. I have several points I wish to take this opportunity of impressing upon you all.

The New Life Movement is a conception in no way remote from everyday life. It is entirely concerned with the general improvement of men's lives and the practice of our moral principles. It aims at the transformation of social customs and habits of mind. We have not only to rouse ourselves but also to rouse others to full consciousness of their duty, to stimulate both ourselves and others. Six years having passed since the inauguration of the movement, it is scarcely necessary for me to dwell here on its theories and program. I wish merely to call upon you to examine your own lives and ascertain how far they accord with New Life conceptions and with what I have called "wartime life." Even the minutest details require attention, and where faults are discovered they should be immediately rectified. Certain concrete measures should be decided upon for the guidance of society and the stimulation of our fellow-countrymen to positive exertion. Our own persons, our homes, and our contacts with society should be so ordered as negatively not to conflict with the demands of wartime and positively to increase the power behind resistance and reconstruction. In simple terms, we must on the one hand make wartime life a reality and on the other exert our best efforts in wartime service. The Headquarters of the Movement has fixed upon five main points as the guiding lines of the work of the movement in its seventh year.

Firstly, to actualize Spiritual Mobilization. The five aims of this campaign which, since its inauguration last year has spread its influence throughout the land, are (1) the reform of living habits, (2) the stimulation of an optimistic spirit, (3) the eradication of evil tendencies, (4) the elimination of injurious plans, (5) the rectification of formless and disorderly ideology. These are all points bearing directly upon symptoms of national weakness. Another function of the campaign is the smashing of the enemy's subterranean designs and his activities in connection with traitors. This has already been clearly indicated in the Citizen's Pact and it is part of the fundamental work of resistance. We have to constrain not only ourselves but also our families and society to unanimous practice of these precepts. All must be called upon loyally to obey the wartime dictates of government and magnanimously make whatever contribution to the national cause is required of them. Public and private life must be tightened up to a high pitch of real austerity and frugality.

Secondly, cooperation among all concerned in the various aspects of military service, including the looking after of wounded army men. We must do all we can to assist in perfecting the arrangements for military service. The "Friends of the Wounded" Movement demands our full support. To men who have so honorably discharged their duty in defense of country and people, we owe both spiritual and material forms of reward. The New Life Movement has already done much to bestir the social conscience to serve wounded men and numerous stations have been set up for the work. On the occasion of this anniversary a central station has been established, having set itself the object of enrolling one hundred thousand "friends of the wounded." I trust that all my listeners will respond by enthusiastically joining up. You will thus directly requite the merits of the wounded, and indirectly raise the fighting morale of the men now at the front. The thorough working out of the system of conscription is a still more important part of national construction. It is for us to lend our assistance to publicity work, to explore all possibilities of seeing that able-bodied men of military age voluntarily enlist, and that each person in the family and society generally does his part in providing for the needs and comfort of men newly enrolled and their families.

Thirdly, cooperation in the task of opium-suppression, for the improvement of national health. The negative course to this end is the eradication of drugs; the positive consists in promoting physical culture. For the attainment of these purposes we have set up the Citizens' Anti-Drug Association and the Citizens' Physical Training Association. You will all be aware that this year the Six-Year Opium-Suppression Plan expires; it has not been affected or retarded by the war. The

Government has repeatedly declared its intention to proceed with its plans to their appointed conclusion. At the same time it requires the wholehearted cooperation of the entire people in the work; only thus can rapidity and thoroughness be attained. I trust that wherever you may be, you will spontaneously encourage one another in observing vigilance and drawing upon the resources of society to supply the clinics with medicine, talent, and expenses, in order to emancipate addicts from their pitiable plight. Moreover it is necessary to awaken our fellow-countrymen in the occupied areas to strive with the aid of one another's good counsel to shatter the enemy's drug dissemination campaign. The spreading of the physical training movement should also be unslackeningly sought in these days of national resistance. I hope that you will all take the molding of citizens' physique as a fundamental part of national rebirth. Hill-climbing, swimming, boxing and modern forms of exercise should, according to circumstances of time and place, be adopted by organizations and enthusiastically promoted, to the end that each individual may become a strong unit in a strong people and our foundation as a strong country be laid.

Fourthly, the stimulation of the national economy and the increase of wartime production. Our material supplies have been subject to obstruction since, as a consequence of resistance, our ports have been harried and blockaded by the enemy. Yet in practice this has afforded us an opportunity of re-creating the economic life of the nation. Our attention is now most urgently required (1) to the use of consumers' cooperatives to adjust supply and demand and effect a lowering of the prices of necessities of life; (2) to the elimination of enemy goods by intensifying the movement for counter-blockade, the absolute cessation of the sale of raw materials and manufactured articles to the enemy, and absolute exclusion of Japanese goods from markets in our territory, in order to smash the enemy's schemes of economic aggression. (3) The increase of agricultural and industrial production. Apart from those taking part in work at the front or in labor corps, every man and woman in the land should choose some variety of productive work in agriculture, horticulture, road-building, transport, or handicrafts, each individual putting all the energy he or she possesses into the activity chosen. All sorts of competitive methods should be instituted with a view to stimulating constant innovations and progress in all phases of wartime work. The Government has already established a thousand or more industrial cooperatives for the large-scale manufacture of all sorts of clothing and foodstuffs. These cooperatives are simple, convenient, very rapidly effective and not dependent upon large amounts of capital. I hope that they will be taken as models for wide development along this line, in order to make the means of productive power penetrate deeply into the countryside.

(4) The stimulation of animal husbandry as one means of increasing tran'sport facilities. It has always been the custom to supplement rural economy with cattle-rearing. The western regions of the rear are famous as natural cattle-raising areas. I hope that provincial governments and individuals generally will exert the utmost of their ability in encouraging poultry and pig raising and especially the breeding of mules and horses. To the economic value of such production there is added the contribution animals can make to wartime transport needs.

(5) The awakening of our fellow-countrywomen and the advance of the women's movement. Half the population of the country are women and therefore in them reposes one half of our national strength. Since resistance began, our women, under the leadership of the Women's Guidance Committees, taking part in war-area service have already established a notable record of achievement. As many as 48 orphanages for the care of thousands of refugee children have now been established. There has also been the foundation of Experimental Weaving Areas and Silkworm Breeding Areas, the organization of the New Life Movement's Women's Handicraft Institutes, and the setting up of Soldiers' Families' Factories. These enterprises have made a very substantial contribution to the increase of production, and are a phenomenon that may well give rise to much gratification. It is, however, strictly speaking, only a very small proportion of our womenfolk who are engaged in such work. We need the mobilization rather of a majority of them to fill up gaps in our national strength; in the family and in society we want them to take part in measures concerned with the improvement of the people's livelihood and the consolidation of the forces of resistance. During the present time we particularly desire to see greater fruits come of pushing the Women's New Life activities.

The five descriptions of work touched upon above have each of them direct bearing upon resistance and reconstruction. I trust that all my fellow-countrymen will display enthusiasm in the cause of saving at once themselves and their country by unanimously putting their best efforts into the carrying out of these projects.

I constantly pass in mental review the aims of the movement, which consist in raising the value and quality of human life and establishing its continuity with universal life. Our lives are just now led under the constraint of Japanese aggression and the history of our people has reached a turning point that will decide its survival or extinction. Only by intensifying our sense of the moral values can we break through the present stormy period. The final military victory in resistance is within reach but we must stretch forth our hands to grasp it, to overcome present difficulties and lay a new foundation for reconstruction. We must all make reforms start from our own lives, bringing ever fresh and stronger exertions to our work. May you all lift up your hearts to press forward to the completion of the mission this age has laid upon us.

The Educator's Mission in China Today

THE future of nation and race is bound up with the quality of the individual and the building up of a sound citizenry must depend upon the principals and teachers at the head of our educational institutions of every description. At the opening of the Third National Educational Conference last year I gave a very full account of my views on the matter. I said I looked to all concerned with education to practise the Three Principles of the People, to exalt our people's traditional morality, to esteem the teacher's calling, to emphasize tutorial instruction, to reinforce the national will to resist and cultivate the spirit of construction—all to the end of effecting a lasting enrichment of the nation's vital force.

I also made a point of telling you to regard the steeling of the national character as the fundamental duty of educationalists. I repeated my insistence upon the four cardinal virtues, and declared the twelve Party Maxims [1] to be Maxims for Youth. At the same time the principals of all Szechwan institutions above the middle grade and personnel in training were summoned to a conference at which the participants were to strive to confirm in one another the revolutionary outlook on life and excite in one another the spirit of patriotism. A year has since made its rapid passage by; now the winter vacations are

A message telegraphed to the principals of all universities, middle schools and primary schools on the occasion of the conclusion of the winter vacations, February 20, 1940.
[1] The Twelve Maxims of the Kuomintang Code:
      Loyalty and courage are the basis of patriotism.
      Filial devotion is the basis of a well-ordered family.
      Goodwill and charity are the basis of harmonious relationships.
      Trustworthiness and uprightness are the basis of a successful career.
      Peaceableness is the basis of getting on with the world.
      Courtesy and self-control are the basis of good administration.
      Obedience is the basis of bearing responsibility.
      Diligence and thrift are the basis of service.
      Orderliness and cleanliness are the basis of physical health.
      Helpfulness is the basis of happiness.
      Knowledge is the basis of helping the world.
      Persistence is the basis of achievement.

at an end and a new term is beginning. This is the time for all educational institutions to review their past work and fix their plans for the future. I particularly approach you educators to dwell once again on your responsibility for the guidance of pupils to progress in their thinking, in their conduct, and in everything that goes to form their physical and moral make-up.

The War of Resistance we are waging today is the most violent struggle for survival to take place in Chinese history; it is a unique turning point on which the nation's rise or decline must depend. The meaning of this war lies, on the one hand, in the withstanding of atrocious aggression for the preservation of our people's existence, and, on the other hand, in the creation during the various constraints and difficulties of wartime of a richly vital modern nation—a nation with a future. With that achievement alone will our responsibilities have been fulfilled. In this connection my first words in addressing last year's educational conference were: "Our education must look as much to what will follow the war as to the war itself." Speaking of the present situation, only a today of concentrated will and awakened spirit will give us the opportunity for a future day of progress. We should take advantage of this critical moment to unify the nation and build up the citizen's ways of thinking, to the end that the youths now studying in our schools may be destined, one and all, to pioneer that national future and undertake the vast work of rehabilitation which must follow the conclusion of the war.

Speaking, again, of the nation's practical needs, not only does the reconquest of our invaded soil demand of our countless citizens a lofty spirit of resolution, but also when resistance is over there will be an even more urgent necessity for all public and private energies to be bent upon economic and productive recovery and for courage and endurance equal to the extraordinary proportions of the task of reconstruction as it will then present itself. In brief, there is nothing we have to oppose to the enemy's aggression but a sound and valiant citizenry standing at the back of our self-sacrificing soldiers, giving them, and reassuring them of, support for their heroic efforts. And if it is not you educators there is none who can so bring up the younger generation as to fit it for the time to come.

Judging from the various manifestations of progress I have observed among our youth and the contrasting insubstantiality and faults of our education as it was ten or twenty years ago, I feel bound to enjoin you with all possible earnestness to make the most of this historic time in the way you dedicate yourselves to perpetuating the glories of China's ageless past and opening the gate on a future of boundless prosperity. I hold that the disabilities of wartime are to be taken as a matter of course; wherever cracks in our material, financial, political and social structure are discovered there can be no question of their being irreparable; above all else in importance is the steeling of the nation's moral fiber and the reward to be reaped from your efforts in this direction will prove beyond all else immense and lasting.

Passing in review all that the years of resistance have brought from devoted and courageous patriots with a deep sense of responsibility, at the front, and others equally self-denying and laborious in the rear, we have only to inquire a little into the lives of the persons most distinguished for their loyal conduct to discover they have benefited in their school-days from invigorating contact with good teachers; and only by virtue of the sound basis given their character could they attain the undaunted spirit with which they have pitted themselves against overwhelming difficulties. Recently the enemy has shown himself exhausted by the state of deadlock in the field; the day of victory is nigh. In the matter of character-building you can and should take a long-range view of the future of national life. I deeply trust that you teachers will shoulder the responsibility of guiding your students' thinking, molding their personalities, ordering their lives, steeling their physique and reinforcing their characters. It is essential to realize that the acquisition of technical and scientific knowledge forms but a single part of education. If it is not allied to a spirit of love of country, people and fellow-men, and made an adjunct to the sense of responsibility for the fate of the nation and the completion of the revolution, to knowledge of the age and the state of world affairs, to a long-sighted view of issues, and to "sinews of brass and bones of iron," a frame equal to all hardships—unless an aspiring inclination to lasting effort is awakened, the acquisitions of the mind may run into any channel fortuitous circumstances present or to waste, and at all events will prove of no value to the nation.

I have devoted a life half spent in military service to the revolution; but from the time of the opening of the Whampoa Academy [2] I have never lost contact with the educational life. I hold that schools owe it to their students to give them philosophic guidance, to eradicate from their minds idle and *laissez-aller* ways of thinking, and to make them all realize that the enterprise of revolution is the expression of

[2] China's foremost military academy, established at Whampoa, near Canton, in 1924 with General Chiang Ki-shek as its principal; now called the Central Military Academy.

China's will as it has lain latent in her for thousands of years. They must accordingly establish in themselves a faith in the Three Principles such that in life or death it shall remain unshaken. In regard to the forging of character, instruction must turn on the commonly prescribed school discipline and the Maxims for Youth, with a view to the cultivation of habits of virtue and responsibility and further bringing out the nation's established moral powers. Thus men may be produced who fulfill the primary duty of unselfish service of others, equal to mastering natural forces and creating a future in accordance with the highest meaning of human life. There must be the inculcation of frugality, of vigorous application, of the will to strive, of prudence and orderliness, of speed and thoroughness, of the strict preservation of discipline and obedience to orders. Men so educated need not be ashamed to take the name of citizens of a modern state.

Reading matter outside the scope of ordinary lessons, the direction of out-of-school activities, the importance to be attached to public morality and philanthropy, and the cultivation of habits of mutual assistance and cooperation, are all aspects of education for which constant attention, similar to that of parents' care for their children, is required, or indeed something of an intimate thoroughness even exceeding that degree. With teacher and pupil in contact from morning to night and sharing all in common there can scarcely fail to be a gradual molding of the pupil's mind by good influence.

The past ten to twenty years have left on our education traces of dissipated and selfish habits of mind such as young students should cast aside and consider the dregs of an age gone by. In all grades of our schools, a single student incapable of patriotism, observance of discipline, respect for teachers, and fellow-feeling for his companions, his headmaster and the teaching staff, should be considered a burning shame to the latter themselves. On the one hand, I look to principals and teachers for conduct in line with what I have consistently enjoined upon them : the giving of a personal example as a way of influencing students towards the good and the production of genuine results to show. Although Chinese education is not universal, the students in our educational institutions of all kinds number not less than twenty millions, who if so educated as to form a sound core of citizens devoted to resistance and reconstruction, would ensure a bright future for China. And when the revolution has succeeded, the Chinese people will undoubtedly have a great contribution to make to world peace and prosperity. You will have firstly done your duty by your country and secondly by your pupils; you will have become strong factors in the creation of the national fortunes and molding of the course of world affairs, worthy of the enduring respect of posterity.

Your calling, for all its hardships, gives you the way to boundless achievement. I trust that you will give heed to my poor words, and make them a living part of your conduct, thereby earning the gratitude of your nation and people.

The Responsibilities of Modern Journalists

DURING the last four or five years Chinese journalism has made very considerable progress—progress that has been only the more marked since the beginning of the present War of Resistance. One outstanding feature has been the widening of the scope of journalists' activities. The modern journalist is acquainted, not only with editing work, but also with the business side of his profession. In the content of our newspapers there is a constantly increasing proportion of substantial reporting and detailed news dispatches to the almost entire exclusion of meaningless social gossip. Technically, there is to be observed conquest of material difficulties, the utilization of inferior and simple equipment, and increase in the volume and rapidity of production. The spirit of service in the profession is meanwhile rendering its members able to endure privations and simplicity in their way of living and giving them the courage to face dangers in the course of their duties.

The work of journalists in the past was confined to the editing room, and the sphere of their activity limited in great part to the clubs, institutions and societies of the large cities. The journalist of today goes out into the countryside of the interior, to the war areas and to the front. In the past a newspaperman was attached to circumstances of ease and comfort; now he seeks the atmosphere of vigor and action. There is a tremendous contrast between the slack and heterogeneous attitudes of journalists in the past and their anxiety today to express the spirit of the age, their regard for the future of the nation, their support of the national policy and their respect for the law.

This progress in journalism is providing a factor in the progress of the nation and people. It is one of the most encouraging phenomena of the war. Dr. Sun Yat-sen once said that publicity is education. This means that the journalist is an organ of speech for the expression of the nation's will; he is a teacher upon whom the people depend for

A message read by Mr. Tai Chi-tao, President of the Examination Yuan, to fifty-two graduates in journalism of the Central Political Academy at a graduation ceremony, March 22, 1940.

their enlightenment. For fifty years the course of national revolution from its inception and throughout its development has been closely bound up with the world of journalism. The vicissitudes of its history have been modified by the standard of intelligence and energy displayed by journalists. Where their efforts have chimed with national policy the revolution has made rapid strides, while where the contrary has been the case its development has been obstructed and delayed. At this time of concentrated national effort in the cause of resistance, the responsibilities of our journalists in the struggle are scarcely less important than those of men fighting and dying in battle.

How the national policy is to be made generally known, public opinion unified, and the wills of all stimulated to unanimous advance towards the goal of national revival, the destruction of the enemy and the rehabilitation of the country according to the Three Principles of the People—all this is contingent upon the positive enthusiasm shown by journalists. I wish to describe in the following paragraphs the nature of the objectives toward which I conceive they should be striving.

One: The fulfillment of their responsibility for widespread publicity. The quantity of news matter distributed in China is far behind that of other countries of the world. The areas served are too much limited to the towns and lines of communication. With the beginning of resistance there began a gradual improvement in this respect. The tendency of the future must certainly be a constant broadening of the field for local newspapers. The production of newspapers in the interior has ever been a matter of difficulty, and if only for that reason it is an enterprise calling for pioneering efforts on the part of journalists, they must plunge into that environment which is no less remarkable for the hope it holds for the future than for the difficulties it presents, and sow there the seeds of culture, to the end of raising the level of popular knowledge and intelligence. It is an ideal we have set ourselves to have for every five or three *hsien* a local newspaper on a satisfactorily complete scale. One need not seek a high finish in printing, but substantial content capable of making up for the deficiencies of social education and acting as a source of local progress.

Two: The fulfillment of journalists' responsibility for making the national policy generally known and understood. In both the editorial and news columns of newspapers the aim should be to stimulate our people's sense of independence and self-respect, to foster in them a progressive spirit, and to urge their accurate observance of the *Outlines of National Reconstruction,* never forgetful of the supremacy of the interests of nation and people. In the analysis of the international situation provided, correct emphasis should be as much a consideration as detail, and everything should be related to the interests of China as a center. Only thus will the reader be made aware of the realities and be benefited. In the exposition of important government decrees, the pointing out of essentials is of greater moment than the mere reproduction of texts; the underlying principles must be explained so that by a full understanding of the law and intelligent talk among themselves the people may come more readily to observe it.

Three: The fulfillment of journalists' responsibility for advancing reconstruction. I hold that China has now entered into a new period wherein real reconstruction is just beginning. The mission of the newspaper is, therefore, also entering into a new phase of its importance. In the past politics formed the main burden of its contents: today emphasis should be shifted to economics and production. In the past government offices and institutions chiefly furnished the newspaper with its material; today the sources should be the rural districts, factories, cooperative societies, and productive organizations generally. The pages of our newspapers should now be filled with practical information regarding economic reconstruction rather than with generalities of no especial concern to the people. There should be discussion of methods of improving production. Such a nation as is our ideal is one wherein production, national strength and the people's livelihood progress in unison. All the newspapers of the country should therefore be working in that direction, leading their readers toward that end.

Four: The fulfillment of the journalist's responsibility for raising popular morale. This is the day of resistance and reconstruction. The people have to be led into the right way, to tread the road of loyalty to the nation and the cause; the traitorous have to be extirpated and patriotic feeling set at the highest valuation. On the one hand, examples of heroic and devoted conduct among the people in the war areas should be extolled to the full. On the other, all light and frivolous writing, all retrograde and aimless habits of mind should be swept away. We must be awake to the fact that seriousness is not just another name for dryness. It is for journalists to find the right ways of rousing their readers' interest in serious subjects. This is highly important as a part of their work in educating the masses.

The above is some description of the mission journalists of today must fulfill, and the direction in which their efforts must be exerted. By passing through this period of hard trial, China will become capable of rising to the status of a great and progressive nation. Not only are we ourselves confident of this but the world too knows that it is so. For more than ten years yet, however, we shall have to strive towards that great end. The active and ever fresh exertions of journalists are required to broaden and accelerate their work of national leadership. Let them with one mind and one purpose bear the nation's destiny forward to its appointed goal: then the people will respond with a like concentration of will and strength in moving toward that goal. To achieve this it will be necessary to keep the newspaper field supplied with fresh talent and new technical ideas. Its duties are incomparably momentous. My desire is that all of you new graduates in journalism should throw yourselves wholeheartedly into the fulfillment of those duties.

No Relaxation of Our Efforts

TODAY we open the fifth full session of this Council. The number of those present is strikingly greater than on previous occasions. This time many who in the past for reasons of distance or health could not attend, have spared themselves no fatigue in hastening to take part. The enthusiasm and liveliness to be seen here today reflects the unanimous will of the whole country to shoulder its burdens. It is inspiring and refreshing in the extreme. In the period of recess which is now at an end, moreover, my fellow-councillors' work has fully displayed our resolution to hold ourselves responsible for the work of resistance and reconstruction. Our Szechwan-Sikang Reconstruction Commission has set up five agencies, and many individual members have been constantly going out to make tours of inspection and report their observations to the Government as a basis for progressive action on its part. Our Constitutional Planning Commission has held several meetings for the close study of various constitutional problems. We have organized a party to travel in North China for the purpose of inspecting and encouraging the troops. It made its way throughout Shensi, Honan, Shansi, and Hopei, conveying to the army and the people its assurances of the Council's sympathy and respect. Some of our members have also taken part in the Inspection Party sent out by the National Military Council to observe the discipline and behavior of the army in the field. That party went to the front and made its contribution to the putting of greater order into military discipline and externals. Respect is due to all of you who, regardless of hardship, difficulty and danger, took part in these forms of work and successfully accomplished your ends.

It is now precisely six months since the Fourth Session of the Council was held and meanwhile the international situation has become tense as a result of the European conflict, while with us resistance has entered a graver stage. By striving onward, however, both at the front and in the rear, with a firm grasp on our established national policy, we have considerably strengthened the foundation of resistance and have achieved

Opening address to the Fifth Session of the People's Political Council, April 1, 1940.

primary results in reconstruction. At this session I wish first to outline what have been the main military, diplomatic, and political features of the last six months.

Let me first speak of military affairs. At the time of the closing of the last full session, I said: "The present fighting strength of China not only exceeds that of last year, but is actually superior to that at the beginning of the War of Resistance two years ago." Reviewing the events of the six months past, I can say that the military strength we are now employing in resistance is sounder than during the previous six months. In all technical matters and in those of organization, progress has been made. The foundation for victory has by now been thoroughly laid. During these six months all the enemy's moves in northern Hunan, in northern Kwangtung, in southern Kwangsi, in northern Hupeh, in southern Shansi, in western Suiyuan have been without exception frustrated by our forces. Recently, the counter-attack on Wuyuan and the recovery of Lingshan and Funan on the Kwangsi front have further demonstrated the debilitated state of the enemy's resources and strength. His defeats in northern Hunan and northern Kwangtung have shown that his offensives no longer have any chance of success. Our recovery of Kunlunkuan has shown how much he may suffer in unsuccessful efforts to hold positions he has already taken. During the last three months the enemy has lost an aggregate of 230,000 men. From now on he has only a further irretrievable decline to contemplate, attended by repeated mortal blows from our forces until he is cut up in detail over the vast expanse of our territory and his armies at last become a total ruin.

Second: In regard to diplomacy, we have been pursuing during these six months a course which I described at our last Session as one of "meeting kaleidoscopic changes with an unchanging attitude"—holding firm to an established policy and following it out consistently. The moment may be one of complication and gravity in the face of international affairs, but our position is quite simple and clear-cut. Those nations of the world friendly to us and clearly aware of the facts of our situation express unanimous sympathy with us. Although war has broken out in Europe, many countries there and on the American continent have been giving us moral and material assistance rather increasingly than otherwise during the past half-year. The United States loan of $20,000,000 has been a great encouragement.

At the time the Russo-Finnish conflict broke out, it seemed that international relations were about to become still more complicated. Now peace has been made between those two countries, the scale of the war in Europe has been reduced, relations between the Soviet Union and

Britain, America and France, it seems, may soon very possibly grow closer. I believe that Soviet Russia, with all the peace-loving countries of the world, will henceforth undoubtedly stand on a common ground of upholding international justice and seeking to carry out its peace policy by restoring peace in the world and in Eastern Asia.

Third: Speaking of political affairs, detailed accounts of the administrative work done during the last six months will be given you in separate reports presented by the various ministries and commissions. What I have now to explain to you all is the aim upon which our administrative plans and measures have been centered during the period under review. Apart from noteworthy achievements made in opium and gambling suppression, the eradication of banditry, the relief of acute distress, the improvement of public health and the promotion of physical training, on the positive side of our work the emphasis has been upon internal administration and economic affairs.

(1) Regarding internal administration, special attention has been paid to the building up of local autonomy and the strengthening of the basic political organs in order to establish a foundation for constitutional government. In September of last year the Government issued some "Essential Rules for All Grades of *Hsien* Administration." On the one hand, provisions were made for the training of personnel for local autonomous governments and on the other hand, practical provisions were made for the collection of necessary funds. It was decided to put all this into practice from the present year. This is of course an arduous undertaking, but it is one into which we must put the utmost determination and energy in order to consolidate the forces of resistance. To see to it that the people have real training in the exercise of their four political powers [election, recall, initiative and referendum], that they are organized, that conscription is made more fully effective, that the resources of local strength are built up, that instruction in citizenship is rendered universal, it is absolutely necessary to put this system into operation. I trust that all of you will do your best to work together towards this end.

(2) On the economic side, special attention must be paid to the development of economic reconstruction and the building up of financial and monetary power. In economic reconstruction, industrial, mining and agricultural production must be increased. In industry and mining, apart from positive application of the plans decided upon, a further plan for widening the scope of development in those fields has just been defined, funds allotted, and a limited period of time fixed for its fulfillment. At the same time it is felt that the consolidation of wartime

166

resources and the commodities of daily necessity to the people must proceed from the development of agriculture. Therefore, measures taken henceforth will be directed to the full development of agricultural economy, and the advance of rural production. The creation of the Ministry of Agriculture and Forestry was aimed at providing an organization whose sole business is with the problems of agriculture, forestry, and land reclamation work. In future, positive progress must be made on the basis of this policy. It is to be hoped that the building up of the national economy and the reduction of unnecessary burdens on the people will proceed alongside the exploration of all possibilities of benefiting our laboring citizenry.

In respect of matters of finance and currency I have to make particular mention of the setting up of a Joint Office for the Four Government Banks. The fact that the basis of national finance has been steadily growing firmer during the past two years and the nation has been able to meet the demands made upon its financial resources is in great part due to the completeness and effectiveness of the groundwork done in pre-war days. Now to tighten up economic reconstruction we have further to concentrate the strength of our financial machinery and utilize it in pressing forward with our whole economic policy. Since the establishment of the Joint Office of the Four Banks it has contributed much to the building and spreading of a currency network, to the stabilization of the basis of foreign exchange transactions, to the absorption of capital in productive enterprise, and to the making available of credit loans. The Four Banks have set up a record of striking achievement during the past six months, and now they must steadily add to what they have done in order to accelerate our economic reconstruction by the acquisition of financial strength.

I have just passed in review the main features of the military, diplomatic, and political scene during the past six months. Let us now look at the enemy's situation. I have already touched on the exhaustion of his military strength. I need not dwell further upon it. The state of internal political and economic life in Japan is such that the country is on the verge of collapse. Economically speaking, the budget has swelled to the figure of 16,000,000,000 yen; loans can no longer be raised; paper money is being recklessly printed; agricultural labor is growing ever scarcer; coal and electricity shortage is obstructing industry; discontent is rife among the people; the foundations of society are shaken; numerous conflagrations have done great damage and other disasters due to natural and human causes have taken place. In politics, the army has its violent, ungoverned way. Yonai has succeeded Abe; Saito has been deprived of his seat in the Diet; wild scenes were enacted in the 75th Session of the Diet. All this has shown that a few irresponsible army men are controlling everything. A second example of such a dark and turbulent state of internal political affairs could not be found in all the world. The reflection of it in Japanese foreign policy is even more confused and contradictory. The one clear intention behind it is to stir up trouble in Eastern Asia by a process the Japanese have the audacity to call "establishing a new order in East Asia." Fully intending likewise to drive out other nations' legitimate rights from the Far East, they try to deceive themselves and others by calling it "cooperation." The fact is that they see in the European War a chance of taking some unfair advantage of the Powers by striking at them one by one. The perfidy of the motives behind Japanese foreign policy is manifest to all.

Let us take one or two examples. Lately, the Japanese have been offering a pretense of opposing Soviet Russia as a bait for America and the European Powers, but the latter did not swallow it. Then they tried to threaten those Powers with a pretense of seeking a rapprochement with Russia, the only result being to incur the contempt of the Soviet Union and utter failure to coerce the European countries or America. Now Japan is again seeking to use the anti-Comintern disguise as a means of currying favor with those countries. This sort of childish floundering naturally excites the lively contempt of the Powers. Towards America, for instance, Japan first adopted a menacing and stern demeanor and then, America being unmoved, turned to promises of compensation for damage done to American property and future respect for American interests in China. Again America was unmoved. The abrogation of the commercial treaty with Japan, the moral embargo, and other steps were taken. Japanese emissaries have been sent out in all directions with some design of persuading a combination of Central and Southern American nations to bring pressure to bear on the United States. Any such pressure would, needless to say, amount to nothing. American public opinion and determination to check Japan has only grown stronger, and feeling against Japan more bitter. In fact, three years of war with us have weakened Japan to a degree that is perfectly well-known to other nations. Her militarists, however, still propose to bully the world with overbearing language. This is bluff that reveals only their own extreme folly. They will bring only ruin upon themselves in this way. The two instances I have given serve to show how Japanese foreign policy is, in the words I used the year before last, a case of "the thing being wrong at the root, no health is to be found in any of its ramifications." It is a matter of course for it to be frustrated at every turn and eventually to end in catastrophe.

Precisely because the enemy is everywhere on the way to ruin in the military, political, economic, and diplomatic fields, he has thought, as a solution to his dilemma, of putting up Wang Ching-wei to form a puppet government in Nanking, and accordingly, on March 30 Wang mounted the stage. He is the center of a collection of shameless rogues who do not hesitate to accept slavery and treachery as their lot. They have made themselves never-to-be-forgotten criminals of the Chinese people and a great blot upon the record of resistance. The law must punish them and the people indict them, but it is not to be supposed they can produce the slightest effect upon resistance in the long run. I long ago said: "Let the enemy manufacture dozens of puppet regimes, and whatever name may be attached to them we shall never recognize them for anything but slaves of Japan. Nothing they do in their internal or external affairs can have any validity whatever or have any ill effect whatever on our Party and nation." The nation has loaded this foul spectacle with abuse; these traitors have long ceased to own the right to call themselves Chinese. They will also fail to deceive any country in the world that is now our friend. This action of the Japanese militarists is doubtless intended as a piece of conjuring for use in dealing with other nations, and towards the people at home as a means of disguising the fact of defeat and palming this off as a substitute for the real successes that are not forthcoming.

For the Japanese trick of clothing this puppet government with all the phraseology of the genuine Kuomintang and Republican Government of China, the motive is to be found in their desire to make this step a means to realizing the dreams of the so-called "Secret Treaty with Wang," [1] the "New Order in East Asia" and "Readjustment of Relations between Japan and China." Everybody knows that Wang's appearance will be but a passing dream. In fact, this is the destiny of the Wang puppet regime. This being the case, his installation at Nanking is a crowning touch to the utter unreality of all the illusions cherished by the Japanese aggressors; it is the knell of their dreams rung by themselves. Japan herself will go into the same grave that is now gaping for Wang. By putting up Wang, the Japanese have made the admission that all their efforts have not sufficed to conquer China, that they are faced by

[1] The secret agreement between Wang Ching-wei and the Japanese, signed on December 30, 1939, and entitled "Outline Governing the Readjustment of Relations Between China and Japan," provided for Japan's domination of China in terms which Generalissimo Chiang characterized as even more severe than the Twenty-one Demands. The text of the puppet agreement was disclosed by two former associates of Wang and was made public on January 22, 1940.

a crisis they know to be hopeless for them. So they have recourse to this weak gamble in an attempt to use a *fait accompli* as an instrument for the extraction of still heavier taxes from their people and still more of the lives of their youths for the satisfaction of their ambitions. In fact, however, the result has been increased dissatisfaction and unrest, for this step can in the eyes of the Japanese people appear only as a confession of defeat. It is certain to arouse greater bitterness and disillusionment than ever. As for its international effects, Wang's debut is an indication to the world of the incorrigibility of the Japanese militarists. Nobody is to be again taken in by a trick they have already used in Korea and Siberia. This is a last desperate move on their part and it will prove one of the most important in accelerating the collapse of Japan. I have often said: "The Japanese militarists can do nothing but what is harmful to their own country, never by any chance something beneficial to it." The present appearance of this puppet government is yet another strong proof of this.

For our part, simply because the enemy is on his way to ruin, we must put especial vigor into our resistance at this time. We have already decided upon a second Three-Year-Plan for Resistance. You must all realize that this plan is at the same time a positive plan for reconstruction. More than ordinary energy, effort, and willingness to accept responsibility in common are called for to build up our political, economic, and military strength. It must be realized that the very fact of the enemy's present hopeless predicament is due only to the struggle we have put up during the two years and nine months just passed. Now that he has offered the whole Chinese people this insult in bringing out Wang Ching-wei, the eyes of the world are turned upon us, not to observe how we deal with this traitor and his crime, for the world knows his utter worthlessness. The U.S. Secretary of State, Mr. Cordell Hull, made a statement on March 31 [1940] which displayed his sense of international justice. He spoke as a representative of world opinion. What the world is interested to see is how the Chinese people deal with those who are behind the pitiful little puppet show—the Japanese militarists themselves. We must now be doubly eager to give of our very best, bringing to bear the heroic revolutionary spirit of resistance to remove this outrageous stain upon our national honor. Our answer to this attempt of the Japanese and their puppets to save their fortunes, annihilate our people and call it by the shameless phrase of "restoring peace" is to put forth all our strength to attack and strike back at them, swearing to drive the enemy from our soil, and create a real and lasting peace in Eastern Asia. To their attempt to use the "Secret Treaty between Japan and Wang" in order to effect a so-called "Readjustment of Relations between the Two Countries" as a device for the annexation of all China, our answer must be to wrest from him the independence, existence, and freedom of our nation. They on their side propose "to build a New Order in East Asia." We on ours must throw the whole strength of our people into the struggle, producing facts wherewith to smash the Japanese ambition of monopolizing East Asia. Until the final defeat of the invader is accomplished, resistance can never cease. We must restore the territorial and administrative integrity of our land, and remove from the world this source of harm and danger to its welfare, demonstrate the splendor of the Three Principles of the People, and cleanse our soil of the poisonous miasma now lying over the occupied areas. Such is the resolve we must set before ourselves today; and it is also the duty we have to fulfill in the cause of world peace.

We can by no means permit ourselves to relax our own efforts because of the exhaustion of the enemy, nor stop pressing him because he is powerless to advance further. Our victory is assured us on condition that we do not cease our efforts but render them more and more vigorous. The greater the exhaustion of the enemy, the more we should be roused; the nearer he is to his end, the more we should ask of ourselves. Since the war began we have made it our plan to prosecute resistance and reconstruction simultaneously. Resistance is our immediate task, while reconstruction is our ultimate goal. Now the international situation is uniformly advantageous to our resistance, and the enemy himself by seeking his own destruction as he has, has done the best he could for our reconstruction. The traitors' puppet-show has reached its culminating point. The basis of our final victory has been strengthened by this event. This is a moment, therefore, from the standpoint of the situation, for us to concentrate all our minds and wills on the work of resistance; from another standpoint, it is the moment for us to give our best positive efforts to reconstruction. We must exert ourselves not only in military matters, but devote efforts at least as determined to matters political, economic, and those generally connected with reconstruction. We are trying to expedite the establishment of the ideal of local autonomy, to build up the basic political framework of national life, to develop the Southwest and the Northwest; we have decided to summon a People's Congress, to bring out a Constitutional Code, to establish the foundation for democratic rule, to have the whole nation, high and low, respecting the national laws, rigidly observing discipline and following out the program of resistance and reconstruction. Why are we doing all this? In order to increase the power of resistance, and also to complete the great enterprise of reconstruction.

I wish to tell all of you present at this session of the Council that while in the first stage of resistance the military aspect of the struggle was perhaps all-important, now after two years and nine months the foundation for military victory has been soundly laid, and we have in future to think not solely in military terms of ultimate victory. It is rather the quality of our work in political and economic reconstruction that will decide the future of resistance. From this moment we must positively concentrate and consolidate our spiritual and material resources. Thus political, economic and social reconstruction will be able rapidly to develop. The establishment of our People's Political Council took place nearly two years ago. Though the Council is held for a certain appointed period of time, we councillors have a duty that knows no bounds. So, far from our duties being near completion, it may be said that the far-reaching and weighty nature of our work is only beginning to appear. I trust that all present here on this occasion will show the utmost sincerity of which they are capable in contributing the best they can towards the success of the gathering. First, there will be a full review of the central items in the administrative measures I have just reported on. Views must be offered as to anything conducive to rapid advance of local autonomy, economy, and reconstruction.

Also, I request you to pay attention to the following three points: First, the Program of Resistance and Reconstruction published two years ago was accepted by this Council as a creed subscribed to by the whole country. We must all examine how much we have achieved of what it requires of us, whether in regard to the Government, to the locality, or to society, or even to various public bodies or individuals. We must ask ourselves if we have faithfully practised it with sincerity and devotion to the public good. Second: The Szechwan-Sikang Reconstruction Commission is an important practical piece of work. I desire an examination of what this Commission has actually achieved towards the actualization of the plans for reconstruction in the two provinces as the base of resistance and a model for all reconstruction. Third: with regard to the laying of a foundation for the Constitution, there must be detailed discussions and practical contributions. We must not limit our attention to the adoption of a constitution; we must proceed to put it into practice. We do not want pretty phrases, but a practicable code, and one that would prove advantageous to resistance and still more so to the future good of the country. Dr. Sun Yat-sen wrote in 1921 a book of *Plans for National Defense*, containing sixty sections, the sixth of which appears in the index under the title "National Defense and the Constitution." This work he unhappily left unfinished, but his obvious purpose may give us much food for thought. In the matter of a constitution for China we need more than to follow out the Three Principles of the People and the division of the Government into five branches. We have also to consider it in relation to national defense. Without sound national defense there can be no foundation for a constitutional country. The code we are now seeking must emphasize national defense, and it will then prove the framework of a sound and permanent national order.

Fellow-councillors, the entire nation has striven together for two years and nine months. Our army and people have provided such a foundation of heroic sacrifice as our victory may easily be built upon. It is a foundation we have all to cherish and reinforce. This session of the Council is held at a peculiar moment in the contortions of the enemy and his puppets. We must exhort our fellow-citizens from now on to exert unprecedented efforts and deal them a heavy blow. It is unthinkable that so advantageous a situation should be let slip by when success is almost within reach. I hope that all will throw into the work all their vitality to aid the Government in giving leadership to society in building up national strength. Our wills and strength being concentrated, a fresh step in political and military progress may be made and economic reconstruction pushed ahead, so that at last the responsibility lying on the shoulders of the whole people may be fulfilled by the discharge of our historic mission of resistance and reconstruction.

People in Government

THE fifth session of this Council comes to an end today. For ten days by day and by night members have been unsparing of their efforts; the Government has withheld nothing from them in the reports it has presented, and in their examination and criticism of the Government's measures members have exhausted the resources of their knowledge and intelligence in making suggestions and expressing their views. There has been collaboration to the full without thought of anything but the public and national good. One may safely say that the session has been richer in spirit and more fruitful in achievement than any one of the previous four. Its proposals and resolutions, moreover, have all been of an eminently practical nature and entirely free from the vague and unrealizable. This is progress and matter for gratification and inspiration to all war-afflicted citizens and the army and people generally. This Council is composed of the elite of the country's leadership and talent: it indeed represents the mind of the nation. With each session it has passed from strength to strength, just as our armies have grown in power with the progress of the war. The Government will undoubtedly embrace the Council's critical observations and proposals and act on them with all thoroughness, while it is hoped of you that you will all use your influence with the public to see your resolutions carried into effect.

It is nearly two years since the People's Political Council was established. The nation has benefited very substantially from its services in many ways. Firstly, it has been an actual demonstration of solidarity; in it the nation has seen a concrete expression of its single-minded devotion to the cause and the concentration of its will and purpose, of its capacity for unity of action and the unreserved sharing of the hardships of the time, and an unqualified confidence of government in people and people in government. Secondly, the Council has confirmed the truly national character of the policy of resistance. At each session it has solemnly expressed absolute adherence to that policy, giving the nation a clear view of its war aims and impressing upon the world a proper esti-

Closing address to the Fifth Session of the People's Political Council, April 10, 1940.

174

mate of the consistency and stability of the national policy through all the changes and difficulties of the course of resistance. Thirdly, the Council is a prototype of future Chinese democratic institutions.

Such were the functions I expected the Council to fulfill when it first assembled, and during the two years that have passed since then my hopes of it have been realized, we have entirely rid ourselves of the defects of past deliberative assemblies, and complete openness and public-spirited sincerity now distinguish the deliberations of the Council. Members have shown themselves emancipated from all petty vanity of their own conceptions—so great a vice of the aristocracy of Sung and Ming times, when cliques and coteries were prepared to sacrifice the nation's interests in the pursuit of their own aggrandisement, dissipating their energies in internecine strife. A complete contrast to this state of things is to be seen in the present assembly. Appeal to the national interest and the necessities of resistance never fails to bring about a rational solution to the differing views of individuals and minorities. This is striking evidence of the progress made by China as a modern nation. I am confident that this progress, if maintained at the level reached in recent years, will raise China to a high place among the nations of the world.

I feel it an immense honor to come before you today as the President of this Council charged with the duty of reviewing its achievements, for I believe them the adumbration of a glorious future before the nation. The numerous resolutions passed by this session may be brought under three main heads; the first being those concerned with the denunciation and exposure of enemy and traitors' designs; the second being with regard to economic development; and the third on the subject of the nation's advance in constitutional method and practice. The Government must attach the highest importance to measures in all three of these categories and the whole country is deeply concerned with all questions falling within their scope. I propose now to arrange my remarks under these three heads.

First: as to an adequate understanding of the plans of the enemy and his puppets. On the second day of this session the Council issued a circular telegram unanimously approved by all in which it recorded its condemnation of the traitor Wang Ching-wei and his administration. This was a stern manifestation of the mind of the whole nation on the point. The telegram summed up and exposed the whole despicable essence of the traitors' conduct in the words "capitulation called national salvation, and national ruin called peace." "What country on earth could make the loss of nationhood an end of its constitutional system?" was a question embodying the firm resolution of all Chinese persons of worth and intelligence, and its sense bears closely on the future of resistance.

To speak in terms of Chinese history, every time that the country has been faced with a great peril the most important consideration has ever proved to be the unequivocal demonstration of the rights and wrongs of the case, and the drawing of a clear line between the plausible and the true. Regardless of national degeneracy and the gravest of threats from without, the point we first look to is the clear and distinct comprehension of the issue. When disaster has occurred it has been due not only to the vain quarreling of the aristocrats and their forsaking the public good for their private interest or to their poverty of moral fiber but also to a general obscurity of moral perceptions in society, the confusion of black and white, right and wrong, and the deadening of men's hearts leading to their unconscious descent to ruin. I invite you all to refer to the history of the Sung Dynasty [960–1276] and there you will see that at the time the Kin troops crossed the Yellow River on their way south it was said: "The southern court has not a man to its name." Reading this expression even at the present day we cannot but feel indignation and shame to think that there must have been at least a population of one hundred millions, though we have no accurate census figures of the time. When the Tartars used this phrase they meant that the nation's standard of upright conduct had fallen low and it had grown careless of moral values; the traitors Chang Pang-ch'ang and Ch'in Ku'ei were intent on capitulation and peace and had no thought of resistance and the preservation of nationhood. In fact there were no men that could be called men or anything worthy of the name of a nation. So it was that the diminutive forces of the Tartars did not fear to invade the splendid territories of China and that they succeeded even in laying her low. This shows that the most essential task before us during resistance is the cultivation and stimulation of the people's sense of rectitude and justice.

The present use by the traitor Wang Ching-wei of the term "peace" to describe his betrayal of his country and "national salvation" to describe capitulation to the enemy manifests his determination to confuse men's minds with sophistries, calling black white. This assembly has with one voice discharged its responsibility of vindicating the distinction of right and wrong, sophistry and truth. This assertion of rectitude has made the whole country aware of the incompatibility of loyalty with treachery and of our cause with the design of the Japanese, thus adding strength to our resolve to oppose the enemy and extirpate the traitors—strength comparable to that of a million men in arms. If all our people possess a thorough realization of the severe condemnation due to treacherous rebels and of the sacred inviolability of China's national integrity, all the might and fury of the enemy will avail him nothing to destroy China. The stern judgment of this assembly has, therefore, done much to take the wind out of the sails of the Japanese and the traitors.

So far as the Japanese are concerned, however, nothing will ever make them understand the measure of the spiritual strength of our people; their ignorance of the age is incurable and of China still deeper. They stop their ears and shut their eyes to the facts, obsessed with their fixed idea of conquest. All they know of our history is the story of the decline of the Sung and Ming dynasties with their defeat by the forces of Yuan and Ch'ing. Their study of the methods used by the Tartars and the Manchus has been profound, but of the recent history of the Republic and its rise they know nothing. They take no account of the way in which the Manchu Dynasty was overthrown or of the course of the Revolution, the Northern Expedition and the present War of Resistance. They are quite oblivious of the highest principle behind our endeavor to regenerate the country—the *San Min Chu I,* the driving force of the Revolution for thirty years.

I think that from your daily reading of the newspapers you must receive the impression that the much advertised dispatch of Abe[1] to China savors of his being conceived as a sort of Korean Viceroy. The very over-emphatic exaggerations of their propaganda indicate their consciousness of their own hypocrisy. What they do not allow for is the stimulus our national and fighting spirit derives from their insults and the store of resentment they are laying up in our hearts. So far from China being, as in Sung times, "without men," the present concentration of the nation's human resources in this assembly is sufficient proof both of their adequacy and of the way the nation can command them to the full in the service of its cause. It shows that the whole people has come under the influence of the nationalist principle and abounds in men of the fiber of the revolutionary martyrs Hsu Hsi-lin, Wen Sheng-ts'ai, Li P'ei-chi and P'eng Chia-chen.[2] Those who think to destroy China will find themselves first destroyed by us. I am ready to commit myself to the bold claim that we are now a nation entirely devoted to

[1] General Nobuyuki Abe, one-time Japanese Premier, was sent as Japan's first "ambassador" to Nanking following Japan's "recognition" of her puppet Wang Ching-wei.

[2] Early revolutionists who paid with their lives for assassinating or plotting against Manchu officials and generals between the years 1907 and 1911.

the Three Principles, capable of planned, intelligent and determined action. Looking at Japan, on the other hand, we see a country of which it is said not only by foreigners but also publicly by the Japanese themselves: "Japan has not a man to her name." I think we can say at least that her present statesmen are all spineless and visionless, while her army men lack character and the true military virtues. You need only look at their behavior since the Mukden Incident, at the Konoye Statement on the "New Order for East Asia" and at the Secret Pact concluded with Wang Ching-wei at the end of last year, and at Abe's dispatch to China on a mission reminiscent of the process whereby Korea was conquered to see how mean, dishonest with themselves and others and brainless are the contemporary Japanese politicians and army men. With these brainless and characterless men in control of everything the country might as well be "without men." You will observe what the future fate of Abe may be. For my part I think that though he cannot stand comparison with the assassinated first Viceroy to Korea, Ito, he may very well meet an end similar to that of the Manchu officials Feng Shan of Kwangtung, Liang Pi of Peking, Tuan Fang of Szechwan and En Ming of Anhwei, all killed in the years preceding the Revolution. Even should he escape a violent death himself, the result of his coming to China will be the ruin of his country at our hands. Abe's present journey to China is evidence both of Japan's "lack of men" and of her complete failure. Contrariwise it indicates that resistance has given China a thoroughly sound foundation for her renaissance and rendered her the protector of all other Asiatic nations' freedom.

Second: with regard to economic development. You have concerned yourselves with the economic problems of this war period in particularly close detail. It has given me the greatest pleasure to observe your enthusiastic contribution to the working out of the problems now confronting the Government. I have, however, certain views I wish to bring up in this connection. The nature of Chinese economy is different from that of any other country and it is not to be regarded from the same point of view as that suitable to any other country. As the war goes on economic difficulties become greater and more numerous; in this respect of course China is in no way exceptional, but the economic situation in China during the past three years of war may be said to be better, generally speaking, from that in other countries at war. Yet it has been no easy task to achieve this in view of the poor and inadequate economic structure of pre-war China. The principal reason for its being possible lies in the fact that China is a country adapted by nature to the waging of a protracted war; its economy naturally differs from that of the industrialized nations. You have expressed anxiety over the problem of commodity prices, but on this point I slightly differ from you. Of course everything possible must be done to stabilize the prices of daily necessities for the people's livelihood, to put a stern check upon profiteering and to improve means of communication and supply, but I hold that there is no ground for uneasiness about the economic future of the country as a whole. Previous to the war I held a similar view of military matters. Our economic position, so far from being hopeless, would be free from difficulty if we could fully exploit our human and other resources. Our land is one of great area, rich resources and numerous population; everywhere food and clothing are obtainable, and shelter is a question readily solved. Clothing, food and shelter are the three great economic necessities of the people; if we properly adjust and manage these matters communications and transport will not present any problem. Therefore, if we exert ourselves to increase production there will be nothing else really worth worrying about. Resistance is of advantage to the development and completion of all our economic plans: the longer the war lasts the more hopeful will our economic situation become.

Moreover, now that we have established our second "Three-Year-War-Economy Plan" I have no hesitation in saying that both government and people should do their best to carry into practice the economic plans already laid down and the resolutions passed at this session of the Council for all to go well. Efforts are called for not only from the Government but also from all citizens, who must urge on one another, and cooperate to see that production is increased and management adjusted as circumstances require. I am sure we shall thus be able to maintain protracted resistance and obtain in vast measure the sympathy of nations friendly to us. Even should the situation become many times more difficult, we shall yet be able to continue building up our economic strength as the war goes on. What everyone must realize is that special endurance and self-sacrifice is demanded of us; we cannot treat wartime by the standards of peacetime. We cannot possibly complain if we are obliged to undergo a little hardship. We must look forward to days to come ten times or perhaps twenty times harder than the present time, and prepare to meet them by establishing the determination to endure whatever hardships, and prevail over whatever difficulties, may come. We must do our utmost to increase production, to promote thrift and to reform all economic procedure. The Government must take its responsibilities with special seriousness and citizens brace themselves to perform their duties with special vigor and resolution. We should take the period of slack indulgence and irresponsibility at the end of the Sung Dynasty as a warning. If at that time there had been in public and private life the ability to endure and strive, the dynasty would not have perished and it is still more certain that, with a foundation now laid for our ultimate victory, the Japanese will never succeed in conquering us unless we throw ourselves into their power through indolence and disunity on our own part.

Third: in regard to the introduction of constitutional government. During this session councillors have brought forward their views on the question of constitution-drafting. Time has not permitted of the reaching of any final conclusion, but we shall be able to carry on our study of the various points raised after the adjournment. The Council intends to submit the draft of its prospecting committee and the views of individual councillors to the Government pending a selection of what it thinks fit by the National People's Congress when it meets to take the final decision. During the last two days of the session I have presented a simple exposition of my own views and I now wish to add something further in explanation.

I think that the questions whether a certain constitution is perfect, whether it is practicable and whether there are the men to make it work are all separate problems. The men who operate the machinery of the constitutional system will be drawn not only from the ranks of the Government; the whole people must participate in the responsibility for its operation and furnish talent for that purpose. The views I expressed I hold not in my capacity as President of the Executive Yuan but simply as a member of this Council contributing to its debate on this question. We are concerned here not with our own position but with the future prosperity and welfare of the nation. It has been my hope and my constant purpose for years to see the Constitution established as soon as possible. Nevertheless I have preserved an open mind free from prejudice. My greatest desire is that when it is established it may function, especially during the first ten or twenty years, with precision, smoothness and without obstruction and embarrassment. It will soon be thirty years since the Republic was established, yet the nation has not fixed upon a democratic form of government; all sorts of involvements have arisen and many of you present here today will have experienced the disabilities of this unsatisfactory state of affairs. Being all of us charged with the responsibility of bringing the Constitution into being and practice, we must not lose sight of the painful experiences and lessons of the past thirty years and still less of the boundless suffering caused our fellow-citizens by the constitutional problem and the immense damage done the nation. There can be no hasty and ill-considered action in regard to a form of constitution such as might cause more damage and suffering. I have, therefore, two points I want to impress upon you.

(1) In the matter of defining the Constitution the whole object in view is the genuine good of the people. We must pay attention not only to the past, but also to the present and future. So far as the past is concerned we have to give due weight to the characteristic features of our nation and its history and benefit from the hard-won lessons learned since the Republic was established. In regard to the present we must take into account the conditions of this period of resistance and reconstruction. Looking into the future, we must anticipate the circumstances that will exist ten or twenty years after the constitution is promulgated and plan for the permanent well-being of the people for an indefinite length of time to come. A detailed consideration is required of all the means to build up the national power of self-defense, develop the happiness of the whole mass of the people and strengthen the citizen's rights. I have often spoken of the meaning of action and of its all-important quality of conscientiousness: whatever course of action is decided upon we shall be able to give constitutional government an unshakable foundation.

(2) Since we are out to make of China a *San Min Chu I* Republic we must implicitly obey the spirit of Dr. Sun's principle of the People's Sovereignty and the Five-Power Constitution. In our adherence to the teachings of the Father of the Republic it is essential to grasp the real sense of the distinction between sovereignty and ability and the creative quality of the Five-Power System, so that no conflict with the provisions of that system may occur. If it is held that objective conditions dictate that necessity of gradual completion and advance, some temporary make-shifts will be admissible but under no circumstances whatever can there be the incorporation in the Constitution itself of any provisions modifying the application of the Three Principles or conflicting with the spirit of the Five-Power Constitution. I am of opinion that there must be the fullest devotion to practicality and due weight given to the unwritten law of precedent. Accordingly, our provisions should not be excessively rigid, but sufficiently elastic to permit of their complete realization in practice.

The above is a review of the most important questions examined by this session of the Council together with some expression of my personal views. This fifth session is now at an end. Within six months the National People's Congress will assemble. The work of resistance and reconstruction becomes more pressing from day to day. There will be many matters demanding your continued efforts after the adjournment. It is not for me to thank you for the courage and self-sacrifice you have displayed in the common cause; the whole people and army have been inspired by your example. In a phrase, what I have to say to you is that in the completion of the great enterprise of resistance and reconstruction practicality and realism are supremely important; of this both you and I need to remind ourselves. The work of national salvation requires of us both physical and mental exertion. We must eliminate all facile approximation. All my life I have put myself on my guard against highfalutin idealism detached from realities. Our highest duty, we must remember, is to secure for China independence, freedom and equality with other nations. With reconstruction incomplete and our people still afflicted as they are, we Chinese, in the eyes of foreigners, are even worse off than conquered slaves. For generations factions have set at nought the interests of the nation and now the enemy desire is to see us divided and weakened by internal strife. The spirit displayed by this Council, however, is in direct opposition to the enemy's evil calculations; it amounts to a powerful counter-stroke aimed at him and the puppets. I hope that you will all continue to exert your utmost for the nation in the manner that spirit suggests.

The Way to Local Autonomy

THE first term of this course of instruction for local administrators opens today. I desire first of all to rouse your liveliest attention to the magnitude of the responsibility public servants must bear for the building up of local political organization and the welfare of the people.

The object of the course is to make of all you men now under training the executors of a sound local administrative system, loyally discharging your duties, fulfilling the provisions of the new *hsien* system, pressing forward with local autonomy, and promoting local commerce and industry to the end that the people of the province may all enjoy a sufficiency of the necessities of life and secure livelihoods. You will then be able worthily to bear the name of followers of the Three Principles of the People and public servants of the present age. The rules and aims of the training given here are all laid down in the regulations. While they will be fully explained to you in due course by your instructors, it is to be hoped that you will also individually give them your earnest study. There is no need for me to enlarge upon them; but, apart from the curriculum fixed by the regulations there are many important points that might easily escape your notice, and these I mean to take this opportunity of bringing before you.

The first question for which we must have a clear answer today is: What is the real nature of the studies you are to pursue here? And the simple answer is: "All the knowledge and abilities needed for the stimulation of good tendencies and the eradication of evil ones in political, economic, social and educational matters, and the cultivation of a spirit of revolutionary reconstruction." This institution was created for the purpose of producing a group of fighters in the struggle for revolutionary reconstruction, equipped to reform the various evils of the past political state of the province, and to proceed to positive measures of rehabilitating local business and advancing the prosperity of the whole population of the province.

An address given at the Szechwan Training Academy on the occasion of the opening of the first term of the instructional course in local administration, May 1, 1940.

A searching examination of the state of affairs existing in the past shows that the most fundamental of our political abuses consisted in the failure of public servants comprehensively to execute their orders. There was also a lack of concern that orders should reach their right destinations, that they should be explained and their efficacy checked. The result was that organizations made a general practice of treating orders as matter for outward conformance and actual evasion, passing things over in any way that best served their turn. There was a complete disregard in issuing mandates to subordinates of the way in which the rulings should be framed in order to secure thorough execution, as to whether the subordinates concerned could understand the intentions behind the mandate on receiving it and how a check on results could be secured. Orders were frequently merely issued and never properly put into practice. Orders originating from the provincial government were often pigeon-holed or side-tracked on reaching *hsien* districts. Not only would local *hsiang, chen, pao* and *chia*[1] authorities often have no idea what a particular order was about, but even heads and members of sections in provincial government departments might be equally unaware of its meaning and importance. Consequently they would dismiss all questions of how it was to be executed and bury it deep. In this way orders excellent, well-conceived and planned in themselves would come to nothing. This evil has remained a rooted one from the end of Imperial times up to the present day. For forty or fifty years there has been no really thoroughgoing effort to reform it. Therefore, in government institutions and in society generally, mandates have come to be looked on as mere documentary red-tape, while reports and the like are even more perfunctorily dealt with. All manner of good laws and administrative measures may thus prove impracticable, and the people's livelihood achieves no progress. All kinds of corrupt political and social practices have arisen from this cause. Were no change ever to be effected our society would perennially be a backward one and our nation never emerge from its semi-colonial status. We must now cleanse the country of this blot and build a new nation on the lines of the Principles of the Three People,—such a nation as foreigners will not only fear to affront but will respect.

The first step must be to form a profound determination to clear ourselves of this fundamental abuse. You who are here today to start

[1] The new *hsien* system of local administration is divided into four grades: *chia*, consisting of ten households; *pao*, consisting of a hundred households; *hsiang* (rural) or *chen* (urban), consisting of ten *pao;* and above that, the *hsien* (county or district) itself.

your training will one day be called upon to make yourselves responsible for putting the affairs of the province into good order. An essential is the cultivation of such a spirit of respect for commands as will lead to their being put as fully as possible into effect. Particular emphasis must be put upon precise provision for the penetration of commands to their appropriate destinations and upon the conditions of time, method and procedure involved. All important mandates, following their issuance, require clear explanation of what they entail, and close superintendence of the way in which subordinates fulfill them. As circumstances may demand, guidance and inspection should be introduced in order that the entire scope of the provisions may be realized. You must all realize that this course is designed to train you in the work of reforming the lower political organization of the country and in advancing the process of establishing local autonomy. The success or failure, the acceleration or delay, of that process will depend upon whether the government's decrees and plans are or are not conscientiously put into practice. Henceforth the provincial government, all its departments and offices, *hsien* governments and all responsible officials of whatever rank, in giving and receiving orders, will do well to adhere strictly to what I have to say today.

Above all, we must have all significant decrees conveyed to the very lowest strata of the body politic—to the *hsiang, chen, pao* and *chia*. The elders of these units must take advantage of the opportunities provided by weekly memorial meetings and monthly citizens' assemblies to call the people together and give them detailed explanation of the intentions underlying important government mandates, and of the methods whereby they are to be put into effect, of the benefits that will consequently accrue to all, and of the harm that will come of failure to put them into practice. At the same time a retrospect should be taken of what orders during the past month have been received, of what orders have been carried into effect and to what degree, a check thus being kept upon the record of achievement, with a view to seeking a final completeness. In future the execution of mandates by the *hsiang, chen, pao* and *chia* authorities should be aided by the utilization of these weekly and monthly meetings as a means of training and guiding the people to regard this as a fundamental part of the approach to local autonomy. The competitive principle must also be employed in order to ascertain which *hsiang, chen, pao* or *chia* has contributed most to the record of achievement, where there has been correct, and where incorrect, conduct, and so on, with a view to appropriate reward and punishment. A close analysis of the situation should be made accordingly, published and made known to the people of every *hsien* throughout the province. The commendable must be rewarded and the contrary penalized that the distinction between right and wrong may be clear and a tendency nourished of being supremely solicitous of the public good. It is thus that progress will be made in local autonomy and a new society eventually constructed, a new nation at last created.

All of you now present must devote yourselves to the development of the ability and mental inclination to reform old evils and get mandates thoroughly obeyed. What I have said about utilizing public meetings for the purpose of keeping a check on achievement calls for your closest attention and most strenuous efforts. It has been laid down that sub-committee meetings are to be held every week to afford you the opportunity of discussing and criticizing at length all the views the people have brought forward on the subject of mandates and plans or on the state of your own work. On your return to your posts you will be in a position to convey the experience you have gained to the authorities of the *hsiang, chen, pao* and *chia,* by whom it may be passed on also to the people in general. For the training you are now to receive should prove something more than merely your possession. After it is finished you are to convey the methods, the spirit, and the way of life you have acquired here to all those public servants who have not accompanied you here; the influence of your training is to go on gradually spreading until the mass of the people is permeated with the spirit of this institution. In this way one of you will come to exercise the strength of ten men, nay, of a thousand or ten thousand men. We shall thus approach the ideal goal of a new China rebuilt on the lines of the Three Principles of the People. When once you have earned the name of practising adherents of those principles, you are to proceed to undertake the duties of reconstructing a new Szechwan and a new China. You must first make yourselves new citizens and public servants of the present age.

To attain this great end, it may be asked, to fulfill this vast undertaking, where is a beginning to be made? and what is to be the center and turning point of our efforts? The answers to these questions are to be found in repeated utterances of mine which have been published in separate form. You will do well to refer to them at length. Apart from the matter of respect for and comprehensive application of mandates, the most vital of the points I have made in my speeches is the necessity of public servants' insistence upon the qualities of unselfishness, diligence, rapidity, realism, fearlessness and honesty in their work. Of these qualities the first is the most indispensable. In my address on

"The Structure of the Three Principles of the People and the Sequence of Steps to their Fulfillment," what I said of "universal commonalty"[2] is the ultimate principle of all Chinese political thought and the highest ideal of the *San Min Chu I,* and it is a fundamental heading under which all political, moral and personal self-improvement may be ranged. Since we are appointed public servants of the nation we must make this quality of concern for the common interest the subject of our most thorough efforts to bring the factual into the closest relation with the nominal. Political corruption and social iniquity with us in the past, the lack of faith in their rulers general among the people, and the consequent backwardness of all administrative, educational, and public enterprises was due to public servants' ignorance or neglect of this quality. The old corrupt officialdom was aware only of its own interests and unaware of the demands made upon it by the public weal and the law. In addition to our future efforts to build up a sound foundation for the political system of the country, to fulfill our revolutionary responsibilities, to bring about a change in modes of social thinking and living, to set up a model system of local autonomy, and to practise the quality of "public-spiritedness," we must by force of example lead subordinates toward the ideal of unselfish public service. It must be realized that the slightest indulgence of self-interest on our part as public servants results in damage not only to the nation but also to ourselves. For the very facts of the aggression from which our country is now suffering and of our social corruption and decadence are traceable to this evil, which is deep-rooted in the mind of China. A change is not to be effected in a day or so, but we must start by devoting ourselves to the nation's interest, making our own conduct exemplary, and thus exercising a moral influence over our subordinates. The confidence of the people may thus be won and the goal of political reform attained.

The way of securing an attitude of devotion to the public good and the sanctity of law among local authorities and especially among the *hsiang, chen, pao-chia,* elders will certainly consist in a display of model behavior on the part of responsible superiors, by our perfectly fulfilling the duty of parental instruction and guidance towards the people. But it is no less necessary that we should make ourselves fully acquainted with the nature of the malpractices I am about to enumerate. We have to realize how perfunctory and slack many of the *hsiang, chen, pao* and *chia* elders now are in the performance of their duties, how frequent are cases of peculation and oppression, how much the execution of

---

[2] *T'ien hsia wei kung.* Translated by Legge "a public and common spirit ruled all under the sky" and by Callery *"l'empire était la chose publique."*

mandates is obstructed and the realization of local autonomy prevented. We must fully appreciate the facts of the situation, for a cure can be devised only when the disease is known. Means can be devised to effect supervision and prevention only when the nature of the case is ascertained. Otherwise an ignorance of the various abuses mentioned below and a failure to reform them will rob us of any sound starting point for more positive action. In the same way an officer in command of troops, were he ignorant of their faults and defects, would find all his own scrupulous obedience to orders and observance of rules of no efficacy, and he would have no success as their leader. We as public servants have also, in what we do to serve society, to know the weaknesses of our subordinates and find the appropriate method of dealing with those weaknesses. Previous to all reform must come careful diagnosis of the disorders concerned.

You have been long serving in various branches of government organization and you come from a great variety of localities. You will undoubtedly know much of the abuses prevalent among the *hsiang, chen, pao* and *chia* authorities. What I wish to do today is to point out some of the most common of those abuses so that you may make a mental note of them as subjects for your future study of concrete and effective means of remedying and eradicating them. Let us enumerate them under four heads.

One: The misuse of public position to serve private ends. Often the elders on appointment set about making their position a source of selfish gain by the abuse of the power it gives them by farming out taxes, managing hotels, and so on. It is a matter of making official position the means of gratifying selfish desires. This sort of conduct is not only an obstacle to progress in local autonomy but it also arouses the antipathy of the people.

Two: The wielding of official prestige as a weapon in oppressing the people. There is a general lack of thorough education in citizenship among *hsiang, chen, pao* and *chia* elders. In their ignorance, they often imagine their appointment a mere way to power and consequence, an instrument not for the service and welfare of the people, but as one for gratifying their own desires in defiance of others. The result is that the mere possession of these functionaries has often been an additional source of affliction for the people. This oppressive attitude is a feature of the past behavior of landlords and squirarchs which has yet to be reformed.

Three: The utilization of the title of *hsiang, chen, pao* or *chia* elder as a means to avenge themselves in private feuds. This is also an evil frequently to be observed. Those who offend in this respect seem to fail to realize that on their assumption of the title they are obliged to set the people an example, divest themselves of all private malice and animosity, and throw themselves wholeheartedly into their public duties. They on the contrary grasp their power as a weapon to use in revenging themselves on persons who have incurred their displeasure. Particularly in cases of the exposure of their own malpractices, they seek to use their influence for the discomfiture or ruin of those opposing their interests, with the result that the people subsequently swallow their indignation and fear to speak out.

Four: A greater evil still arises from the abuse by elders of the power, to a great extent in their hands, of engaging labor for public works and of recruiting soldiers. In this connection opportunities arise for all sorts of cruel exactions from the poor and for illegitimate exemption of the rich and consequential. On the one hand merciless extortion and on the other absolute immunity—this sort of social injustice represents the damage *hsiang, chen, pao* and *chia* elders are capable of doing to the *pao-chia* system. How, while these wrongs are perpetrated, are we ever to make available to the people the benefits intended in the measures and laws prescribed by the government? How are we ever to fashion a modern nation? Therefore your especial attention will be required in the matter of ways and means of preventing the elders from maltreating the weak and well-intentioned while they servilely permit the powerful wrongdoer to have his way.

The four main descriptions of corruption I have just enumerated are common phenomena in the *hsiang, chen, pao* and *chia* districts of China today. Szechwan is naturally no exception. On your return to your *hsien* district to train the elders under your supervision, you must make absolutely clear to them that, if they commit these criminal errors, not only will the Principles never be realized and the nation never be delivered from its pressing dangers, but the whole *pao-chia* system with all its excellent provisions will be ruined by them, local autonomy will be put beyond all hope of realization, and the people will never see the day of release from the burdens now weighing on them. Their conduct will be equivalent to that of traitors and their offense against Party, nation and people be mortal. It is above all desirable to stir them to a thorough awakening, bringing about a reversal of their former conceptions of their duties. Only then will these malpractices disappear and the full efficacy of the *pao-chia* system be exploited. In regard very particularly to the raising of labor and recruiting, equity must imperatively be sought and abuses purged with especial severity. The elders must forget they are private individuals susceptible to flattery and intimidation, and see only with eyes for rectitude in the public interest. If in the course of faithfully fulfilling their duties and upholding justice they encounter opposition or slanderous attack from the landlords and squirarchs, we should furnish them protection. They must not be involved in trouble because of their devotion to duty in such a way as to discourage them from continuing in public service. On the one hand we must keep a close watch over our subordinates and see that they have full scope for the performance of their duty; on the other hand we must make ourselves responsible for preventing their being in any way socially ostracized or penalized by small groups of individuals maligning them and opposing them for what they do in loyally obeying government orders and carrying out the new system of *hsien* administration. In this way zeal will be stimulated, habitual malpractices eradicated, a firm foundation laid for local autonomy and the Three Principles of the People genuinely realized.

Next, in our work henceforth for the advance of local autonomy, the most important point is our applying ourselves realistically to the problems involved. Every day's work should yield its definite measure of progress and every step lead to a definite result. In our way of going about things we must especially emphasize the quality of precision. In the past we had plans, rules, and regulations and all sorts of organizations, yet everything undertaken came to nothing because nobody knew how to make a realistic approach to the work. You will do well to make a close study of what I have said in this respect in my lectures to the Central Training Academy. I spoke, however, only of certain general principles of procedure. The actual application of these principles in specific cases would, of course, require the vigorous exercise of your own discretion according to circumstances of place and time. One description of procedure would call for the application of one particular principle, on the basis of which concrete steps would have to be resolved upon. Regular and steady progress may thus be made. Otherwise the best of methods and intentions will prove totally ineffective in the absence of realistically conceived and practicable procedure. It is indispensable that you should be acquainted with scientific principles and with the use of scientific methods. There is a booklet in which I have fully explained the significance of scientific principle, and to this I would call your earnest attention. Its contents call not only for your individual efforts at full comprehension but also for conveyance by you to the knowledge of *hsiang, chen, pao,* and *chia* elders. I believe that apart from utterly degenerate and self-forsaking elements with whom nothing can be done, all other men with even only the most elementary ideas of nationhood and progress will certainly consent to proceed along scientific lines for the sake of greater efficiency in their work. We may have principles, organization, rules and regulations, but effectiveness and success in our undertakings have yet to be attained.

Among ancient Chinese statesmen previous to Ch'in and Han times, Duke Chou may be held supreme; thereafter Wang An-shih is the figure I most admire. He proved himself capable of designing on the basis of our Chinese political axioms plans that corresponded exactly to the evils of the age. He devised a new political system, remolded society, and reconstructed the economic structure of the country in order to relieve the poverty-stricken condition of the Sung State of that time. His deficiency, however, lay in his failure to provide himself with sound executives and to give his attention to problems of training personnel. The result was that his plans were not carried into effect and were completely nullified. It is for us to treat his failure as a warning lesson in respect of training executive personnel. On the one hand we may well model ourselves upon his disregard of merit and demerit, his fearlessness of fatigue and malice, and his patriotic fervor. On the other hand we must make amends in our own proceedings for his faults of inattention to methods of approach, and to the training and supervision of subordinates. In pushing forward with local autonomy, we want, in addition to organization and regulations, thorough exploration of ways and means to the end. If only we have those ways and means clear, funds, where there may appear a lack of them, can be produced, manpower can be found, enterprises at first apparently of great difficulty can rapidly be brought to success. There must be preparation, method, and training before we can successfully reach our objective.

Again, in conducting local autonomy, and indeed in all political work, a single individual of us has to concern himself with scores, hundreds or thousands of his fellow-men. It is naturally incumbent upon him, therefore, to understand the nature of guidance and leadership. For that he needs to know how to supervise, for leadership and supervision are mutually interdependent and supplementary. The former presupposes the latter: without supervision leadership will inevitably fail. General neglect of this fact in the past, the reliance upon mere giving of orders without going on to see to it that they are carried into practice, frequently caused such orders to prove quite ineffectual.

Such conduct cannot be tolerated by any nation of the present age. In a modern nation men do not talk and issue orders and leave it at that; they go on to see that those responsible execute those orders to the full. Only then do they consider their duty done as the originators of the orders concerned. As the public servants and citizens of a modern nation, to whatever sphere of administration we may belong, we must follow up all the orders and plans we make by strict supervision of subordinates—particularly of the basic executives, *pao-chia* elders and their various subordinates—to make sure that they exert themselves energetically in order to put fully into execution the sense of plans and mandates.

In regard to all descriptions of work, therefore, it is essential to consider how efficiency is to be checked. The process of such "checking" consists in "making the nominal and the actual agree" and in seeking factual reality. Right and wrong, merit and demerit must be reckoned on grounds of actual results. This ideal of making the nominal and the actual coincide does not permit of favor being shown to those from one's native place or to relations, of saying things are done when they are not or work finished when it is not. Only unselfish public service and uniform obedience to the law will now enable us to set China on the right road to political well-being. In managing the affairs of the masses control and guidance are indispensable, and to develop the capacity for guidance thorough supervision is essential. If supervision yields results the nominal will necessarily be brought to agree with the actual, and that will imply just and unfailing apportionment of praise and blame. This is an important requisite of our future work. There is no more important feature than this of the knowledge you are to acquire in this institution.

On your return to your posts you will have to set a personal example to your subordinates and the people. You must start by establishing a reputation for integrity. By unselfish devotion to the public interest, patient endurance of toil and ill-will, and by constant care over every detail of our daily lives we should attempt to furnish the people with a model of correct conduct. Our especially close attention must be given to the poor, the old, the children, and all in the district open to oppression and maltreatment. They demand our very closest care and protection to the end that each and every one of them may obtain a satisfactory place and livelihood in society. Our ancient Chinese political order made its main principles "selection of the wise and able" and "the observance of pledged faith and the cultivation of cordial relations with neighbors," but a principle exceeding even these in importance was that of respect for age and protection of the young. These principles form the course we must follow if we are to set local political organization on the right road. The ancients said: "A hamlet of ten houses must yet possess men of loyalty and good faith." It is for us to learn how to seek out such men of excellent qualities in the localities under our care; those with signs of promise should be displayed as a standard for society, and those with ability be given the opportunity to undertake enterprises in the neighborhood. As a consequence the whole business of local autonomy would achieve redoubled success for half the trouble. Wherever we may be we must show respect for and treat with distinction the old when we encounter them, and in the case of unemployed young men and unschooled and unfed children we must try to find means of rescuing them and caring for them. If we provide an example, the influence of it will necessarily extend downwards, and the *hsiang, chen* and *pao-chia* elders will not dare to take advantage of the old and weak or frustrate men of qualities and ability. Our object of reconstructing Szechwan will thus be gradually approached.

It is undoubtedly known to you that every *hsien* district of the province possesses inexhaustible resources. The earth might be supposed paved with gold. Not only are the cultivated areas of rice and wheat-fields immense, but every stream in the province contains the yellow metal. With land and resources of such richness and with a population so numerous, if we government administrators put forth all our energies to explore the possibilities, striving with patience and endurance and making use of all the manpower available in order to develop these limitless resources, there would be no question of unemployment or illiteracy for anybody and every man and woman would have his or her sufficiency of clothing and food. Yet, under the existing circumstances there are not only unemployed young men and uneducated children, but there is also general poverty among the people, even to the point of starvation and death. This cannot be described as anything but a disgrace for public servants of Szechwan. Having this vast manpower at our disposal, we fail to turn it to account; provided with such rich resources we fail to develop them. This means that the Government has not fulfilled its responsibilities. It is an indication of the fact that we public servants of the province lack ability and devotion to our duties.

Henceforth we must all give advancement to those of good qualities and abilities, cultivating good faith and cordiality in our relations with the people, allowing everybody the fullest opportunity of contributing what he can to the service of the public. At the same time we must exercise respect for the aged and care for the weak until there is no single member of our society who is shelterless and neglected. This is the most important end local autonomy sets out to attain and it constitutes the fundamental work for putting the Three Principles of the People into practice. I hold that if you will energetically pursue the policy and follow out the methods I am defining for you today, not only will every inhabitant of Szechwan within three years have food to eat and clothes to wear, but within ten a splendid, strong, prosperous new China will be created.

Now I wish to pass on to some other descriptions of important work for the successful accomplishment of which I intend to hold you responsible and to which it is my hope you will apply yourselves with all possible seriousness. Firstly: fitting distribution of material resources and stabilization of commodity prices. From the *hsien* government down to the local *pao-chia* unit all are concerned in this responsibility of adjusting supply of commodities to the demand and needs of their localities. The quantity of goods stored up has to be investigated and means devised of stabilizing the prices of things in everyday use, and of preventing hoarding and speculation with consequent sharp rises in price levels. These measures are required for the security of the people's livelihood. The Government is about to issue a number of effective measures which I hope you will give your constant attention and vigorously execute in such manner as circumstances of time and place may dictate.

Secondly: let there be set on foot a movement to improve and strengthen means of transport. It must be realized that while transport is not properly managed satisfactory distribution will never be attained however much production may be increased, however plentiful commodities may be rendered in particular places. The price problem turns on this matter of distribution and transport. Dr. Sun said: "Let the best be got out of things and the flow of goods be accelerated"—that is, transport facilities must be exploited to the full; the methods and means of transport in various localities differ according to local conditions, but all that is essential is a complete resolution to effect improvements and remove obstacles. There will always be found room for increase in efficiency. Henceforth all grades of government administration and local autonomous institutions must give their especially close study to increasing transport facilities and accelerating the flow of goods from place to place. *Hsien* governments must consider in the fullest detail the actual nature of local conditions and lay down concrete plans for thorough application.

Thirdly: this year the Central Government ordered the Bank of China, the Central Bank, the Bank of Communications and the Farmer's Bank of China to make available one hundred million dollars' worth of credit loans for farmers. If this immense sum of money is put to proper use it will undoubtedly bring about a vast increase in happiness for all our fellow-countrymen of Szechwan. Therefore to see that these loans are rationally paid out in order that the agricultural population may get real benefit, rural economy be developed, and rural production be advanced, is the obligation of all grades of government organization and all ranks of public servants must work out practical plans and make themselves responsible for their execution. It will not do for things to proceed as in the past with the banks or cooperative societies lending money to the farmers in ways that brought them no practical advantage, but rather even the ills attendant upon high-interest loans.

Fourthly: in the program of local autonomy there are two items that are of particular importance in regard to the province of Szechwan. Of these one is the accurate measurement of land and another the reclamation of wasteland. The process of obtaining accurate figures of landholdings in the province must be accelerated. What might have been thought two years' work must be carried out in one year, and what might take three years be done in eighteen months. The intrinsic difficulty of this is not important: what is lacking is good contact between government and people and its consequent failure to mobilize their strength. Putting local autonomy into force implies uniting government and people and ending the divorce prevailing between them in the past. I hope for your thorough realization of this. We must do all possible to develop wasteland. At present not only are there many of the more remote *hsien* districts with much land lying waste but also in even the rather less accessible spots nearer at hand there is soil to develop for which there has not been a proper effort. There lies before us the necessity of studying how the power of the people can be put in motion for the purpose of measuring acreage and reclaiming wasteland, the aims being the increase of funds needed for local autonomy and the relief of the afflictions of the poor and wretched among our fellow-countrymen.

The points I have made above all belong to the sphere of economics. We must not suppose that because we are administrators economic reconstruction is no concern of ours but of experts. It must be realized that local autonomy is just as dependent upon a good economic foundation, as the whole political system of the nation. While land lies waste, local economy is undeveloped and the people lack food and clothing, local autonomy is scarcely a thing to be talked of. In promoting political advancement we have first to lay a good economic foundation. That entails the above-mentioned work of distributing material resources, stabilizing commodity prices, improving transport services, facilitating the granting of agricultural credit, measurement of the land, reclamation work, and the increase of public funds.

You have come here today to be trained not merely in how to organize the *pao-chia* system, collect statistics and in similar knowledge and functions connected with local autonomy. Such is simply the scope of the management of local autonomy, whereas our ultimate aims in promoting local autonomy are economic development and the enrichment of the people's livelihood. Those great aims demand of every individual among our people endurance with fortitude of the hardships that may fall to his lot and the exertion of his full strength and ability. Only thus can a rich and powerful country arise.

In these three years to come we must see to it that every inhabitant of the province has clothes to wear and food to eat. Nothing in the world can be attained without exertion. If for instance farmers are to reap a rich harvest in the autumn they have to make great efforts in their spring ploughing and summer weeding; for without these efforts there would be no harvest. If we are, therefore, to establish local autonomy and reconstruct the province of Szechwan, it is imperative that we should set about our work with all our might. It was anciently said that "it is from labor that the wealth of the people comes." If we do not call forth the people's fullest capacity to labor, how are they ever to have a sufficiency of food and clothing? Particularly today in the first stages of the establishment of local autonomy we need a spirit of "thought only for tillage, and not for the harvest."

Finally, there are a number of other descriptions of work which still await our further efforts for their completion: (1) the strengthening of the system of military service, (2) cooperation in the work of bandit suppression, (3) the registration of weapons in the possession of private individuals among the people, (4) the extinction of opium and drugs. In respect of the first—to strengthen the system of military service it is necessary to reform ingrained abuses, to do all possible to secure equity and to encourage the people in spontaneously enlisting. In regard to the suppression of banditry, it is necessary to exploit the strength of the *pao-chia* system, to get the people of a locality to keep watch upon one another, voluntarily carrying out inspection work, so that lawless elements have nowhere to hide. In regard to the registration of weapons our best course is now to exhort the people rapidly to make a voluntary declaration of the weapons they hold, in order that a formal record may be made of them, while those that have already been recorded are to become perpetually at the disposal of the locality for purposes of militia defense. As for opium-suppression, it has already gone far but has not yet reached complete success. If the people of Szechwan can continue with the vigorous efficiency they have shown during the last six months in the work of opium-prohibition they will demonstrate how great a power lies in the Chinese nation, a power capable of achieving anything it makes its object. It will also prove an indication of the fine capacity for local autonomy and the spirit of service among the inhabitants of this province. If only this spirit displayed in the task of opium suppression can be thrown into other work, not only will local autonomy be accomplished within the period stipulated but economic reconstruction also will make flying strides of progress, and the future of our country present a prospect of limitless splendor.

The four points I have just mentioned are very intimately related to local autonomy and economic reconstruction. I hope that all of you while you are here will study and discuss them before later going out to do your practical administrative work. Strive together and urge one another on to the end of final and total success. In conclusion you must all grasp the meaning behind the formation of this class of which you are members, putting your utmost into the task of making of yourselves sound local administrators, casting out the bad habits of the past, and working up a revolutionary spirit, in order that you may eventually undertake the responsibility of making an absolutely fresh start with local administration and the prosecution of local autonomy. Then we shall be able worthily to bear the name of modern citizens and adherents of the Three Principles of the People, and the province of Szechwan will veritably become the base of a reawakening China.

Manchuria: Hell on Earth

FELLOW-COUNTRYMEN, today is the ninth anniversary of the day on which the Japanese invasion and occupation of our Northeastern territories began. Since that thunder of gunfire in the north and the fall of Mukden, since that outrage and affront was laid on our entire people, nine years have rapidly passed away. The babies in arms of that time are now school-children, while the school-children of then have reached adult years. Yet the liberation of our Northeastern fellow-countrymen and the recovery of our territorial sovereignty over the lost land have still to be achieved. This means resistance has not gained its ultimate goal, and the souls of those martyred lack consolation. We find ourselves on this anniversary day with the same uncured pain at heart and the same heavy responsibilities on our shoulders; I take this opportunity of speaking to all of you and especially to North-easterners about certain matters of the utmost importance. I trust you will engrave on your hearts the determination to strive together in the cause.

I have frequently had occasion to remark on the sort of hell-on-earth life has become for our fellow-countrymen in the Northeast under the enslaving and debasing oppression of the enemy. A month ago I heard a friend just returned from actual observation of the conditions describing what he had seen and heard with his own eyes and ears. The people now living under the puppet Manchurian regime have no security for life and property and no freedom of movement; the whole power of giving and taking life or anything else rests in the hands of the Japanese. The slightest motion cannot escape their strict surveillance and control. Here are some of the more striking features of the situation:

(1) It is estimated that there are now some 5,400 administrative officials of the puppet regime. Of these 3,300 are Japanese, and among the higher ranking officials there are only a small number of sub-

A message to the people of the Japanese-occupied Northeastern Provinces of China, and to the nation in general, published September 18, 1940, on the occasion of the ninth anniversary of Japan's invasion of Manchuria.

servient puppet figures. All the law-making authority of the regime lies in the grasp of the Japanese whose most lightly expressed desires define the scope of laws. In local districts vice-mayors are always Japanese and in police posts the greater number of men are Japanese. The officials presiding over smaller administrative units, the "street" and the village, are selected by the Japanese from among the most servile traitors. They heap upon the people further repression and supervision. Any individual wishing merely to move from one village to another must obtain the requisite permission and even movement within a village is subject to surveillance. Census-taking is usually done at night so that it is forbidden to fasten doors. This gives the Japanese freedom to pass in and out of houses at will and commit acts of indecency and rape. Special permits have to be obtained by the people for marriage and giving in marriage. Women married and unmarried are equally at the mercy of the lusting Japanese: there have been cases without number of those who have died or killed themselves for shame, and of others who have known the even crueller plight of desiring death but failing to obtain it.

(2) There is in Manchuria a so-called "national system of military service" under which the Japanese regard all men over 19 years of age as liable to compulsory service. On being called up the more robust are set to hard labor like convicts, and sent off to unknown destinations beyond all reach of inquiry after their fate. As for those recruited into the puppet troops, they are watched over by Japanese instructors. The observer mentioned saw a detachment of puppet troops one day drawn up at a railway station. The corporals were all Japanese and orders were given in Japanese. The men seemed between the ages of 16 to 20; their features bore an impress of suffering intolerable to behold. The Japanese officers would strike them at random as though they were so much cattle. There is also the practice of pressing men for work on fortifications upon the completion of which their names are inscribed on wooden slips and they are held answerable indefinitely for the repair of any damage their work may afterwards sustain.

(3) The Japanese inquisitors established in all the puppet police-station imprison and kill innocent people as a daily occurrence. In their dark dens there is no room for talk of law or humanity; ill-usage of every description, torture by unheard-of instruments, leave the questioned half-dead or crippled at the end of their ordeal. The search for members of the volunteer anti-Japanese armies offers a pretext for all manner of oppression and atrocities. People may be herded into one village, or village A amalgamated with village B, or several small vil-

lages made into one, and then the whole property of the falsely accused unit burned. Firearms in the possession of the people were long ago thoroughly rummaged out by the Japanese, but the discovery of a single remaining cartridge-case means a death sentence.

(4) The people are good for nothing but labor service, as beasts of burden; it is not for them to carry on private business enterprise. Industry, small and big alike, has been removed from the hands of indigenous owners by compulsory purchase or confiscation, until it is now all under the control of Japanese "trusts." The treatment of the rural populace has been even more relentless. The farmers' land has been confiscated without any pretense of rhyme or reason. The rather more fertile tracts along the South Manchurian Railway line have been entirely seized for the settlement of the so-called Japanese "colonists." Wherever these "colonists" appear, in their wake arise opium and gambling dens, brothels and wineshops, and trade and the professions, down to hairdressing, laundering, cooking, and errand running, are totally monopolized by Japanese. The original inhabitants—that is, our fellow-countrymen—are driven into the cold climate of Jehol, there to take to soldiering or manual labor. Not only their land but also their houses are taken from them: the very ground is cut from under their feet: even burial space is denied them.

(5) All commodities come under the control and manipulation of the Japanese. Control over industrial products is exercised by a so-called "Daily Necessities Trust" and an "Import Trade Alliance." Weighed down by oppressive and extortionate taxation, the people have little capacity to buy from them; even so, they are faced by all sorts of restrictions if they make the attempt—even cloth, shoes, and stockings are virtually debarred them. Among comestibles for instance, Chinese people are absolutely deprived of the right to purchase rice and flour. Even maize and kaoliang are rigidly restricted in the quantities allowed. In the larger cities and towns a common sight is the face dehumanized with hunger. Near Liaoyang a certain peasant whispered to this traveler that for three years he had not set his eyes on white flour. Only at the New Year was it permitted to purchase a nominal amount of nine ounces of flour per household. The state of things in other respects may be readily imagined. The Three Eastern Provinces are rich in soy bean production, yet the country people find themselves without bean-oil to eat or lamp-oil to burn. The wretchedness of our Northeastern fellow-countrymen being like this, each day that passes before we can deliver them is a day of responsibility undischarged.

(6) In the sphere of education, most intellectuals have been arrested

or done to death. In educational institutions above the middle-school the teachers are Japanese. Many of the schools conducted by missionaries have been forced to close. The puppet administration has initiated a so-called "Teachers' Training Class" for the carrying into effect of slave-education. Teachers in primary schools are required to have a thorough knowledge of Japanese and in such schools there must be eight or more hours weekly devoted to Japanese lessons. The qualifications for entrance to the primary schools are subject to rigid restriction. Films come under the control of the "Japanese Cinematographic Trust." In libraries none but slave-literature can find a place. Two years ago the Japanese set up a "Committee for Investigation into the Manchurian Language," for the purpose of designing a system of phonetic symbols similar to the Japanese "kana," to be given the misnomer of a "Kana for East Asia." In August of this year the committee issued an approved system and this was conveyed to all puppet organizations and to schools for compulsory use and study. The Japanese are clearly out to destroy the Chinese language and culture in their extinction of the Northeast as a part of China.

The above points are but a sketch of the features of life in the Northeast. In short, the Japanese treatment of Chinese people there has exceeded the brutality and malignity of even their treatment of the Korean people. Beneath this foul oppression the Northeasterners have no freedom of residence, livelihood, speech, education, or of marrying and burying: the slightest movement, and what is more ghastly to relate, even life and death are not of an individual's choice. One Northeasterner said to the investigator I have quoted: "I would have you convey a message to fellow-countrymen south of the Wall: we too desire, tell them, to die as befits Chinese, but it may be judged how imperative it is to make one's sacrifice for the country in due time by the fact that we in our position find it no simple matter to die an honorable death fighting against the enemy." These words, in their simplicity and reserve, give us a picture of the minds of more than thirty million Northeasterners.

On this important day of commemoration I want to call upon all of you to give thought to the sufferings of the people of the Northeast, and I especially recommend to your attention the solemn words I have just quoted. Of course we are all concerned about the situation of Northeasterners; for the nine years of struggle of which the last three of resistance are but a part, our aim has been to recover our national independence, sovereignty, and territory, thus delivering them. Cut off from us by distance and the Japanese hordes as they are, we know, perhaps, only a tenth or so of the truth about them. We must, however, take their fate as a warning in the sense that "sacrifice to save the country must be made in due time;" those who would give their lives for their country must give them while they still have weapons in hand; if you would kill the Japanese, it must be under the leadership of the Government that you serve; the giving of strength and money to the national cause must be done while you yet have freedom and time. With the Northeasterners the case is that all their weapons have been taken from them, control and supervision over troops is infallibly thorough, so that, though their spirit is not dead and many an heroic death-blow has been struck, they have little else but bare fists wherewith to strike. Infinite dangers and difficulties confront them in any such move, and under these conditions the driving out of the enemy from within is a task all but to be despaired of. Therefore we must realize, subject as we are to the enemy's bombing, his incendiarism and destruction from the air, how much better we are situated than the Northeasterners who, as it were, gaze up to us from earth to heaven. Our sympathy for them and our sense of our responsibilities towards them should be correspondingly intense; now or never must we exert ourselves and omit no sacrifice for the sake of the happiness and freedom of succeeding generations of our people. The Japanese slogan "New Order in East Asia" covers only a design to reduce all the population of China to the same state of slavery as the Northeasterners find themselves in: it means Japanese control of East Asia by means of the annexation of China. Actually, however, the Japanese are forging for themselves fetters from which they will never free themselves; they are moving towards their own destruction and collapse. The beginning of that collapse will mark the deliverance of the Northeast. It is for us to do all we can by the firm and courageous prosecution of resistance to hasten the approach of the hour of Japan's collapse.

What I can reassure our Northeastern fellow-countrymen of is the constant thought of them and the resolution not to fail them in the minds of our entire army and people. Three years of war have established a noble and splendid record of achievement. More than 1,500,000 of the proud and reckless Japanese armies have been laid low; Japan has been plunged into a profound abyss of peril. Such is the achievement of the undaunted, all-enduring, unyielding spirit with which our soldiers and people have devoted themselves to resistance and which gives them their title to hold themselves the "hands and feet" of you Northeasterners. The outrageous conduct of the enemy wherever he has penetrated has been faced with stubborn composure by men, women

and children alike, who for the sake of final victory have resigned themselves to whatever sufferings were asked of them.

In recent months the embarrassment and frustration of the enemy
have led him to resort to a policy of intensive bombing and incendiary
air-attacks with a view to intimidating the heart of our people. These
prodigal raids have been aimed exclusively at such non-military centers
as Sian, Paochi, and Ankang in Shensi Province; Chian, Iyang,
Kweihsi and Yingtan in Kiangsi; Hengyang, Yuanling, and Chih-
chiang in Hunan; Kweilin, Liuchow and Ishan in Kwangsi; Shaokwan
in Kwangtung; Lanchow in Kansu; Loyang in Honan; Chuchi,
Kinhwa, Ningpo, Chenhai, and Shenghsien in Chekiang; Chengtu,
Luhsien, Chichiang, Hochwan and Nanchung in Szechwan. The
ferocity and frequency of these raids have produced enormous damage,
yet rather a stimulating than a frightening effect has resulted, rather
increased firmness than submission, so far as the mind of the populace
is concerned. In the stricken areas there are those who have lost home
and all else, who have suffered exposure and hunger, yet with calm
and equanimity. People of all ages and both sexes have merely borne
in mind the account to be settled with the Japanese, but remain unconscious of panic or fear. All those serving in relief work among
air-raid victims have thrown themselves into their duties with extraordinary vigor and disregard of personal safety, in supporting the old
and weak and succoring the dying and injured. This display of robust
and steady national striving imparts a unique and unprecedented distinction to all concerned.

There will undoubtedly be felt by fellow-countrymen in the Northeast and in the war areas anxiety as to the effect of the enemy's bombing of our rear; in fact it has served only to steel us to greater national
unity and a deeper sense of indignation. Since the Government began
last year to evacuate the cities and expand the rural living capacity,
the city populations have widely experienced the horrors of air-attack,
but in point of spirit the more we are bombed the stronger we grow,
and in point of material considerations we have come lightly to regard
our losses. We bid the enemy go on squandering his aerial strength in
the blind and indiscriminate dropping of costly projectiles. His menaces
and his destructiveness fall flat and we are content to await the time
when he has used up all his American oil, engines and parts. The real
measure of his strength is a matter of common knowledge; no one
is any longer intimidated by his threats. Our shattered walls and charred
remains of buildings may for the moment stand as a striking reminder
for us of the cause for which we must fight, and as a monument to the

senseless barbarity of the Japanese. Those whose homes have been destroyed have moved out into the far-flung countryside; indeed we are presented with an opportunity to achieve a great development of productive power in the rural areas, and thus attain the objectives of our people's economic reconstructive movement. You Northeasterners and people living in the war areas need not, therefore, be disturbed or anxious on account of the news you hear of bombing in the rear. It has proved only evidence of the strength of the people's spirit there; that it is not inferior to that being shown by officers and men at the front. With the exception of a few wretched traitors such as Wang Ching-wei, the entire nation is inspired with an inflexible spirit of "preference for jade in fragments to a tile unscathed;" everyone is prepared for suffering and sacrifice for the sake of final victory; at the thought of our Northeastern fellow-countrymen's sufferings, we discount our own; at the thought of how they seek both life and death in vain, we feel we ought to accept whatever sacrifice may be imposed upon us. We are one and the same people as they; we are as the hands and feet of one body—breathing the same breath—we all bear the same responsibility for national salvation, but it is we "south of the Wall" who must feel it weighs most directly upon us. This is a point on which I wish especially to reassure Northeastern fellow-countrymen.

Since the loss of the Northeastern provinces nine years have elapsed, and during that period we have to recall unprecedented calamity not only for you but also for the whole country. Before final victory is won there may well be a time of still greater difficulty, but with the experiences of the present and the past in mind, we are in a position to grasp the supreme truths upon which success and failure, victory and defeat, depend; to have confidence in final victory; and to be aware of our responsibility as seen in the vast perspective of history.

I have three points to make in what remains for me to say today.

Firstly: The occurrence of September 18 nine years ago formed a prime factor in upsetting international peace and order in the world. The present war in Europe may be put down to the Japanese militarists as the prime movers responsible. Now, the wilder they wax the more diplomatically isolated the Japanese become, and the course before them the more perilous. The saying, "The perpetrator of many wrongs must at last bring on his own ruin," will apply to the inevitable outcome of Japan's actions—her boundless ambition will issue in self-destruction. It is for us at once to be revenged and to rid the world of this universal enemy.

Secondly: During these nine years past and especially since the

European conflict began, international events have proved that any people, if only capable of exerting itself to develop its own strength, and of confronting all the difficulties in the path of its national rehabilitation, can in time convert its weakness into strength. An unyielding spirit has been shown to be the main element in overcoming a foe and commanding victory. Once the spirit submits, a nation is laid open to boundless pillage and irrevocable submergence in the tide of fate. If we, therefore, look out into the world of today and are aware of the duties naturally imposed upon us, we cannot but observe that of all experiences submission is the most painful. The only result of it is destruction. It is only necessary to look at the situation of the Northeasterners. On the one hand there is the solid resistance of Free China; and on the other their constrained and tragic struggle against impossible odds. In the light of this contrast we must conceive the efforts we are putting into resistance not only as our appointed duty but even as matter for rejoicing. Even if we die of cold and hunger, or perish in battle, it is not to be reckoned cause for sorrow while the spirit is unsubdued. Only the loss of the nation's vantage ground from which to re-establish its freedom and equality with other countries, only the descent to utter dispossession of its rights may be called genuine pain. When the Northeasterners desire to seek opportunities of killing the enemy and dying honorable death, they find such hard to come by. I would have you think this over repeatedly.

Thirdly: There is evidence to be found in recent international events for the belief that nations reap as they sow in victory or defeat. Behind us we have the five thousand glorious years of our history; before us, there are the untold generations of our descendants. A little more hardship endured and energy expended today will mean as much more happiness and well-being for our descendants. Another year of persevering resistance will mean at least a hundred years of freedom for them. Now the victory that will bring recovery of the Northeastern Provinces is at hand. It is my fervent desire to see all China's people and soldiers, whether north or south of the Great Wall, at the front or in the rear, advancing with one purpose towards that victory and the wiping away of disgrace from the country's name, for the accomplishment of the mission imposed by history upon us.

The International Role of the Republic

THIS is the twenty-ninth anniversary of the day when the Republic came into existence. We celebrate the occasion this year with resistance in its fourth year and at a time when tremendous changes are sweeping over East Asia and the whole world. These circumstances charge the day with a significance out of all proportion to that it bears in normal times. It is all the more necessary for us to be deeply aware of the aims of China's nation-building and to go about the fulfillment of our duties with the mighty spirit of the revolutionary martyrs.

Recalling the course of the establishment of the Chinese Republic, we are all bound to think first of our late Tsungli, Dr. Sun Yat-sen, who strove his whole life for the Revolution and whose great leadership, together with the magnanimous sacrifices of numberless martyrs twenty-nine years ago, brought about the overthrow of the Imperial system and the creation of the Republic. The events of 1911, however, only set in motion the enterprise of national construction; they were but the first step in the course of the Revolution. The aim of that national construction and that Revolution is the realization of the Three Principles of the People. On the one hand, the goal is to secure for China independence and freedom and give her a permanent place in the world as a strong and prosperous country. On the other hand, "having attained a good for oneself, desiring to convey it to others," we proceed to bring to bear on the advancement of peace and happiness for all mankind the great moral ideas our people possess, in order to fulfill China's responsibility towards the world.

Since our country belongs geographically to East Asia our first desire is to ensure its tranquillity. Peace in the world at large can be assured only if tranquillity prevails in the Pacific Ocean. Simply, therefore, we aim at home to build up our national defenses that China may have the means to freedom and equality with other nations, and abroad to stabilize the affairs of the Asiatic continent with a view to true world peace. Such are the aims the Tsungli set himself in his lifelong struggle, and such are the ideals of 1911.

A "Double Tenth" message to the army and the people, October 10, 1940.

Nearly thirty years have passed, but the aspirations of Dr. Sun and the revolutionaries are yet unattained. We cannot but feel immense compunction at our vacillations and inconclusive efforts. However, the greatest obstacles in the way of the still halting and delayed progress of the Revolution have been and are due to external causes, above all, to the Japanese militarists. They are the mortal enemies of national construction in China; their aggressive policy and the Three Principles of the People are incompatible forces, one of which must yield to the other. Their aims are the destruction of China, the enslavement of East Asia, and the conquest of the world. The first step in the Tanaka plan [1] was the conquest of China, and "what is most to be feared," wrote Tanaka, "is the awakening of China; if China were to become united the consequence would be industrial development; it is necessary to control Manchuria and Mongolia and then to use them as a base for the seizure of all China's wealth and resources." These are not merely the wild words of an individual. They represent the consistent and fundamental policy of the Japanese militarists. Ever since the Revolution of 1911 they have been ceaselessly interfering with and obstructing the unification, economic revival and national defensive measures of China. Previous to the time of the Northern Expedition they practised political sabotage, produced civil strife, sold drugs, and promoted smuggling in China. They left no device untried for the injury of our national unity. After 1928, the violence with which they went to work and the obvious nature of their intentions were only the more striking.

Nine years ago they invaded our Northeastern Provinces and then the climax came with the Lukouchiao Incident of 1937 when they commenced aggression on a scale calculated to strike at the very foundation of China's national existence. It is clear enough that the present slaughter and pillage perpetrated by the enemy is due to the Japanese militarists; but the same is no less true of all the chaos and tragic suffering our country has endured for the last thirty years. We are fighting now not only to clear and revenge ourselves of disgrace, but as a necessary means of attaining our national ideals, for the completion of the revolutionary enterprise set on foot in 1911 and the realization of the Three Principles of the People. Out of this war must come the recovery of our sovereignty, independence and territorial and administrative integrity and the contribution we have to make towards the strengthening of standards of international conduct, human equity and world peace.

[1] The Tanaka Memorial, presented to the Emperor of Japan on July 25, 1927, by Premier Baron Giichi Tanaka.

The former is absolutely the most essential and most elementary condition for national construction, while as I have often brought to your attention, the indestructibility of the conception of equity and the inevitable victory of justice in the world are facts of which we can never obtain too close a grasp.

The Japanese themselves avow the boundlessness of their ambitions. The center of those ambitions is the conquest of China but they include the overrunning of all East Asia, the carving up of the whole Pacific area, and unlimited aggression throughout the world. The attack on China, therefore, cannot be considered apart from the worldwide aggression contemplated by the Japanese militarists. Whether they say "a conclusion to the China Incident," or "to the south the defensive; to the north the offensive," or "to the north the defensive; to the south the offensive," it is all only a matter of sequence in the steps of their great scheme. Tanaka declared: "If China be completely conquered by us, Central Asia and Asia Minor, India and the South Seas, with their heterogeneous peoples, will certainly fear and yield to us; the world will be given to understand that East Asia is in our possession." He also spoke of the inevitability of war between Japan and America and Russia. "The rich resources of China," he wrote, "will become instrumental to the conquest of India, the South Seas, Central Asia and Asia Minor and Europe."

The minds of the Japanese militarists are crazed with this sort of dream. Their so-called "New Order in East Asia" is the phrase in which they express their determination to see all the countries on the shores of the Pacific and all the peoples of Asia acknowledge their overlordship. So they plunge into mad adventures and throw themselves toward ruin. Their nature, however, is such that save on the point of extinction they will never realize the error of their ways. Aware of this, China is resolved to fight not only to smash their scheme of conquest insofar as it applies to her, but also to shatter their hope of subduing the rest of Asia. China is the most ancient and the largest Asiatic country. Without her, East Asia would dissolve. She has not, therefore, shrunk from assuming responsibility for the stability of East Asia.

Since the outbreak of the European War the Japanese, despite the little strength left them after fighting three years with China, have been thinking constantly how they may take advantage of the situation for purposes of expansion southwards. Following the reverses suffered by Britain and France their "New Order in East Asia" suddenly became a "New Order for Greater Asia." The announcement was made that "Greater Asia" included the South Seas and frequent mention was made of a "new world order." Then came the compact engineered with Germany and Italy. Action no less extravagant than the mental ebullitions of the Japanese is clearly to be expected. It matters little to us whether they expand northward or southward; all their moves spell danger to China. China is inveterately opposed to both the "New Order in East Asia" and the "New Order for Greater Asia," and she will never cease her struggle, whatever the future difficulties, until her people have attained their national ideals.

Any country recognizing Japan's right to a "leading role in a New Order for East Asia," I unhesitatingly declare, will come eventually to regret having been a tool of Japan. Any treaty concluded with Japan in regard to Eastern Asiatic affairs, if China opposes it, will prove as worthless a scrap of paper as the treaty made between the Nanking puppets and their Japanese masters. I also declare that if only we persevere in resistance the Japanese scheme behind the Triple Alliance will be utterly frustrated. Every day that passes without a pause in Chinese resistance is another day without a solution for the grave emergency in Japanese affairs. The main Japanese motive, indeed, for entering into this alliance lies in the "urgent desire to bring the China Incident to a close." China, however, is engaged in a life-and-death struggle. As long as we have not reached the goal of resistance, no matter whatsoever threats and tricks he may employ, the enemy will never succeed in causing us to swerve a hair's-breadth from our purpose. If we analyze it objectively, this Triple Alliance is seen to be, as it were, a pit of self-destruction in addition to the shackles the enemy has already forged for himself with the "New Order in East Asia."

Everyone must understand that into whatever part of East Asia the enemy leaders may carry their aggression, it is all part of their criminal design to destroy China. Every move is a mortal blow aimed at the nation which we are planning to build and which will never be built without the dissipation of the Japanese dream of a "New Order in East Asia." At a time when the Japanese are exposing themselves to fresh risks it is opportune to strike them with the utmost severity. Thus we shall not fail to observe the directions left us by the Tsungli, as well as China's responsibility towards East Asia.

In this period of urgency for resistance and of unprecedented convulsions for the world, it behooves our devoted army and people, holding fast to the Tsungli's teachings, with firm faith in their cause, to exert intensified effort. To drive out the enemy and carry to completion the unfinished work of the revolutionary martyrs we must draw on their revolutionary and fighting spirit. Recall the circumstances of their heroism : those circumstances were certainly no less arduous than ours, yet they were infinitely the worse off. They defied death, returned ever to the charge, and fought even with bare fists and weaponless in creating the Republic.

Dr. Sun said: "At Huanghuakang three hundred men faced thirty thousand, pitting pistols and grenades against rifles and artillery. In the rising at Wuchang the odds were five hundred to one. Such contests are unknown in the annals of ancient and modern times, in the military art at home and abroad. Only revolutionary history could have put them on record. . . . If we would bring China into line with other nations and secure for the Chinese people an everlasting existence among mankind, we must emulate the revolutionary martyrs' conduct, make them our standard, be ready like them to sacrifice everything in single-hearted devotion to national salvation. There is no other recipe for the spirit that should animate the Kuomintang but this : fearlessness of death." This spirit of selfless patriotism dwells in the foundations of the Chinese Republic.

No revolutionary endeavor in the world that answered natural and human needs and laws has failed. The building of a nation, however, is always attended by numberless trials and sufferings. With other nations it has ever been that revolutionary endeavor has met immense obstacles and steady endurance has been required. American independence encountered numerous setbacks and material difficulties greater than China's today. Eight years of bloody conflict went to the making of the present spectacle of a strong and prosperous United States. The Russian revolution was hindered from without by foreign intervention and blockade and internally by reactionary elements, with the addition of grave natural calamities. It kept, however, to a steady course towards a defined goal, and at last repelled the foreign invader and pacified the land, leading to the construction of the imposing state of today. The revival of Turkey, again, took place when the Powers had just imposed upon her crushing terms of peace. Mustapha Kemal Pasha set about the salvation of his country at a time when its territory was daily diminishing, its economic strength was steadily declining, the army was falling to pieces and internal administration was in confusion. He cut a way through these overwhelming difficulties, leading the Turkish army and people to war for the recovery of the lost territory and national liberation. Subsequently, he threw himself into ten years of intense work to reconstruct the country and army and to institute all kinds of reforms, until the great enterprise of rehabilitation was at last completed.

These are all examples worthy of our emulation. The present European War may serve to impress on us the importance of concentrating our resources for the strengthening of national defense, but also the fact that such efforts must be seconded by the ability to maintain a struggle without wavering, no matter how long it lasts. At the same time, we should observe how any nation, to whatever degree favorably circumstanced, if it falls into ways of dissipation and easygoing self-seeking may perish in a flash. On the other hand, in circumstances the most perilous, unity and determination of a people's heart can save the situation. Our nation now hangs between life and death. Resistance is at a critical and arduous stage of its course; yet we are far better off than were the revolutionary martyrs or the builders of other nations at the commencement of their task. There is little difficulty in comprehending this truth: we confront a foe who has on all sides of him enemies other than ourselves—the rapidly weakening Japanese; while at our side are ranged the nations working for justice and existence in co-operation with others. In the last resort, all these nations desire to see in Asia a free and ascendant new China which, after winning the War of Resistance, will be able to assist in world economic cooperation and in the establishment of true world peace. The question now is, therefore, whether we have confidence in ourselves, whether we still possess the revolutionary spirit of 1911, and such a spirit as all countries have displayed in their periods of national construction.

Long ago I expressed my acute sense of the dangers and difficulties that must beset resistance. I have been equally emphatic in asserting that resistance is bound to be victorious, reconstruction bound to be successful. I have pointed out that the fundamental error of the Japanese permits of no good coming of whatever they undertake. Dr. Sun said: "Conduct that goes against the dictates of justice and humanity will sooner or later be defeated." Let the enemy contort himself as he may, his ruin will be only the more catastrophic the greater the adventures in which he indulges. On another occasion I said: "No matter what changes may take place in the international situation, they will be found essentially favorable to our resistance." For we have all along maintained the initiative; we have put the war on a basis of self-reliance and self-help. Advantageous to our cause have been the recent increase of other countries' assistance to China and measures against Japan, but they belong merely to the outwardly apparent indications of a trend in the international situation the impalpable significance of which is even more important for us to realize. That trend is day by day more closely approximating the aims of our resistance in its direction. During this period of resistance and world upheaval the Tsungli's ideal of national and world salvation will gain universal recognition and eventually be wholly realized. We are resolved to exert ourselves only the more vigorously should international events appear to turn an unfavorable face on our cause.

With the Triple Alliance the Japanese seem to have emptied their box of tricks. The Chinese people stand sublimely aloof meanwhile, growing stronger as the war proceeds. Our part in responsibility for the security of East Asia and the world lies heavily upon us; but, unless we are remiss ourselves no force can injure us, no power prevent the attainment of our national ideals. On the Double Tenth of the first year of resistance I remember telling you that "this war will not be a matter of six or twelve months." Today, our struggle is still in progress while the whole world has begun the general settlement of accounts that must precede the dawn of new hope. Re-reading the teachings bequeathed us by the Tsungli we cannot but feel that our road is lengthy in proportion to the importance of the journey we are making. Thousands of years of Chinese history show that as a people we are peculiarly gifted with a capacity for endurance and the overcoming of all descriptions of difficulty. It is not for us to waver in the face of trials, to be bewildered by perils, to lose heart at reverses, to be weakly fascinated by world changes and fall in the midst of difficulties into *laisser-faire,* irresponsible and compromising habits of mind.

For China to accomplish her own task of resistance is for her to discharge her responsibility to the world. For the individual to stand to his post and energetically do his particular duty is his way of making the greatest possible contribution to the nation. From the whole army and people there must be loyalty to the nation, loyalty to duty, loyalty to the Principles, loyalty to the law; and courage in unselfish patriotism, courage in bearing pain to serve the public interest.

In life a man's self is both his greatest friend and his greatest enemy. With self-reliance and self-exertion he has no enemy he cannot put to rout; while if he lets himself slide he courts his own destruction. Similarly, the ghastly injuries we have been subject to may be put down to the dissipation, folly, and selfishness of the past, while the rigor, bloodshed and striving of the present will go to the making of future prosperity and happiness. This gravest crisis in the history of our nation is also an experience fateful for Asia and mankind. It is the most serious trial history has ever made of the Chinese people's qualities. Extraordinary times have their extraordinary difficulties and these require extraordinary power to overcome. The strength and splendor of the national character must come into evidence now if ever. Our people will assuredly be steeled in this blood and fire; they will develop a pioneering spirit of endeavor for the opening up of the way to national construction and revival. I demand of army and people: at the front, vigorous fighting; in the occupied areas, sabotage and frustration of the enemy and sworn resolution not to compromise with the enemy and his puppets; and in the rear, self-denial and frugality, sturdiness and enthusiasm.

The Tsungli, in painstakingly setting down the plans for national construction, anticipated such a unique opportunity as presents itself today. This is the time for us to concentrate our will and strength and lay a sound political foundation for the country. The blockade we must turn to advantage by striving to counter it with the energetic development of production, and the promotion of research and invention with a view to establishing a robust and independent economy. We must exert ourselves in building up the army, in social training, in the completion of the new system of *hsien* administration and local autonomy, in stimulating industry and developing communications, all in order to reinforce the foundations of national defense.

The whole army and people, and especially those individuals gifted with special knowledge and technical skill holding positions of leadership in the various spheres of life, must realize the nature of our responsibility which extends to the fate of East Asia and the world. It is a responsibility not to be shirked but to be upheld with a courage equal to the immense and noble enterprise. The ancients called thirty years a generation and with next year the Republic will have attained that age. It finds itself still menaced and the work of reconstruction still lacks an adequate foundation. A barbarous enemy confronts it meanwhile. Things being so, we have to reflect upon our unworthiness of the sacrifices made and the distress suffered by the Tsungli, the revolutionary martyrs and innumerable other fellow-countrymen. The situation with us and in the world is now at a turning point. Our efforts and devotion were never more urgently required. I trust that you will all display a spirit such as may benefit those to whom has fallen the duty of executing the Will[2] and following in the steps of the Tsungli

---

[2] Dr. Sun Yat-sen's Will reads:
"For forty years I have devoted myself to the cause of the people's revolution with but one end in view, the elevation of China to a position of freedom and equality among the nations. My experiences during these forty years have firmly convinced me that to attain this goal we must bring about a thorough awakening of our own people and ally ourselves in a common struggle with those peoples of the world who treat us on the basis of equality.

and those who created the Republic twenty-nine years ago and initiated the noble mission we have to bring to completion.

"The work of the Revolution is not yet done. Let all our comrades follow my 'Plans for National Reconstruction,' 'Fundamentals of National Reconstruction,' 'Three Principles of the People,' and the 'Manifesto' issued by the First National Convention of our Party, and strive on earnestly for their consummation. Above all, our recent declarations in favor of the convocation of a National Convention and the abolition of unequal treaties should be carried into effect with the least possible delay. This is my heartfelt charge to you."

The Function of Revolutionary Discipline

I T IS the 27th of January; the rapidly passing days have already carried us far from the New Year's Day of the thirtieth year of the Republic. In the few days that yet remain of this month all Party, government and army men must, no matter how busily occupied they may be, scrutinize the record of their past year's work and duly report upon it. In regard to the work of the year before you it is still more important for you to lay down solid and definite plans preparatory to pressing forward to accomplish more and make better progress than last year. Our advance to victory has arrived at a highly critical stage that requires of us more than ordinary vigilance and circumspection. It calls for unusual exertions if the final success of resistance and re-construction is to be secured. Only by eliminating all negligence and irresponsibility that put the issue in jeopardy can we do our duty by the nation's soldiers and citizens who have bled and suffered for the cause, and solace the departed souls of the Tsungli and every martyr of the Revolution.

Speaking of the international situation it is no exaggeration to say that scarcely a day passes without some development to the advantage of our cause. With the Japanese the recent re-assembly of their Diet has afforded a dismal spectacle of dumb acquiescence, evidencing only the almost utter destruction of its constitutional framework. In the speeches delivered by Konoye and Matsuoka we can readily discern their sense of impending ruin. Matsuoka made clear only the tendency of his dreams of aggrandizement to grow in extravagance with the approach of the day when disaster and defeat will shatter them all; this time he expatiated on the phrase "co-prosperity sphere of greater Asia," saying this sphere must be taken to embrace the South Seas generally, and yesterday he went so far as to declare Japan requires control of the whole western Pacific area: the Philippines, Guam and Midway islands, Australia, Vladivostok, the northern part of Sahkalin and the maritime province of Siberia were all to be brought within the sphere of Japanese influence.

A speech delivered at the Weekly Memorial Service of January 27, 1941, being Generalissimo Chiang's first public reference to the New Fourth Army Incident.

During the past two weeks the Japanese have been playing up the New Fourth Army Incident by the fabrication of a great batch of fantastic rumors aimed both at sapping the strength of our fighting spirit and at misleading world opinion with insinuations of disunion in our ranks. These rumors may be divided roughly into two categories. In the first place they state that since the Government took action in regard to the New Fourth Army there has been resulting dissension to the point of civil war. In the second place they claim that on account of the incident nations favoring and assisting us are about to change their attitude towards China. A close examination of the incident concerned and of its falsified interpretation in the rumors will show that the motive really lies in the apprehension aroused among the enemy by the determination we have displayed in the strict maintenance of military discipline. Everybody knows that since the war began the whole Chinese army and people have unanimously devoted themselves to struggle and sacrifice with a common allegiance to one command, one discipline and one policy. Only a negligible minority of degenerate traitors such as Wang Ching-wei have chosen to throw themselves under the dominion of the enemy and organize their slavish puppet regimes, dressing up their treachery the while in talk of feud and faction. The traitors and puppets, however, are now all living under the aegis of their masters' power. With the defeat of the Japanese, we shall also have procured their destruction.

Apart from them there are no phenomena in the China of today to which the name of internal disruption could be given and still less anything that could be called civil war. Questions of wartime discipline and obedience to military commands have nothing whatever to do with such possibilities. The Government's disposal of the problem presented by the conduct of the New Fourth Army was simply and solely a matter of enforcing military discipline: there can be no room for doubt on this point in the minds of Chinese or foreigners. The affair was unambiguous; the issue was uninvolved; the incident not abnormal. Disobedience and insubordination among army men naturally bring down punishment upon them. Acts of revolt, attacks on comrades-in-arms, the forceful occupation of territory and other actions obstructive to the prosecution of the war still more certainly demand the disembodiment of the troops concerned. The most rudimentary conception of the principles essential to military command would require it. Only minds to which the ideas of law and discipline are equally foreign such as those of the Japanese Junior Officers' Group would perceive anything extraordinary in action so obviously necessary; none but they would think of exploiting it as material for malicious exaggeration in propaganda.

Turning to the international aspect, I may observe that the record of four years' sympathy and assistance from friendly nations has shown them uniformly desirous of seeing strict discipline enforced in our armies as a means of rendering them efficient in resistance. There has been no instance of their finding cause for suspicion and dubiety in our checking insubordination for the sake of that very object. On the contrary, they will be gratified to see us do so. Perspicacious statesmen of nations friendly to China will express only approbation for action lending strength and progress to our national armies. For those nations help us because they hope we can display a spirit of robust self-mastery; they expect to see us able to carry our own laws into full effect and keep order in our armies. Reckless disorder in civil life or lawlessness and insubordination among our soldiers would mean a people without national spirit and an army without discipline; were we deserving of this description no one would care to assist us, and resistance would have been quite out of the question for us. The various rumors propagated by the enemy are such, in the light of these facts, that nobody of the slightest intelligence can fail to understand the nature of the motives for their fabrication, not to speak of swallowing them. Since the war began a number of cases of disobedience to orders and defiance of discipline have had to be dealt with; Han Fu-chu, Li Fu-ying and Shih Yu-san were three instances.[1] The behavior of the New Fourth Army, its disregard of orders, attacks on comrades-in-arms and even acts of mutiny and sabotage had necessarily to be put an end to; it was purely a matter of the assertion of military law. There was not the minutest admixture of issues belonging to the sphere of politics and party relationships. This is the first point that must be clear to the minds of all.

With the three men I have just mentioned, the offense began and ended in the person of the individual. Let us now inquire why in the case of the New Fourth Army punishment had to extend to its abolition as a unit of the national forces. I will explain the distinction. Han Fu-chu, Li Fu-ying and Shih Yu-san acted solely on their own responsibility when they disobeyed orders. They did not incite their men to mutiny or lead them against another section of the national armies. The first of them was executed because he failed to obey the Govern-

[1] General Han Fu-chu, Governor of Shantung Province and Commander of the 3rd Route Army, and two other generals, courtmartialed and executed in 1938 for dereliction of duty in the War of Resistance.

ment's order to hold his ground in eastern Shantung and instead wanted to withdraw westward into Shansi. Li Fu-ying was shot for his persisting in retreat when retreat had been forbidden him. Shih Yu-san was ordered to move his forces into western Honan, whereas he remained in the eastern parts of the province, imposing meanwhile upon the people of the area. The officers and men serving under these three offenders took no part in the insubordination of their superiors; they fully comprehended the principles at stake and concurred in the change of command, and the Government accordingly preserved them intact.

With the New Fourth Army it was otherwise; in November it was ordered by the High Command to move northward to engage the enemy in a certain appointed area. It elected not to respond, but waited until after the expiry of the period of time allotted, then made an arbitrary move southward, executing a premeditated maneuver leading to an attack in broad daylight upon the headquarters of General Shang-kuan Yun-hsiang in command of the 40th Division. This plainly mutinous proceeding caused its disbandment as a disciplinary necessity. The incident has its place in the category of similar action taken on other occasions during the war. There are now a dozen or so high-ranking commanders in confinement as a result of sentences passed on them for acts of insubordination, and of these some are men distinguished for their former zeal and merit who could be in no way thereby exempted from the penalty due their guilt. This is evidence of the undiscriminating severity of measures taken to maintain discipline in our armies. They depend for their very life, the nation depends for its very existence, and resistance for victory, upon the allowance of no indulgence to violators of that discipline, upon the Government's never overlooking such offenses. At the same time we have to avoid all over-hasty conviction of those under suspicion of bad intentions lest injustice should be done them. The Government, therefore, limited itself last year to adjurations, calling upon the New Fourth Army to have done with its constant failure to comply with orders. It obstinately persisted, however, in its evil courses and at last went beyond all bounds. The situation developed in a way imperatively demanding the most rigorous action.

My own feelings were of acute pain and shame, for the errors and failings of subordinates are to be laid at the door of their commanding officer. I felt personally responsible for this unhappy affair, wherein you must none of you find any cause for gratification. Although the incident has been disposed of, it remains a blot on the glorious record of resistance. In my capacity of Commander-in-Chief I am sensible of a distress exceeding that of any other person concerned. This is the second point I would have you all clearly understand.

Now let us ask what is the value of the rigid maintenance of military discipline. In it reposes a principle vital to the preservation of an army and a nation. Victory or defeat for resistance will turn upon the state of discipline in our armies. The mutinous attempt of the New Fourth Army to break away from the restraint of that discipline is a test of the Government's ability to keep it inviolate: it is, therefore, also an episode fraught with immense consequence to the nation's being. I acted as I did with the determination to protect army and nation from a threatening disaster. The alternative of letting things take their course, of giving mutineers their head, could but have resulted in military defeat and national ruin. Should I, charged with the duties of Commander-in-Chief, for the sake of a transitory avoidance of the disagreeable, nourish in my bosom the viper of disaffection, imperilling the integrity of the national forces, I should be guilty not only of dereliction of my duty but also of betraying every fighting man and every citizen who has made sacrifices for the cause of resistance. In the strictest sense of the words I should be leading my followers to destruction; my offense would be the greatest a Commander-in-Chief could commit. I am resolved to demonstrate to the nation the essential qualities of sound discipline. It applies to all equally; it is a rule to which no exceptions are permissible. This is my third point.

At the beginning of the war several friends spoke to me in the following sense: "The unification of the country is not yet complete, its military preparedness is inadequate, the international situation is unfavorable, there are many doing lip-service to the idea of resistance who are not really ready to support the Government's policy. We cannot fight Japan; for such a venture defeat is to be expected." My reply was to the effect that their attitude was wrong: they failed to realize the revolutionary character of our present government and fighting forces. Our armies drew their strength not only from their weapons and equipment in matching themselves against the Japanese. We need not concern ourselves with difficulties that might possibly arise after the war. The relevant question was whether we possessed revolutionary principles and revolutionary discipline; what was the quality of our revolutionary spirit and determination. If we were confident, I said, of having such principles and discipline, such a spirit, and the determination to make sacrifices, if we had ascertained the sincerity of our intention to fight for the existence of our nation, we need not hesitate to throw ourselves into the struggle. As for the international situation, the hope of favorable changes in that must depend on our own showing; to wait for them to come before entering upon resistance would mean the indefinite postponement of success for the Revolution. We have ourselves to compel modifications in the attitude of the world towards us. A policy of wait-and-see in circumstances of such national peril would have meant waiting helplessly for death to claim us. For resistance is a stage in the process of Revolution: it is not some merely incidental adventure. At that time I expressed myself in these concise terms: "Essential to resistance is deliverance from fear of internal strife; fear of it would incapacitate us for resistance." When those friends observed my resolution they offered their unfaltering support, and now that the war has been in progress for nearly four years, the enemy is well on the way to defeat and we are within sight of victory, the complete soundness of my views and decision has been vindicated.

You must all grasp the two elements of our attitude: Towards the world, a proper dignity and self-respect, and efforts to deserve well of friendly nations; towards home affairs, strict discipline, the building up of our strength by all means with the aim of standing firmly on our own feet, our minds purged of any apprehension of internal disputes. In the event of an instance of rebellious conduct in the army it must be rigorously checked and the whole affair put in order, so that the evil may not impair the integral health of army and nation. I trust that no individual or party with the cause of national salvation and regeneration at heart will entertain any doubts as to the propriety of action taken by the Government to enforce discipline. While we oppose to the enemy the fullest possible measure of our strength, our serried ranks must answer to but one source of command, observe a common discipline. That is a basic condition for the attainment of victory.

You are all aware that the Government of China is a revolutionary one that can shatter any outward obstacles and suppress any internal rising against its authority. Had we during the years 1924-1926 laid aside our revolutionary mission for fear of internal opposition the Northern Expedition would never have been embarked upon. Every true revolutionary meets the obstacles and setbacks in his path with calm confidence in the fullness of his preparations. Revolutionary armies anywhere in the world have rarely been exempt from insurrectionary episodes; we need only ask whether a government claiming to be revolutionary has the ability to deal effectively with disaffection. If it is seen to go about the matter with a revolutionary vigor, especially where rebels are in arms, and uproot the evil, it will have achieved a victory that will contribute to the general success of its revolutionary endeavors. Now I can solemnly assure you our Government has both the determination and the ability to put down any incipient rebellion long before it could develop into civil war. That determination and ability are all the more certain at such a time as this when the whole people is pervaded with patriotic enthusiasm and loyalty to their fighting Government. We all share in the national life and honor we defend, with the exception only of traitors like Wang Ching-wei who pretend to represent a faction of opinion in the country while they go about the purely private pursuit of gain at its expense. Apart from these criminals, there are none so mad as to will the defeat of resistance.

There is yet another reason for the fact that the action taken against the New Fourth Army was unavoidable. Since the incident occurred the Japanese militarists have been rejoicing over the opportunity they think it provides them of fomenting sedition in our ranks. They are always on the look-out for signs of slack discipline and insubordination among us that might lead to national instability and eventual collapse. If we had not acted resolutely an indirect result would have been encouragement of the Japanese contempt for our national integrity and revolutionary spirit and a fillip to their lust for conquest. Actually the course we took was a downright shock for them, putting their tricks at naught and giving them disagreeably clear evidence of the revolutionary discipline and spirit, and the conception of nationhood prevailing in our armies, in contrast to the enervation of which they hoped to take advantage. Let me assure the Japanese militarists that their interests will in no way be served by the Government's procedure in regard to the New Fourth Army and that on the contrary it will brace up our discipline and invigorate our fighting spirit. The outcome will be quite the reverse of their expectations and all to their disadvantage. Speaking in terms of our internal necessities, the Government had necessarily to assert its authority in an unequivocal manner to safeguard the essential conditions for successful prosecution of the war.

By now I think you will all have absolutely clear in your minds the outstanding fact that the incident under discussion was a normal, ordinary and indispensable case of the functioning of military authority. I am convinced that all exaggerative and malicious deductions representing it as something more are to be attributed to the enemy. I also trust that no citizen with love of his country and loyalty to the cause of resistance will permit himself to be fooled by the Japanese rumors or be influenced by them to take any disproportionately grave view of the affair. When the order for the disbandment of the New Fourth Army was about to be issued attempts were made in quarters connected with it to extenuate its offense by means of a variety of insidious and far-fetched arguments. I then dispatched representatives to make an indirect appeal to them not to add error to error but to lend the true support due from all Chinese citizens to the interests of national resistance. The Government at first refrained from publishing the facts concerning the New Fourth Army's culpable disregard of orders and this I told them was out of consideration for them, not weak procrastination or fear of consequences. If they were to add to their former misdemeanors the mendacious vilification of superior commanders and the Government without thought for the good name of their country in the world's eyes their conduct would be universally condemned as conduct to be expected only from China's enemies and traitors, or at least calculated to give the Japanese every satisfaction. They would not only fail, I warned them, to justify their misdeeds thereby but would also make themselves abominated by all their fellow-countrymen. True patriots among us must respect the law and obey commands, conform to discipline and free ourselves of all disingenuous dealings in our devotion to the cause, I declared. Subsequently the vindictive talk ceased, and I now believe no son of Han will serve the interests of the Japanese by echoing their exaggerated versions of the incident.

You must all realize that we did not immediately make the matter public because the New Fourth Army was a section of the national revolutionary army, of which I am the Commander-in-Chief. I have often compared the army to a family wherein I look upon the soldiers under me as a father regards his children. If his children behave well the father feels they reflect honor upon him; if badly, they disgrace him. I attempted to discharge my responsibility towards the New Fourth Army in the past by repeatedly warning it and imploring it to make a fresh start in the genuine service of the nation. I feared a premature revelation of its misdeeds might cut off its way to reform. My solicitude failed, however, to move them; they interpreted it as weakness and even timidity on the ground of their threats of precipitating civil war. Who will say that there could be any possibility of tolerating the perversity and reckless selfishness of men prepared deliberately to expose to the sight of the enemy the weaknesses of their own army as a means of intimidating their superior officers? In point of fact, however, the Japanese were no doubt well informed, perhaps better informed than we, regarding the actions of the New Fourth Army. It was certainly not, therefore, for fear of letting them or the world know that we abstained from publishing the state of things for so long. All along the motive lay in the moral precept, held so important in Chinese society, of "keeping evil out of sight and bringing good to the fore." I have always observed this principle in my dealings with men in general and only the more studiously in dealing with soldiers under my command, to whom I feel bound in an intimacy equal to that of family relationship. The honor of my subordinates is as my own; their merit or demerit as my own. With this sense of personal responsibility for their misconduct I am ever reluctant to make it known. On this occasion, however, there came a point beyond which it was totally impossible to conceal the ugly facts. All of you will recall the New Testament teaching of forgiveness unto seventy times seven. The misdeeds of the New Fourth Army even exceeded that number; there was no further room for pardon, if I myself were not to become criminally negligent of my country's welfare.

Discipline is to be thought of as a bond of faith uniting all ranks of the army; its nature permits of no exceptions or partial treatment. So far as it is concerned all soldiers from Commander-in-Chief to private are on an equal footing. To feign blindness to its violation would mean my complete unworthiness of the trust reposed in me by the army. Only under the guarantee of its inviolability can all strive together for the sacred cause of resistance.

You are all acquainted with the fact that Japan finds herself in her present plight simply because her army men have set legality at naught and made a sport of discipline while her government has been powerless to uphold the law and enforce discipline. The Mukden Outrage came about as a result of the arbitrary action of the Japanese Junior Officers' Group who disobeyed their Emperor's commands and disregarded their government's directions pursuing their ambitious schemes free from all restraint. Consequently there followed the Tokyo Incident of May 15, 1932, still without the government exercising any check on those responsible for the bloody event of that day. Then again in 1936 there was open rebellion in the Japanese capital, the killing of elder statesmen and cabinet ministers and the overthrow of the government. Finally, with the Lukouchiao Incident war on a scale unprecedented in the Orient was brought about, threatening the destruction of world civilization. All this can be put down to the Japanese government's inability to maintain its authority and punish insubordination. The fact that the Japanese army can still continue its war of aggression in China, however, is due to the measure of disciplined habits preserved by the

High Command. War-weary as they may be and ill-disposed to continue the war, they must make the best shift they can to obey orders. This indicates the vital character of the observance due to orders that suffices to keep the spiritless Japanese army in the field as nothing else could. With the very different motives and spirit animating our forces it is nevertheless imperative that we show the same unquestioning obedience to commands.

If henceforth all sections of our forces carry out their orders, adhere strictly to the plans laid down by the High Command and fulfill the precise duties allotted them, the Government will naturally look upon them with undiscriminating solicitude for their well-being, providing each an opportunity to make its full contribution to a victory in the glory of which all will share equally. Now the New Fourth Army has been abolished, the question has been settled and no other question remains. Our Government has always been liberal and considerate towards all sections of the national forces, while I regard my soldiers as the members of a family of which I am head. An affair involving unbeseeming action causes me pain and shame, and all of you too will, I hope, consider this incident as a great disgrace to the Revolution, an incomparably regrettable page in the history of resistance, and take it as a warning example of the consequences inevitable to such conduct, encroachment upon areas not assigned to you, obstruction of the movements of other troops, the seizure of their arms, the confiscation of the people's weapons and food, and so on. You must moreover see to it that, on the contrary, troops function to the advantage of the people and give stability to the social order, especially in areas behind the enemy lines where solidarity of army and people is so essential. Let this affair be a stimulus to our faith in resistance and reconstruction; let good come of evil.

In conclusion, the incident is not to be considered as something negative, but as of positive value. Firstly, it has proved a sharp disappointment to the enemy's hopes of seeing internal disruption weaken the strength of the nation's will and ability to resist. Secondly, it has produced a vindication of the quality of our discipline, with an invigorating and salutary effect upon the morale of our forces. Had the action not been taken the Japanese would have felt more sure than ever of our worthlessness and of the feasibility of their aggressive designs. All our troops having been made aware of the motives of the Government in at first refraining from publication of the facts and of its subsequent severe procedure, they will know that all was done in the interests of resistance and they will be warned of its determination to act with similar resolution in any similar case.

Discipline is a criterion whereby the efficiency of the Government as a revolutionary and fighting government may be judged and the degree of soldiers' sincerity in devotion to the defense of their country be assessed. Apart from the preservation of sound discipline, no other issue whatever was involved in the Government's action. Nor did the behavior of the New Fourth Army have any connection with other parts of the national forces. The incident was entirely free from any political character. The Government is absolutely committed to the respect of all groups and parties that conform to the provisions of the program for resistance and reconstruction; it legally safeguards their rights of freedom and independence. An infringement of the law by them would of course require the exercise of the law to restrain them. I constantly say to friends that though victory is near the country is not yet past the period of danger and while the crisis lasts people in all positions throughout the land should observe particular caution to avoid giving rise to obstructions to national unity and effort. The Government, however, cannot neglect its most important duties or fail in its responsibilities for the sake of such caution, though to the limited extent possible it kept silence for this reason in regard to the activities of the New Fourth Army.

My hope is that the whole country will of one accord observe strict discipline, obey orders and throw its whole weight into the strength to accomplish our revolutionary mission.

National Defense First

THE second session of the People's Political Council assembles today for the first time. I am here as the representative of the Supreme National Defense Council to say a few introductory words and first of all to extend a warm welcome to all you Councillors present. We may well congratulate ourselves upon the patriotic and public-spirited enthusiasm that, with the war in its fifth year and all the national energies concentrated upon the struggle for survival, has brought Councillors together from all parts of the country, some, in particular, having made their difficult and dangerous way here from provinces in the occupied areas. Scarcely anything more glorious and memorable will be recorded in the history of resistance. The Council has met five times since it was originally convened on the occasion of the first anniversary of the outbreak of war and during these three years it has afforded the Government highly valuable assistance in the execution of the national policy of resistance and reconstruction. It has been a great force working for solidarity which has attracted the attention of the whole world and inspired our whole army and people.

The world situation is now more critical than ever and the importance of resistance looms larger from day to day. The present session of the Council, therefore, has not only to carry on the work of the previous session but also to anticipate and provide for the needs of a new situation. Your fellow-citizens and the Government cherish correspondingly greater expectations of you.

I propose today to present you a succinct report on the course of government administrative measures since the Council last met and on the more significant aspects of the current phase of the war. I wish also to take this opportunity of voicing my own personal faith regarding the future.

Since the Provisional National Assembly of the Kuomintang passed its resolution sanctioning the Outline Program of Resistance and Reconstruction and the first meeting of the People's Political Council

A speech given at the inaugural session of the Second People's Political Council, March 1, 1941.

unanimously expressed its approval and support of the Government's policy, the Program has become a creed universally subscribed to by the entire army and people, and the basis of all national policy. On each occasion it has met, the Council has framed important resolutions in accordance with the requirements of that Program. For three years, it may be said, the work of the Government has been exclusively guided by its provisions and by the desire strictly to adhere to the suggestions of the Council. Ministers and other responsible officials will give you detailed reports of what has been undertaken and achieved since the Council last adjourned. Generally speaking, the main aim of all the Government's measures has been the strengthening of the country's power to resist and the establishment of a sound framework for reconstruction. Among the preliminaries in reconstruction much has been done to hasten the day of rule by law, to prepare the way to constitutional government and to build up the system of local autonomy in districts smaller than the *hsien*; production has been stimulated, communications developed, economic control rendered more effective. Objective limitations and fluctuating war circumstances have caused our achievements in many respects to fall short of what had been hoped. These deficiencies the Government is determined to do its best to remedy and in its efforts to do so it is eager to have the full cooperation of this Council.

Of the situation as things stand between the enemy and ourselves it may be truly said that it conforms now, and has conformed during the past two years or more, to the course we anticipated. From the time when the war entered its second stage with the fall of Hankow the Japanese have gradually come to find themselves at a military disadvantage. We on the contrary have been constantly recruiting fresh strength, acquiring the will and the ability to take the offensive. It is true that after the winter of 1939 the enemy made two reckless forward moves in his penetration of southern Kwangsi and western Hupeh, but in the autumn of last year he was compelled to withdraw ignominiously from Kwangsi and in Hupeh he has fallen into a position wherein he has the utmost difficulty in maintaining himself. Taking a comprehensive view of the military situation, we see the enemy debilitated and discouraged by the long-drawn-out inconclusiveness of his operations, while the Chinese fighting strength and spirit are still mounting. The defeat of the Japanese is all but consummated, both in the field of battle and in the sphere of diplomacy. Their refusal to admit and realize their military failure has enhanced their diplomatic ineptitude; in vain have they thought to find a way out of their difficulties in diplomatic trickery, by alternately threatening and bribing various countries of Eastern Asia. All Powers on friendly terms with China have come fully to realize that there is no room for compromise with such insatiable aggressors as the Japanese. They also now have fresh faith in the certainty of Chinese victory. So far from yielding to the bullying or blandishments of Japan they are increasing their aid for China's cause. All nations whose interests are affected by events in the Pacific are by now aware of the boundless extent of the Japanese ambitions, they are taking firm and concerted action, and there is consequently a rapid clarification of the Pacific situation proceeding such as the Japanese militarists have always feared. And this is, moreover, a sign of a coming worldwide clarification of issues.

In his political offensive the enemy for two years or more past has, both by the continual manufacture of peace rumors and by recruiting the services of traitors, tried to shake the will of the Chinese people and influence the established policy of the Government. In March of last year he formally set up the puppet administration in Nanking having a short time previously published the long "secret" pact with Wang Ching-wei. China, however, is united in purpose and growing in strength; her whole army and people stand four-square and proof against insidious Japanese tricks and rumor offensives. The world's contempt for the Japanese militarists has increased in proportion to its better acquaintance with their motives. Because in the first period of the war we strove alone but undismayed, confident we were fighting a force that imperilled justice and peace throughout the world we now find our resistance the concentration point of efforts exerted by many other countries in the Pacific area.

Coming to speak of internal events and conditions in Japan, we observe that political bankruptcy has led to the appearance of a "new political structure" and economic bankruptcy has produced a "new economic structure"—both names for desperate remedies that are bound to prove quite ineffectual as means of averting Japan's national ruin or even prolonging her uncertain hold on life. The likelier effect of these devices will be to render the final collapse of the militarists more shocking and catastrophic. During the twenty-four or so months past we have succeeded in laying the foundation of victory and that has not been the work of any limited group of men but the outcome of all the courageous efforts and sacrifices of army and people. To this achievement have contributed numberless episodes, recorded and unrecorded, of heroic devotion to the cause, at the thought of which

I, as Commander-in-Chief, am profoundly stirred, and long worthily to act up to my fellow-countrymen's hopes of me.

The facts I desire now to call your attention to are: the inevitability of the enemy's defeat and the general advantageousness of the present situation in all its aspects. We cannot permit these facts, however, to weaken our determination to be prepared to face the worst eventualities conceivable; we must rather intensify both our caution and vigor as the day of victory draws near. We need a thorough grasp of the significance of the present world scene, and it is with that necessity in view that I propose to give you an account of my own beliefs regarding the future founded on my observations of that scene. Following the outbreak of the European conflict the evil of war has been steadily extending its shadow over a greater area, and the horrors produced by the use of modern weapons and the overthrow of countries small and large have astounded the mind of humanity. Nations everywhere have been impressed with the urgency of defensive measures to preserve their independence and freedom. A tide of nationalistic feeling is rising and as yet has only begun to inundate the world. We are convinced that the tendencies apparent in the march of world events accord with the traditional conceptions of the Chinese nation and that they are certain eventually to advantage our cause.

At the same time we must not lose sight of the fact that in this warring world survival is impossible to a nation not resolute and strong enough to defend itself. In Eastern Asia there can be no taking Japan's designs and ambitions lightly or ignoring the way in which she is constantly scheming to make the European war the means of giving substance to her dream of conquest despite failure in China. The recent tentative steps of the Japanese towards invasion of the South Seas should put us on our guard; we must bear in mind that this is only a feint, their real object still being the destruction of China. They will certainly make a final attack on us during the initial stages of the southward move; in fact, the new campaign would be inseparable from the old. The creation of "Manchukuo" and the recognition of Wang Ching-wei outraged us sufficiently, but the so-called "New Order for 'Greater' Eastern Asia" and the "'Greater' Eastern Asiatic sphere of co-prosperity" are still more atrocious insults to China and the whole of Eastern Asia. The addition of this word "greater" to these phrases has been made presumably to forewarn all concerned of Japanese claims to proprietorship over the vast resources and territories of the South Seas, of their intention to tighten the blockade of China and carry out other parts of their program for domination in the Pacific.

You are all aware that for us the South Seas are not merely the second fatherland of some ten million fellow-countrymen resident there; their fate is bound up with our own existence and security. A Japanese attack on the South Seas would undoubtedly imply a grave menace to China. The enemy, despite his non-success, is yet far from regretting his folly; and, the European conflict has whetted his appetite anew. He is speculating upon the chances of a bold throw, by risking all perhaps to gain all. We have not only firmly to maintain resistance in the defense of our soil but also to protect the world and the Orient from the most vicious of aggressors. The present time is a period of transition in the development of the world situation and it is also the final stage of our struggle with the Japanese.

We find ourselves at this historic point of time possessed of prestige won in more than three years of bloody warfare, and charged with responsibility heavier than ever before. For the past ten years China has been repeatedly warning the world that the maintenance of world peace depends upon the restraint of Japanese aggression. Because the warning went unheeded the world has been plunged into the present ocean of calamity. When China took up arms in solitary opposition to the Japanese militarists' formidable power and succeeded in pinning down forces of which they might otherwise have made predatory use elsewhere in the Pacific, she was playing the part of prophetical leader in the cause of peace and at the same time was the vanguard of action to vindicate that cause. That is now an evident fact. The world has awarded us its sympathy and confidence and our relations with countries sharing interests in common with us have been rendered closer. Chinese resistance has ceased being isolated and unilateral, becoming rather a pivotal factor in world security and order. Under these fresh circumstances, I ask all you Councillors to carry your efforts a step further, keeping before your minds a clear conception of the great goal to be attained.

Let me describe that goal. Firstly, resistance must issue in victory, in the final victory that will smash the "New Order for Eastern Asia" together with the "New Order for 'Greater' Eastern Asia." Our standpoint has never shifted. We intend to fight Japanese aggression to the point of exhaustion, restore the integrity of our territorial sovereignty and permit ourselves no rest until the day of the extinction of the Japanese militarists' ability to threaten the peace of the world. There is no room for compromise with our present antagonist. Secondly, national reconstruction must give the country such defensive preparedness as can guarantee it absolute security. The Three Principles of the People demand a state with solid provision for national defense, with developed democratic institutions and a prosperous livelihood for its whole people. The Principles conceive of national defense as having only the protection of the State as its object; it cannot possibly conflict with the people's authority and livelihood which indeed it exists to safeguard. Today our national strength is making rapid strides and the international situation seems entirely favorable to us, but in order to win final victory, respond to the demands of our part in world affairs and fully acquit ourselves of our weighty responsibilities we have yet to work for the thorough awakening of our people to the realities of their position. Our past efforts, we must realize, are inadequate in the face of the needs of today and tomorrow. The completion of our national defenses is an indispensable prerequisite for the completion of the work of national reconstruction as a whole. Therefore all reconstructive activities at present must be subordinated to the requirements of national defense and the entire people must adopt a military cast of life.

Only the capability for self-defense can safeguard democracy; without the will to strive there can be no real democracy. Taking these maxims as a text I wish to bring forward the following views which I hope will find their way through you to the ears of my fellow-countrymen generally.

In matters political, all my fellow-countrymen must have their minds quite clear regarding the fact that political partisanship and ideological bias to the so-called "left" or "right" are now the outworn and useless lumber of a past age and utterly incompatible with the realities of the day. Let us face those stern realities and learn from our experience in this war to make our first aim the building of absolutely reliable national defenses. The European War has demonstrated that only nations with the will and the ability to strive can be sure of survival and avoid conquest and enslavement. A modern nation moreover when once conquered by an alien power finds, by reason of the present highly developed technical nature of the military art and the inexorable rigidity possible to modern methods of economic control, that it will never be able unaided to recover its lost independence. Nations conquered today are powerless ever again to assert themselves; this is a point of dissimilarity btween conditions now and those obtaining twenty or thirty years ago. Only a political system adapted to the strains of war is serviceable in this new age. A democracy unable to defend itself is a contradiction in terms. What democratic institutions remain to a conquered nation? The capital and labor alike of a conquered country belong to the conqueror, and in such a country all political opinions and programs are equally valueless. The Kuomintang is working for a republican revolution of which the aim is national salvation. It is seeking to secure for China freedom and equality of status among the nations of the world and its consistent policy is to solidify the strength of the people and build up national defense. It has always loudly declared to the public the importance of national defense and it is now leading the nation in a tremendous campaign of national self-defense such as has never before been seen. In order properly to fulfill this duty it has freed itself of all party prejudice, appealing to all citizens simply and solely for action to protect their country. It is adjusting the functioning of Government with a view to raising the standard of administrative efficiency; it is hastening the institution of local autonomy with a view to establishing a sound basis of democracy. The postponement of the meeting of a national convention only renders the more pressing the Government's responsibility of bringing into existence a strong basic political organization of local representative machinery. The tide of events forces upon the Party an unprecedentedly heavy burden of responsibility. It has to call upon everyone to recognize the supremacy of the nation's interests and abandon old notions out of place in these days in order to make the nation a strong and unified fighting body—a China equal to the task of defending herself and vindicating justice.

The Party demands of everyone better knowledge and faith, fitter thought and action, in all that concerns national security. The very center of national reconstruction in future must be the building up of the army and it is necessary to organize the political, economic, educational and cultural life of the nation and even private life on a war footing. On the one hand, the training of troops will be strengthened, the conscription system improved, military training rendered universal, and fighting technique raised to a higher standard. On the other hand, the people's sense for the needs of national defense will be sharpened and fighting discipline better enforced. This is the time to establish an economic basis for national defense. Economic measures taken for this purpose now are not to be limited to the present period of resistance but carried forward until the day the nation can feel perfectly safe in its defensive preparedness. The Government must take steps to adjust production and finance, improve communications and methods of transportation, ask of the people frugality and hard work, and concentrate the country's capital resources. The Government and the people must work in unison to conserve those resources, develop war industry, raise the national power of production, extend effective control over all economic activity, nourish and stabilize the people's means to subsistence. Beyond the needs of our own defense and progress I believe that the reinforcing and development of China's economy will be of immense benefit to the whole world. At the end of the first European War Dr. Sun drew up an industrial plan [1] which can not only serve the Government well as a fundamental policy for the reconstruction of national defense, but is also, when the broadest and longest view of affairs is taken, seen to be indispensable as a guide to future economic policy in general. Today a war of dimensions far greater than those of the last European War is in progress and it will bring about correspondingly more far-reaching changes. If at its conclusion China can obtain modern machinery and technical skill for the development of her economic possibilities she will be in a position to relieve the distress and chaos produced by world economic maladjustment and give the Orient a foundation for lasting peace. For this, however, to come about it is first necessary to make sure of her ability to stand the economic strains of the present time. A nation incapable of bestirring itself on its own behalf has no right to expect foreign financial and technical assistance and collaboration on a basis of equal and reciprocal advantage. We must be absolutely clear on this point.

In matters of education and culture, of private and public life, greater efforts are required to conform to this conception of the dominant needs of national defense. We must elevate the moral quality of national life, stimulate the pursuit of scientific knowledge and skill, make elementary education universally available, and encourage labor and service until every citizen is able and willing to play his full and proper part in national defense and reconstruction. Support for the wounded and relatives of the fallen, relief of distress, protection of those unable to shift for themselves, improvement of public health and physique are aspects of the work necessary for the security and soundness of the population. Without effective national defense there can be no State, no livelihood for the people. The whole spirit of the Three Principles of the People lies in their emphasis upon national defense as the guarantee for national prosperity; it must be the focus of all policy and planning, the criterion for all political activity. The individual must restrict his personal needs as far as possible and develop his energy to the utmost. We must throw aside all out-of-date and narrow ideas of the conflicting interests of groups and reform habits

[1] Dr. Sun's plan was embodied in a book entitled *The International Development of China*, published in 1922.

of indulgence, slackness and idleness. I am convinced the nation is capable of far greater concentration of purpose and action in mobilizing and organizing its strength. At the same time it is no less imperative for us to work in the closest possible cooperation with all other countries that oppose Japanese aggression.

Looking at the world today we see vast changes going on: the moral and material life of humanity will undoubtedly be profoundly modified by them and all political and economic theories will be recast as a result. One thing, however, appears certain: that a nation must be armed and organized with modern efficiency if it is to survive, while thought and action incompatible with national fighting strength stand to be eliminated by the demands of the time. Looking at China we are aware of her excellent natural advantages, the fighting spirit of her people, and the generous aid and sympathy for her cause extended by countries friendly to her. Japan we see internally exhausted and externally menaced on all sides. Our national future may be said to be richly promising. The key to victory, however, remains in our ability to grasp the new realities and make new efforts. On this occasion of the Council's meeting I have given you this account of my beliefs in the hope that this session will work with a due sense of the present state of world affairs and national needs, contributing to the best of its ability to national leadership to the end of final victory by the completion of the task of building up national defense.

Again National Solidarity

I INTEND, as a representative of the Government, to explain today its attitude toward the conditions laid down by the Communist members of the Council. Before I make any report I wish to state that the Government did not originally intend to declare publicly its stand on its relations with the Chinese Communist Party. Now that the latter has, however, formally telegraphed these demands to the Council, which is an organ of national opinion, it has acted in a manner quite unlike that usually characterizing its words and deeds. It is, therefore, incumbent upon the Government and the Council to make a formal declaration of their attitude in the interests of the nation, the War of Resistance and the future of national reconstruction. A nation, and more especially when it is engaged in mortal combat with an aggressor, depends for its very life upon the maintenance of discipline, order and the necessity of the Government's writ being obeyed. Given a sound framework of discipline and legality it will be able to overcome whatever perils and difficulties come in its way. If, on the other hand, its military command is not unified and its authority questioned, it will meet with defeat no matter how strong its armed forces may be. We are now pitting the whole strength of the nation against the Japanese militarists in a life-and-death struggle. The fate of our nation is hanging in the balance. It is a time when we must give the most scrupulous attention to the upholding of order and authority in the State. In all matters—whether political, social or party problems—not involving conflict with, or obstruction to national order and authority, there is room for frank and open adjustment of differences in search of rational solutions. This has always been the policy and attitude of the Government in relation to the Chinese Communist Party; the achievement of unity by means of mutual concessions in the face of external aggression and the attainment of success in resistance and reconstruction.

In this message, delivered on March 6, 1941, Generalissimo Chiang explained to the People's Political Council the Government's attitude towards the Communists' demands the satisfaction of which they required as a condition for the attendance of their members of the Council.

I understand that the Secretariat of the Council has received two sets of demands from the Chinese Communist Party entitled: firstly, "rehabilitation measures;" and secondly, "measures for a provisional settlement"—each set containing twelve points. I can assert that though these demands were received by members of the Council before it assembled, no government institution or individual member of the Government, nor I myself, received them. Now that we have seen them we are, first of all, astonished at the wording of the titles and next, at the formal resemblance of the contents to the demands made by the Japanese prior to the Lukouchiao Incident. One is particularly and painfully reminded of the so-called "Three Principles" announced by the Japanese at that unhappy time. The Chinese Communists are as much citizens of the Chinese Republic as we all are, and yet their presentation of such demands at such a time as this would seem clearly to indicate their intention of taking up a hostile attitude to the National Government and the People's Political Council. We think, therefore, the least said the better, and do not regard it as necessary to rebut each point in detail. It is sufficient to classify the sense of the demands into three main categories of "military," "political" and "party" affairs. The first eight points of the first set of demands regarding "rehabilitation measures" and the first, sixth, seventh, eighth, ninth, and tenth points of the second set regarding "measures for a provisional settlement" belong to the category of military affairs. The ninth and twelfth points of the first set and the third, fourth and fifth points of the second set belong to the category of political affairs, while the tenth and eleventh points of the first set and the eleventh and twelfth points of the second set belong to the category of party affairs. A brief explanation of the bearing of the sense of the demands under each of these three heads upon resistance and reconstruction is indispensable.

Firstly, the demand is, in effect, that the Government should not suppress disobedient and rebellious troops, that government authorities should be punished for so doing and that the losses of the mutineers in such rebellions should be compensated.

Secondly, the implication is that the Government should establish special areas outside the sphere of its authority, recognize the existence of anomalous political organizations and restrict its power to check illegal activities on the part of organizations or individuals. Recognition of a so-called "democratic authority in the enemy's rear" is also demanded. The logical outcome of all this would be disaster,—such a disaster as must invariably follow any attempt by a party to take advantage of enemy invasion in order to seize supreme power.

Thirdly, the sense of the demands is that the Communist Party should enjoy a special status and special rights and that the Government should not deal with the Communist members of the Council on the same footing as it deals with all other members belonging to other parties or to none. The Government not being ready to comply, the Communists have refused to attend the present meeting of the People's Political Council. In essence this is really what the demands amount to. I think that when the Communist Party produced them it did not perhaps realize they were of so drastic a nature. But were the Government to accept them without protest, China would scarcely be any longer worthy of being called a nation or the People's Political Council an organ of the national will.

Now I shall further expound the attitude of the Government towards these three categories of demands.

In the category of military affairs the consistent policy of the Government has been to nationalize our armies. That is, under the supreme command of the National Government there is but one system of national armies, and there can be no second system of armies under the control of individual parties or private persons. I can categorically assure the Council that the national revolutionary army is the army of the State and in no way the army of any particular party whatever. It is, therefore, absolutely out of the question to regard a section of it as belonging to the Communist Party. There can be but one source of command. Should a second presume to assert itself, it would be indistinguishable from the "military council" of Wang Ching-wei's puppet regime and accordingly detested and abjured by the whole country. It is inconceivable that the Communists, if devoted to the cause of resistance, should take up such a position.

Next, the political principle of the Government is to democratize the national political system. All citizens, individually or in organized bodies, while they conform to discipline, should shoulder their responsibilities, fulfill their duties and enjoy their rights, possess all due freedom of action, but sovereignty is indivisible. If a second source of political authority were to be allowed to exist outside the Government —such, for example, as might be called by the name of a "democratic authority behind the enemy lines," mentioned in these demands—it would not differ from the traitorous administrations in Nanking and Manchuria. Not only would the Government find it intolerable, but the whole country would see in it an irreconcilable enemy.

Although as a result of the nation's historical development there is now but one party exercising administrative power, while others of varying size and permanency are "in opposition," yet all parties exist in a spirit of equality with one another, this being nowhere more markedly visible than in this democratic institution, the People's Political Council. Here all are equal rather as citizens than as parties. There could be no room for a special status of one party or demands for special rights, such as would vitiate the sprouting of our democratic institutions. I hope that all of you councillors will fully comprehend the nature of this considered and unvarying stand of the Government regarding its relationship with political parties.

Now I would like to elaborate somewhat upon the military aspect of the matter. From the time in 1938 when the 18th Army Corps, in defiance of the orders of the High Command, arbitrarily withdrew to the right bank of the Yellow River and forcibly carried out an illegal occupation of the Sui-Teh district, the Government has been loath to consider this move as instigated solely by the Communist Party, or to hold that party guilty of sabotaging resistance; nor did it think that any such motive was necessarily behind the 18th Army Corps' insubordination. Nevertheless, the effect extended even to the rear where it created general uneasiness on account of the potential dangers it threatened. The result was highly damaging to the whole prosecution of the war, putting a weapon into the hands of the enemy and imperilling the nation in the gravest manner. During the past two years or more the Government has been simultaneously unifying the fighting efforts of the whole army at the front and stabilizing the internal condition of the nation in the southwest and northwest of the rear. It is an exceedingly distressing fact that while all other countries in the world present a united front to external aggression, with us the Government finds added to the task of waging war on an invader that of settling internal troubles. Surely such a state of affairs is not to be paralleled in the history of any other revolutionary country. However, the precautions taken by the Government have been such as to avert any disaster either at the front or in the rear and the country may reckon this as great good fortune. Despite this danger, we find our capacity to withstand the enemy strong enough to ensure our final victory and also a sound and formidable foundation laid for stability in the rear. Had it been otherwise and had timely measures not been taken, by now the provinces of the south and northwest, if not long overrun by the enemy, would have been ruined by the escapades of rebels and anti-social elements; and the people in the rear would be living in such insecurity as those suffer in provinces behind the enemy lines, in Hopei, Chahar, Shantung and Kiangsu where the National Government and its armed forces cannot protect them from the double oppression of the Japanese and the puppets.

However, the fact remains that the forces of resistance are considerably weakened by the enforced retention in the rear of large numbers of troops who might be fighting at the front. This also imposes a grievously depressing weight upon the spirits of the whole army and people. The problem is one that is really not difficult to solve. All that is required is a complete change in the attitude and actions of the Communist Party, in no longer regarding the 18th Army Corps as its peculiar possession or as an instrument for the obstruction of other sections of the national forces to the detriment of resistance. Let the Communists carry out the declaration they themselves made in 1937 wherein they said: (1) Dr. Sun's Three Principles of the People serve the needs of present-day China and the Chinese Communist Party is prepared to strive for their complete fulfillment; (2) they would abandon all violent action and policy aimed at the overthrow of the Kuomintang, the movement for the propagation of communism in China, and the policy of violent confiscation of landowners' holdings; (3) they would abolish the then Chinese Soviet government in the Northwest and work towards a united democratic government for the whole country; (4) they would abolish the name and status of the Red Army and permit its incorporation into the national revolutionary army under the command of the National Military Council of the National Government.[1] If they would now but faithfully carry out their original intention to comply with these conditions and move all the troops connected with their party according to the plans laid down by the National Military Council into the areas appointed for them to defend, the whole country could be united to meet the invader, there would be an end of internal obstacles and anxieties, and it would be possible to deal the exhausted enemy a tremendous blow which I am convinced would bring about within a short time a most sensational victory. At least we could restore the lines held in the autumn of 1938; of this the military authorities are in no doubt. Then lost territory would be recovered and our fellow-countrymen delivered from their sufferings. This would be an immense contribution of the 18th Army Corps to the national cause and the whole country would admire the patriot-

[1] See Generalissimo Chiang's statement on "National Solidarity," issued on September 24, 1937, subsequent to the United Front pledge given by the Chinese Communist Party.

ism of the Communists. Our Government has no other demand to make of the Communist Party and the troops connected with it save this one fervent wish that they will carry out the obligations into which they themselves freely entered and support the Program of Resistance and Reconstruction to which the People's Political Council gave its unanimous endorsement. It merely hopes that the Communists will cast off all party prejudice and put the interests of the nation first by obeying orders, maintaining discipline and working in harmony with all their comrades-in-arms.

There are also two other groups of these demands which have an intimate relation with military affairs: what the Communists call the "prevention of provocation," the "withdrawal of the anti-Communist forces in Central China" and the "immediate cessation of all attacks on us." These three points call for some remark. This sort of senseless, mendacious, misleading and malicious propaganda vilifies our Government and deliberately injures the sacred mission of resistance, but, more than that, it offers insult to the pure spirit of the whole country's united battle against aggression. I need scarcely assert that our Government is solely concerned with leading the nation against the Japanese invaders and extirpating the traitors, and is utterly without any notion of again taking up arms to "suppress the Communists." It desires never again to hear of that ill-omened term which now has a place only in Chinese history. Let them obey orders, give up their attacks on their comrades-in-arms and cease all their provocative acts; the Government will then treat them with all possible consideration. The Government is, moreover, desirous of showing generosity and of letting bygones be bygones. In defense of our national interest it cannot, however, fail to punish and check insubordination, for it would otherwise fail in its duty to the nation. For loyal soldiers it has such a loving solicitude that the charge of provocation and attack is absurd. I can make myself responsible for the statement in your presence that at no future time could there conceivably be another campaign for the suppression of the Communists. I hope that you will address an appeal to Mao Tse-tung, Tung Pi-wu and the other Communist members of this Council to effect a change in the attitude of their party so that we can discuss here all together the questions they have raised and arrive at some reasonable solution of them. You represent the will of the nation and your bounden duty is to strive for the success of resistance and reconstruction and national unity. If the Communist Party will only accept your advice, and say and do nothing in future contrary to the Program of Resistance and Reconstruction and their own manifesto of 1937,

240

the Government will undoubtedly respect whatever resolutions you may adopt for the settlement of the incident and see that they are carried fully into effect without delay.

In conclusion, provided unity can be preserved and resistance carried on to the end, the Government will be ready to follow your directions in the settlement of all outstanding questions. I call upon the Communist members of the Council to realize the national danger at this time of mortal combat with the invader and, acting in the spirit of the saying "brothers quarrel at home but go out together to repel assault from without," to accept the judgment of this Council and make their contribution to national solidarity. This is the fervent prayer of the whole people, and it would moreover deal the enemy a mighty blow. Out of solicitude for the Communist Party and in the desire to see it play its full part in the history of this life-and-death struggle of our country, we beg it to continue in its mission of reconstruction and resistance against aggression.

Bonds Between China and America

AFTER thirty-three years in China Ambassador Johnson is about to leave the country to take up a fresh post. For the valued guest and his hosts alike this time of parting is fraught with many and varied thoughts and feelings. Mr. Johnson has been American diplomatic representative in China for more than ten years, since, in fact, the National Government was set up in Nanking. His relationship with the Chinese Government has been peculiarly intimate, his acquaintance with the Chinese people far-reaching and profound. I and my revolutionary colleagues deeply regret that so good a friend is leaving us. I propose this evening to make the traditional friendship between the Chinese and American nations and the responsibilities that today and in the future must be discharged in common by the two great peoples who dwell on the eastern and western shores of the Pacific Ocean the theme of these words of farewell.

China and the United States have common interests in the Pacific Ocean. More cogent still is the consideration of their responsibility for the maintenance of an order of peace and justice in the Pacific and the characteristic attachment to upright and peaceful conduct that they have both made the spirit of their nationalism. In America that spirit is expressed in the principle of government of the people, by the people, for the people. In China it consists of the Three Principles enunciated by Dr. Sun of nationalism, democracy and livelihood that demand China's independence, equality and freedom among the nations of the world. As Dr. Sun explained, independence means the people in possession, equality the people as sovereign, and freedom the people satisfied, or in other words government of the people, by the people, for the people. In short, in both countries political principles turn upon the will and the interests of the people. The Three Principles of the People are really one with the democratic principles of America. Because both China and the United States are devoted to this democratic spirit of independence, freedom and equality they have never for all their vast area, resources

An address given at the farewell dinner to Ambassador Nelson T. Johnson on May 10, 1941.

and population given thought to any attack on others, but have rather presented positive opposition to aggression. In the eastern and western hemispheres they have become two pillars supporting the peace and well-being of humanity and a unique foundation whereon may be built the universal brotherhood that was Dr. Sun's highest ideal. Such is the spirit of the two nations and such their responsibility. It is the great mission they are striving together to fulfill.

Peaceful order in the Pacific has been utterly shattered by the Japanese militarists. At a time when her armed preparedness was inadequate China became the object of their aggression, but she has sworn to persevere indefinitely in her endeavor to answer their challenge to peace and justice. The government and citizens of the United States have from the beginning made clear their deep sympathy with our cause. In the face of this unbridled aggression the historical and geographical relationship of the two countries, the international agreements to which they have both subscribed, and their common interests and responsibilities all make a blow struck at one also an injury to the other. Neither can conceivably be an indifferent spectator of the other's distress. That is a matter of plain and indubitable fact. There is no occasion to have recourse to any remote historical proof of this. As recently as the 30th of last month an official mouthpiece of the Japanese Foreign Office, the "Japan Times and Advertiser" came out with a "World Peace Plan." We need not concern ourselves with what this had to say of the European and African continents; let us merely note its references to the Pacific and the United States and we shall observe that Japan's aggression in China is but a preliminary to attack on America. The first point of the "Plan" calls for the demilitarization of British and American naval bases in the Pacific. The second is that the United States shall not seek hegemony on the American Continent. The third demands that American influence shall not extend further west than the Hawaiian Islands. The fourth suggests that all Pacific islands shall be incorporated in the Japanese sphere of co-prosperity. These four points are sufficient to show that Japan, with China still an unsettled issue, is already busying herself with American territory and rights in the Pacific and planning to achieve a complete nullification of American power. While this Japanese dreamtalk is beneath the contempt of any intelligent person, Japan having grown steadily weaker in her years of inconclusive war with China, it is the expression of a firmly established policy and traditional scheme of aggression. Could the Japanese militarists manage in some way to dispose of their China problem, they would certainly proceed to attack America. If we imagine the eventuality of a

Chinese defeat, we see in this Japanese paper's "Plan" the way in which Japan would then set about dealing with America.

We are, therefore, justified in holding that victory or defeat for Chinese resistance will be also an American victory or defeat, and a victory or defeat for every nation in the Pacific. A Chinese defeat would result in the expulsion of British and American armed forces from that ocean and of Soviet arms from Vladivosiok and Siberia. The "World Peace Plan" resembles the Konoye Statement on a "New Order for East Asia" issued on November 3, 1938. As that was addressed to China, the present "Plan" might be called a "New Order for the Pacific" addressed to America. The proposal to bring all Pacific islands within Japan's "sphere of co-prosperity" simply means that all American territory in the Pacific should be brought under Japanese control. The aggressive policy of Japan is revealed in its every feature and each practical measure she undertakes corresponds to some specific part of that policy. The Japanese official organ also mentions in this "Plan" the banishment of Soviet Russian influence from the Pacific; Siberia and Vladivostok are to come under Japanese control. Britain, fully occupied as she is with the European War, is of course the object of more measureless exactions. Australia, New Zealand, Malaya, Burma, India and all her Far Eastern territories and rights are to be stripped from her. Such being the character of the Japanese scheme of aggression, it is clearly imperative that all friendly nations should thoroughly comprehend and squarely face this menace.

Nearly four years of Chinese resistance, however, have so exhausted Japan that at present she is powerless to move further towards the attainment of the fantastic goal of aggrandizement I have just described. She is therefore resorting more and more to bluff and all manner of devious devices to procure disunity among the peoples of the Pacific. By threats and blandishments she is seeking to gain her ends by disintegrating the ranks of her desired victims to facilitate a process of gradual absorption. Every nation concerned should be on its guard against this insidious design.

If all nations friendly to us will, in the name of justice, live up to what is expected of them in supporting Chinese resistance by supplying us with war material and economic aid, China is prepared to undertake singlehanded the task of putting down this enemy of all who would dwell in peace on the shores of the Pacific. Expeditionary forces or naval action is not asked of them. This claim is no mere verbal boast; it is the resolve and the faith of the whole Chinese army and people. It rests moreover on the solid showing of four years' fighting. At the same time the support we need forms, whether we think of the interests common to China and America or of the status the two nations have to maintain in the Pacific, an inalienable responsibility for those who are in a position to give it.

Chinese observers of the world situation as it has developed during the last eighteen months of the European conflict see among the dozen or more shipwrecked and ruined nations of the West the imposing and solitary survival of Britain. They compare the spectacle to that of China's stand in the East. The two countries share a unique record of inflexible determination to defend themselves and their independence. They both have interests in common with America and their fortunes are bound up in such a manner that the distinction of East and West has virtually disappeared. The world war of today has become a simple struggle between equity and force, between liberty and evil. Our confidence in victory for resistance comes of the principles of national independence, liberty and sovereignty for which we are fighting and the ideal ground of human welfare, right-dealing and peace in which our faith is rooted. This confidence in our own cause leads us to believe that America also is bound to stand forth as a protector of the same ideals. The greatest respect has been engendered in the hearts of the Chinese army and people by the present policy of the American Government, by the firm and upright attitude and its courageous determination. The mind of the American people is becoming more and more clearly made up to check aggression: their resolve to defend the spirit of democracy against the forces of tyranny is now such that they will support the policy of their government to the point of war. One need not hesitate to assert that America has thus brought perceptibly nearer the day when the world will again enjoy peace. That she is a decisive force working for peace in the Pacific is still more obvious. Japanese aggression has now neither the strength nor the audacity to risk a clash with this American buttress of peace. I am prepared to express the conviction that any country in the world matching itself against American democracy would meet with certain destruction. The inconsiderable caliber of Japan would make nonsense of an attempt on her part to grapple with the United States.

The unequivocal assurance which I can today give Ambassador Johnson is this: the Chinese army and people regard the situation in the Pacific created by the preparations underway in various countries, by the present policy of the American Government, and by what we have ourselves achieved in four years of war, as affording full grounds for confidence that Japan can be overthrown without any direct naval action

245

on the part of any nation or nations committed to the support of our cause. We believe our ultimate victory can be secured on the mainland of Eastern Asia alone provided the American people second their government's policy without reserve and bring their full weight to bear in support of Chinese resistance. If, on the other hand, the nations of the Pacific are careless of their responsibilities, each waiting for others to move first, exhibiting afresh the *laissez-faire* and slothful conduct of the past, ignoring Japanese designs and ambitions and failing positively to assist Chinese resistance—then a great war involving the whole Pacific area will ensue with consequences that do not bear thinking about.

Mr. Johnson has had more than thirty years' experience of life in China and he is a loyal friend of China. Following the establishment of the National Government in Nanking one of the first issues it took up was that of the annulment of the unequal treaties whereby our Customs Administration was lodged in foreign hands. At that time America lent the force of her example to this end by first concluding with us a treaty providing for our autonomy in Customs administration. We remember Mr. Johnson's efforts during the time of his ambassadorship to bring about cooperation between China and America—efforts that laid the foundation for the present development of that cooperation. At some future time when China and America again play their part in a peaceful order of Pacific affairs Ambassador Johnson's contribution to the traditional friendship of China with America will be recalled with a due sense of the value of his services. He will undoubtedly convey to his people on his return home, previous to assuming his new post, the fervent expectations entertained of them by the whole Chinese army and people. He will thus add still more to the close and friendly relations existing between the two countries. That responsibility remains with him and we are convinced of his will and ability to fulfill it. At this moment of separation I have only to add an expression of my best wishes for the prosperity of American and Chinese national fortunes, for the health of President Roosevelt and of the departing Ambassador.

A Balanced Development in National Finances

TODAY we are present at the opening ceremony of the Third National Financial and Pacification Conferences. You have just heard the President describe the great significance and weighty responsibilities of these conferences and you will certainly be fully aware of the importance of your duties here. I have a few words to add to the President's remarks and some views to which I wish to call your attention.

The Financial and the Pacification Conferences have much in common and the work of each has considerable bearing on that of the other. Both are concerned with the harmonization of military and political affairs in the rear and the strengthening of the foundation of resistance and reconstruction. I desire to bring up today certain fundamental issues and it is my hope that those of you delegated to the Pacification Conference will also be attentive to what I have to say and active in lending your assistance.

Since the Central Government was established there have been two financial conferences, the first of which achieved the abolition of the *"likin,"* [1] while the second dealt with other local oppressive and multifarious taxes. These two undertakings removed immense obstacles from the path of national economy: the people's livelihood was enabled to develop freely; a great reform profoundly affecting national reconstruction was achieved. The good fruit of those two conferences, however, was of a negative character, consisting in the "removal of abuses." The nature of our duties at this Third Financial Conference differs; it is the work of positive reconstruction, the putting of national finance and economy on a thoroughly firm foundation. We have to devise comprehensive planning of national finance and its rational control. We have to remove from national economy and provincial reconstruction in

An address delivered at the Third National Financial Conference in Chungking, June 16, 1941.

[1] A tax on goods in transit first levied in the imperial days and abolished by the Government in 1931.

general the irregularities of the past which permitted of excessive wealth in one place and excessive poverty in another. The aim is to reduce all to uniformity and set in motion a balanced development. The Government has therefore set itself two immediate objectives: (1) the balancing of the national budget and (2) the equalization of the burden of taxation on the shoulders of the people. These are fundamental features of the Government's policy in resistance and reconstruction. All of you must accordingly keep clear in your minds the way in which this conference differs from others called in normal times. It is distinguished not only by its determination to apply the policy of nationalizing land taxes and to set up a national fiscal system, important as these two undertakings are, but also by the whole spirit and fundamental quality its deliberations must display and which will relate them to the future of the people's livelihood and national reconstruction.

Looking back over the time that has elapsed since the National Government was established, we see the great difficulties and perils through which Chinese finance has passed and yet now after almost four years of war it is not merely sound but growing more and more robust. This spectacle should reassure us of the vast potential economic strength of our people. It proves on the other hand the worth and accuracy of the policy the Government has been pursuing. You must not fail to realize that this precious and hard-won gain as well as the achievements of prolonged resistance we owe in large measure to the success of the monetary policy, which in turn may be defined as the success of Dr. Sun's "monetary revolution." When I came to Szechwan on a tour of inspection in 1935 I was appalled at the chaos of local currencies to be observed. It led me to a consideration of the distress and squalor for which this chaos was largely responsible, and thence to the thought that should war come economic catastrophe must result. Unity of currency was imperative; only by making one monetary writ run the land could the people be released from the exploitation to which they were subject and in wartime from the effects of chaotic currency and finance. At that time, therefore, as soon as I had arrived in the province I decided that it must accept the same currency as the rest of the country. The policy of unified national currency had been in operation since 1921, but it was generally viewed with misgivings and doubts of its practicability. What no financier had dared attempt before our financial authorities then set indefatigably about doing in accordance with the principles of Dr. Sun's monetary revolution. And at last they fully succeeded with the result that resistance has been able to attain all it has. When this policy was in its beginnings there was apprehension among financiers, monetary experts and commercial bankers that it would be sure to damage their interests. All sorts of rumors were heard, and great opposition manifested. Public confidence was shaken. And yet when the policy had been translated into fact it was discovered that so far from doing the bankers and dealers in exchange any harm, business was intensely stimulated and commerce expanded. Public and private enterprise alike was so benefited that the country seemed to have derived a new lease of economic life from the unification of the currency. We are close to victory now, but the difficulties that yet remain to be overcome require our attacking them with penetrating vigor. Let us recall the obstacles we have already surmounted and the unification of currency achieved in 1935 that for centuries had been impossible. Bad conventions of long standing were successfully broken down; one money flowed through the financial and commercial veins of the country. Confronted by such a scabrous and tangled problem we were yet able to solve it to complete satisfaction. How then can there be any further problem so arduous as to daunt us?

We must bear in mind that this progress has been a general advance of the standard of national intelligence and of financiers' and businessmen's breadth of vision, of their sense of justice and support for the Government's policy. From our experience in the matter of unified currency we can form the axiom that "everything making for the good of the people is necessarily to the good of the individual." The Government is bound, therefore, whatever may be the difficulties encountered, to pursue to its logical conclusion any policy conducive to the advantage and happiness of the country and the people. Any such policy is likewise bound to succeed.

If we are to set up a sound basis for financial reconstruction, all revenue from taxation of the land must accrue to the State. A sharp distinction must be drawn between the national fiscal system and the locally autonomous ones. Thereafter the State may be modernized. With regard to land taxation, I shall speak later. With regard to fiscal systems, if a clear line of demarcation can be drawn between them there will be an assured source of finance for the public enterprises of local autonomous units, and the way will be smoothed for the full application of the new system of *hsien* administration to the destruction of the old conformity in name but not in substance. At the same time when a national fiscal system is inaugurated not only will the Central Government's financial position be strengthened but provincial enterprises, especially those connected with economic defense, will be able to make real progress. There will be an elimination of the unstable and unsound conditions of the past that rendered remote and sparsely populated districts incapable of contributing anything to the forces of reconstruction. These two measures are therefore essential to the whole livelihood of the people. They will have effects beyond the scope of finance; you and all central and provincial officials must realize those effects will extend to the questions most closely touching the lives of workers, farmers, students and all other members of society.

Resistance and reconstruction are essentially one and the same thing. We are fighting the war for the sake of reconstruction and it may be equally well said that we are reconstructing for the sake of resistance. When the war first began we laid the groundwork of reconstruction, and while it has been proceeding we have done our best to continue the work. Three concrete lines of policy were resolved upon: (1) The application of the new system of *hsien* administration and the advancement of the local autonomy. If the new system of *hsien* administration can be applied as its plans and objectives dictate and local autonomy made genuinely effective the State will be provided with a firm political foundation, and the whole work of national reconstruction will be brought to success. (2) Balancing of the National Budget and the equitable distribution of tax burden. To achieve the former end the Government has simply to keep strictly within the limits of its budgets and final fiscal statements and to do its utmost in developing sources of revenue and restricting public expenditure. The latter duty is of immense importance: in this time of war we cannot tolerate refusal of the wealthy to make their contribution to the cause while the indigent masses are obliged to support the finances of the State. This thoroughly unfair state of things must be radically reformed and to bring about the desired equalization of tax burdens taxation must be regularized according to a comprehensive plan put into universal execution by the Government. (3) The application of Dr. Sun's land and food policies. In the teachings bequeathed us by Dr. Sun there are defined three essential courses of action in regard to financial and economic policy during the revolutionary period: (i) For the fulfillment of the Principle of People's Livelihood there must be a "monetary revolution," or unification of the currency system. (ii) In both peace and war time there must be "food control" with a special bureau in charge of this. A country without food control will be without assured supplies of food for people and army, and will never attain the status of a modern nation and will lose its independent existence. (iii) Equitable disposition of land ownership, and the implementation of land policy. The land policy must be thoroughly applied in order that the Three Principles of the People may be fully realized. These three revolutionary tasks the Tsungli expounded in a way that leaves me no necessity of going into details here. Since 1935 when the present national currency came into use the first of these tasks —the monetary revolution—has been in the main completed with success. The other two tasks, the control of food and the equitable distribution of land ownership, are focal ones for both peace and wartime finance and economy and demand our strongest efforts. If we cannot now carry them into effect, there will never be a second chance. Moreover all should know that if the land policy is not put into effect and food not controlled, our people's livelihood will decline from bad to worse and eventually to ruin. No matter what hardships we may have to suffer, we must realize these are tasks calling for the utmost striving on the part of the nation, society and the individual, in the same spirit as that displayed in the process of unifying the national currency, until we can truly say: "My neighbor's interests are mine and mine his; the home and the nation exist for each other's good." Then the leaders of the nation will worthily bear the name of leaders of a nation equal in stature to the urgency of the hour. Otherwise our national economy and political system will be perpetually condemned to remain that of a semi-colony and our descendants will never raise their heads again. Perhaps land and food are the most important of the matters before the Conference. Success with regard to them will be a proof of China's capacity to become a truly independent and free nation. I trust you will exert yourselves to the utmost over them.

Next, in regard to land taxation I have some points to make. From ancient times China's State revenue has been derived from land taxation. So it was with the Republican government until the establishment of the present Central Government when it was decided to allot revenue from the land to the provincial authorities—a decision that in retrospect gives rise to much regret. The essentials of a State, after sovereignty, are land and people. And these two elements are bound up with each other, just as the people cannot leave the land, for it depends on them for tillage. If land taxes are allotted to the local governments, this virtually separates the people and the land from the State; it leaves them with only a local consciousness, without a national one. In order to make citizens understand that the reason for their payment of land taxes lies in the welfare of the nation as a whole and that the rights of citizenship belong to them by virtue of the contribution they make to the maintenance of the State, the revenue from land taxation must go to the Central Government. This is essential for the development of the people's sense of nationhood and constitutes a fundamental principle of policy. Two other great sources of State revenue in the past were the customs and the salt tax, which have, with the exception of a small portion still obtainable from the interior, passed out of the control of the central authorities since the enemy attacked the coast where the lack of naval power made inevitable this loss. But China is an agricultural country. The national finances should in both peace and war time rest upon agricultural sources of revenue. During this war national finance has made, as it were, two discoveries—of the land and of food—and they have become its strong supports. The depth and wisdom of Dr. Sun's teaching has been fully revealed and vindicated. I have already said that this Conference must be one devoted to positive reconstruction. You must devise concrete methods of improving the food situation and the administration of the land. A point I desire to impress upon you with especial emphasis is that this move of appropriating the land tax to the Central Government is taken with a view to the good of the whole fabric of national economy and for the security of the people's livelihood. The aim is not merely to increase the Government's income. For during these four years of war, had China been financially circumstanced as most countries at war are, she would have already been bankrupt. In fact, Chinese finance through the efforts of our financial authorities and your exertions, and with the assistance of friendly nations has been maintained and it never stood on a firmer basis than it does today. That being so, the future may be faced with confidence. In your work here you must treat these two undertakings of change in the system of land taxation and the strengthening of the fiscal system as essential features of future policy involving the success of national reconstruction in its entirety rather than as mere financial expedients.

With regard to the food problem I have some suggestions to make. Local feeling on the issues is diverse, but there is universal agreement upon the gravity and urgency of the question. Everyone's attention is fixed upon the question how food supplies are to be collected, and what standard is to be followed in collecting them, but there is a lack of clear conception as to the central essence of the matter. I hold that it is a question of how we are to put into practice the Tsungli's teachings on the methods of food control in a rational and profitable way. All comrades must understand that the success or failure of resistance and reconstruction is deeply concerned in this as well as the well-being and very existence of the people. All social problems depend for their solution upon the solution of this food problem. Those who possess land and food will not be able indefinitely to go on eating with indifference to those others who have nothing to eat. It is for those who possess to give whether at the front or in the rear, but especially rich landowners in the rear who depend upon the protection of the armies of resistance and of the Government's administration of the law for the freedom in which they live and freely express their views. What freedom of expression have people in the Northeastern Provinces, in Hopei, Shantung, Suiyuan, and Shansi? There they restrict the supply of food absolutely necessary to your sustenance and they confiscate your own food. Perhaps our wealthy proprietors in the rear have not thought of these sufferings. Should we be defeated the people both in the war areas and the rear will lose all security of existence, be robbed of all their possessions and fall into the same state of slavery as the inhabitants of the Northeastern Provinces. We must realize that the present security of our lives and property comes entirely from the Government and revolutionary armies and if you will not obey government orders and support the Government's policy, you are pulling down the very fences that stand between you and the arbitrary ruthlessness of the enemy and the puppets. You and your descendants will be enslaved for ever.

The Government is preoccupied with its strenuous efforts to win the war, but it desires in the interests of the whole people and of those of our fellow-countrymen who are suffering affliction and poverty to avail itself of public opinion and it wishes wealthy landowners to understand that in levying a quota of ten or twenty per cent on their stocks of food it is doing this not to damage their interests but to afford them protection. If they balk at this contribution and display indifference to the hunger of the people and army, and the defeat of resistance they will find their food confiscated in entirety by the enemy. They must fully comprehend this point and then they will understand the Government's present policy and how it is directed to the protection of the interests of the ordinary man and landowner alike.

If however those holding stocks of provisions think only of their own selfish gain and ignore the demands of patriotism, disregarding the Government's food regulations, the Government will be obliged to take strong action against them whether they hoard, speculate or indulge in any other illegal proceedings. It will act fearlessly of any evil forces arrayed in its path. I have long resolved upon a final solution of this food problem; I shall not be hindered by any further uncertainties. The Northwest and Southwest are agricultural areas fully capable of producing all the food required; there is no fear of our being unable to obtain the quota exacted. The Government hopes and expects, however, that local landowners will spontaneously do their best to fulfill the provisions of the mandates issued, that they will all act as duty and the high interests of the nation dictate. The Government has resolved upon this food policy with unmixed concern for the public good. It will bring it into operation without fail when the autumn harvest comes round; there can be no delay until next year. The maxims set for the citizen's patriotic duty in the past were "those with money, give money" and "those with strength, give strength." To these we must now add "those with food, give food." If landowners selfishly fail to give the food demanded of them they will be acting criminally. They will put themselves in the same class with oppressive landlords and corrupt officials. The Government will show no clemency towards them.

With regard to the control and management of food, the course adopted may be the issuance of "food treasury notes," a subject upon which there is also a great division of opinion. Some landholders, lacking patriotic vision, will insist upon equating these notes to national currency. At this time of national crisis it is utterly distressing that there should be people capable of minutely calculating their own gain rather than thinking of the country's good and the giving of an example to society. Whether we issue such notes or collect taxes in kind the object is to obtain a specific amount of food for the purpose of adjusting the supply of food for people and army. In the future the Government will redeem the notes, which will constitute what may be called a "compulsory loan." They will not, however, legitimately be reckoned functionally equivalent to national currency.

At this time, if we are to call ourselves worthy citizens of an independent country we must respond with implicit obedience to the Government's commands. In the execution of both its food and land policies the Government is out to put army and victory first and take measures of the fairest and soundest kind; the duty of all citizens is magnanimously to obey the letter and the spirit of these measures. To methods of food control the Government has given its especially close and earnest attention. Its demands of the landowners and food-dealers in the rear are lenient, and when we compare the food control measures of other countries at war with ours, the latter appear kindly and tolerant in the extreme. It is to be hoped that fellow-countrymen generally will take account of the Government's solicitude and carry out all government orders with punctilious loyalty, with the ultimate object of bringing to fulfillment the Three Principles of the People.

The Central Government is now engaged on the one hand in leading the revolutionary forces of the nation in resistance at the front to drive out the invaders, and on the other hand in directing the efforts of the masses of the people in the rear in the work of reconstruction for the establishment of a firm foundation for a new *San Min Chu I* nation. It is therefore not to be deterred by any sacrifices or obstacles. My hope is that the whole country will act with a full sense of this truth and everyone will urge obedience in a spirit of revolutionary and patriotic zeal to the Government's provisions, eliminating all evasion and connivance at evasion. Henceforth if there can be a thorough solution of agrarian and food problems, other wartime military, political, financial, economic and social questions will be readily solved. The ancients said: "Enough food and enough soldiers" were the two essentials upon which equal emphasis should be placed. In our present War of Resistance, to have "enough soldiers" will not suffice if we have not also "enough food." So it is that we have created this maxim, "Those with food must give food." Supplies of food for the army alone will not do if those of the people are inadequate. The work of farmers, industrial workers, merchants and students should be thought of as identical to that of soldiers. The sustenance of the whole people must necessarily engage the attention of the Government as closely as that of the army. All citizens with common knowledge of modern conditions will be aware of this. In regard to the solution of the present food problems everyone is most concerned with the security of the people's food supply, because arrangements to feed the army had long already been made. In fact there is really no reason to separate military and public supplies. To allow uncontrolled business dealings in food in these days is quite incompatible with modern ideas.

The above observations regarding the appropriation of land taxation by the Central Government, the establishment of a national fiscal system, and the institution of measures of food control are all fundamental issues in resistance and reconstruction and policies essential to the fulfillment of the Three Principles of the People. I look to all of you here today to follow out the points I have made in your close study of the situation and take effective action. Moreover all responsible men in Party, Government, army and other positions must diligently and courageously devote themselves to the completion of the great task of resistance and reconstruction that we may worthily fulfill our revolutionary mission.

The Northeast and Territorial Integrity

TODAY we commemorate the day of national humiliation that occurred on September 18 just ten years ago. For a decade our Northeastern fellow-countrymen have endured under the oppression of the Japanese a hellish life of spoliation and outrage. In indignation at the intolerable wrongs done them, the whole people under the leadership of their government went through a period of energetic preparation to the point of entering upon their crusade of resistance. Losses without parallel in history have since been incurred and today the war continues, the will of the nation unanimously prepared to make all the sacrifices required. This is because we are resolved to assert and maintain the absolute inviolacy of China's territorial severeignty to recover the lost territory of the Northeastern Provinces and to release their inhabitants from the atrocious miseries of invasion. There will be no cessation of resistance until the Japanese armies are wholly expelled from the land and the thought of conquest utterly eradicated from the minds of the Japanese, until the freedom of the Northeasterners is regained and their provinces restored. It is a matter of the loss to China of an area geographically essential to her national defenses, where there are resources equally indispensable to us. We can go so far as to say that if liberty and independence cannot be won for the thirty million Northeasterners the whole country will eventually also be enslaved beyond all hope of deliverance. Their lives are one with the lives of all other citizens and the soil whereon they live is one with the rest of the country; there can be no separating any portion of Chinese territory from the whole. Surviving, we shall survive together; or, if we perish, we shall perish as one man. This we must hold an unassailable axiom of our policy.

The boundless sacrifices of the past decade have been made for the sake of achieving the complete liberation of the Chinese nation and people and of securing for them a status of true independence and equality among the nations of the world.

A message to the nation on Sept. 18, 1941, the tenth anniversary of occupation of the Northeastern Provinces (Manchuria) by Japan.

In the Northeast there dwell thirty millions of a fine and sturdy population; there are 240,000,000 *mow*[1] of farmlands; there are 200,000,000 *mow* of fertile land yet uncultivated; there are 700,000,000 *mow* of standing timber; there are 8,000,000,000 tons of unmined metal and other minerals. Some of the resources most important to our people's livelihood are to be found there; all the conditions essential to the reconstruction of a modern nation prevail there. The ports, strategic positions, mines, railways and other lines of communication detailed by Dr. Sun in his plan for industrial development were largely centered about the Northeast. Its abundant material and human resources touch the life of the nation closely; without them it can scarcely be preserved. They are certainly not to be given up to the enemy for use against China and the world. Taking a world view of things, we see that the Northeast, apart from its bearing upon Chinese national survival, of the first consequence to the safety of East Asia and the entire world. As long as the Northeast remains under the control of the Japanese the peace-loving nations of the world can know no immunity from their acts of aggression. The proposal to "disarm the aggressor nations" will all the more obviously be impracticable while Japan is still in possession of such a source of strength.

The prolonged hardships and heroic deeds of the Northeasterners are of a significance and value to the whole nation as it strives to bring them relief. In fact the sum of all that the rest of the nation has endured and lost may a thousand times exceed that of their sacrifices. They should be thereby inspired to greater efforts in the struggle against the enemy in his rear, in the endeavor to render his occupation of the territory as little profitable as possible to him. That is the minimum measure of responsibility which they can hold as theirs. If they can fulfill it they will be effectively seconding the splendid work of resistance in all other parts of the country, and we shall all be marching together on the sure road to our goal.

It must be realized how closely relevant the fate of the four Northeastern Provinces is to the advance of the revolution and the development of world events. In 1914 I had an opportunity for careful study of Northeastern conditions, and in a memorandum I then presented to Dr. Sun I wrote: "The Northeast is rather the destination of the Revolution than a starting-point for it. The area involves problems affecting the whole international situation. Its problems are not to be solved during the initial stages of the Revolution but to be approached

[1] One *mow* is equivalent to one sixth of an acre.

as the Revolution nears completion." I again emphasized the international character of the Northeastern question at the time the Mukden Incident occurred, and since resistance began I have frequently reminded you that "the life of the entire nation being committed to this bid for survival, there can be no compromise short of the goal." I further made clear that "the duration of the war and the nature of its conclusion will be determined in conjunction with the general restoration of world peace and security." When I said that it was fully evident that Japanese ambition and European quarrels had rendered inevitable a second world war, I also said: "China's resistance will be resolutely fought on, becoming a part of the world conflict, and concluding when Far Eastern and European problems find a common and integral solution." These words of mine command the assent of the entire nation.

The decade that has elapsed seems to me but as the passage of a day, for from that time I have considered it my peculiar responsibility to see the nation's honor vindicated and vengeance for the outrage exacted. It became my conviction that a long war must be waged if a genuine settlement of the issue was to be bad. On the one hand I perceived the extremities of enemy ambition and brutality; on the other I reviewed the geographical, international and other features of our national position. Then I defined the national policy of resistance to Japan as follows: Firstly, China's territorial sovereignty and administrative integrity must be preserved intact; secondly, respect for international justice and equity must be enforced and the forces of aggression overthrown in order to establish permanent peace in the Orient and the world. For ten years our attachment to these principles has brought with it confidence in their attainability.

The origins of the Japanese ambition to conquer China are to be traced far further back than September 18, 1931. Even in Ming times the predatory proclivities of the Japanese had become fully apparent. In those days Toyetomi Hideyoshi gave expression to the idea of "crossing the mountains and the seas, entering the land of Ming and making ours its four hundred counties." Later there was wild talk from one Shusin Soejima of "seizing lands from Ching (the Manchu Empire)" and of "making one province of the Ching domains a base on the Continent." So we see that the covetous desire for Chinese soil took root some three hundred or more years ago. At the time of the invasion of Korea and during the subsequent war with China the Japanese made the possession of our Northeast their objective. When in 1904 they entered upon the war with Russia they were intent on the same prize. The humiliation to which they have subjected China goes back three centuries to the days when their pirates marauded on our coasts; tales of their deeds are still current among the people of those districts.

September 18, 1931, however, is a date that marks the point at which Japanese aggression took on full definition of its enormous scope, being seen, as the Tanaka Memorial put it, to seek "the conquest of China, Asia, India and the South Seas" and "the domination of East Asia as a means to conquest of the world." The first step was the seizure of the Northeast to serve as a field headquarters in the campaign of global aggression. The history of conflict between China and Japan is written about the theme of the Northeast. Those powers resolved to prevent Japan's encroachment upon Asia and other parts of the world can ill afford to neglect the importance of the Northeast. That the leaders and publics of all countries should be properly aware of the relevant facts is as necessary as knowledge of them among the Chinese people. The loss of the provinces to China would inhibit her national reconstruction, and in Japanese hands they would be utilized not only in the destruction of China but also in the prosecution of aggressive expansion elsewhere in the world. Our survival and world security alike demand the expulsion of the invader from the Northeast and its integral restoration to the Chinese state.

These ten years have been years of trial and sacrifice for our armies and people. Today we find our cause has won due appreciation of its merits among the peoples of the world. Great indeed is the contrast between China's circumstances in 1931 and the position in which she stands today. Since then the nations friendly to us have added practical action to verbal expressions of sympathy. America in particular, under the leadership of President Roosevelt and Mr. Cordell Hull, has proceeded from the "non-recognition principle" to one of drastic sanctions against Japan and material aid on a large scale for China. Other countries, such as Britain and Soviet Russia, are acting with a proper sense of their common interests in a similar manner and in collaboration one with another. All this has deeply gratified and elated us.

Though it has been our resistance that has drawn the acclaim of the just-minded and consigned the Japanese to irremediable isolation in the Pacific, this state of affairs is to be referred at bottom to the action of the Japanese themselves in making enemies of China and the powers when they set out on the career of aggression that began with the Mukden Incident. At that time, in a letter to the then War Minister Minami, Honjo[2] wrote: "China's revival and the progress of America

[2] General Shigeru Honjo, commander of the Japanese Kwantung Army which invaded Manchuria.

and Russia are equally inimical to the national policy of Japan. Preparatory to war with the United States, China and Russia must be crushed and a separate country made of Manchuria and Mongolia under Japanese occupation. The next step must be invasion of Siberia in order to convert both the Seas of Okhotsk and of Japan into Japanese territorial waters. Going on, we must drive the Americans east of Hawaii and the English west of Singapore. In this way the Dutch East Indies, Australia and New Zealand shall all come under our hegemony." So we observe that Japan was in those days already bent upon bringing Britain, America, Russia and the Netherlands within the scope of her aggression. On September 18, 1931, the Japanese initiated the unfolding of a tremendous scheme comprising their Continental and Oceanic policies, the development of which whether to north or south has been prohibited by our resistance. They are pinned down and deprived of all freedom of movement as a result of the spiritual and military endeavors we have made in this decade of struggle. Today there is no "divine breath" to blow them the good fortune they experienced at the conclusion of the previous European War; they are irresolute and perplexed; they dare not repeat their former reckless feats of outrage to the interests of the Pacific powers. We ought therefore to keep in mind how great is the achievement that has rewarded the exertions of resistance, how immense the contribution made to the good of the nation and the world. On the one hand we are full of confidence in the nations friendly to us and supremely optimistic regarding the future of the fight against the aggressors. On the other hand we believe a place of high honor and renown in the pages of human history is reserved for the part we are playing in that enterprise.

Fellow-countrymen, resistance has now reached a stage anticipated three years ago, and we have in our grasp the destiny of the Northeast. I wish you fully to apprehend the meaning of the phrase I used: "The Northeast is the destination of the revolution." The success of the revolution and all that will attend upon it can be attained only through united and persevering devotion of the national energies to that end; indolence or complacency cannot be permitted to impair that constant devotion. Remember: "Heaven helps those who help themselves" and "others always help him who helps himself." Until all lost territory is recovered victory will not have been gained. The favorable aspect of international affairs should only move us to enhanced self-mastery and self-reliance. So far from inducing any mood of relaxation and sanguine expectations of the best, we must continue in the spirit of independent renascence evoked by this war, being prepared at all times for the worst possible eventualities. From height to height, slipping only to regain a new foothold, we must press forward to realization of our unvarying policy and the fulfillment of our responsibilities.

On so solemn a day as this I would have every citizen search his heart and reflect upon the record of action and endurance this decade and especially the years since 1937 have laid up. It is a record of blood and tears shed without distinction of place or person. The waves of a flood of national wrath have beaten on the aggressor's ranks and are washing away the miasma of invasion and the fetor of treachery, dispersing the vapors that would threaten to obscure the hope of peace for Asia and the world. The story is one of the noblest and most moving in the annals of mankind and it has been written, we can plainly inform both friends and enemies, that the independent existence of the Chinese people as a nation may be preserved together with our territorial sovereignty and administrative integrity. Death shall not daunt us nor difficulties obstruct our utter determination to free the Northeast and its inhabitants from the oppression under which the land has groaned since 1931. With a status of true freedom and equality China shall take her place in a system of lasting peace in the Orient and the world reestablished on foundations of justice and equity. Failing that end, there can be no cessation of resistance. While a single man of the invader's forces remains upon our soil and the slightest infraction of our territorial sovereignty persists, resistance cannot halt. I am sure that the Pacific powers friendly to us will continue a steady tightening and strengthening of the cordon of restraining pressure they have drawn about Japan; that in no case will they slacken it. For our part we shall go unwaveringly upon our way. In the course of the ten years past and under the blows of our prolonged resistance the criminal initiator of aggression in the Far East has been weakened to the point of collapse and awaits the consummation of his ruin. That is the reflection that should hearten and spur us on as we commemorate this day of national mourning. Fellow-countrymen, let us endeavor for every day each of us has to live to show our sense of the sacrifices made by those who have died for the cause, and worthily to display our feeling for the loyal citizens laboring under the tyrannies of the enemy in all we do to discharge our responsibility towards mankind and its ideal of justice among nations.

The Engineer's Role in National Crisis

I T HAS been a great pleasure to hear that you are holding the Tenth
Annual Meeting and simultaneously commemorating the thirtieth
anniversary of the founding of your Association. Valuable results are
sure to come of this gathering of engineering experts from all parts of
the country for the purpose of discussing the present phase of national
reconstruction.

Although modern Chinese engineering began in days prior to the
Republican era, it was really with the founding of the Republic and
the inauguration of your Association that serious progress commenced.
During the thirty years that have since elapsed China, despite the handicaps that have prevented her development on a scale comparable with
other modern nations, has at least laid the groundwork of her material
reconstruction. Communications, mines, shipbuilding and water conservancy, and the industries related to national defense, have engaged
the active attention of our engineers, with results they deserve to be
well congratulated upon.

Our deficiencies of men and resources, our poverty of experience in
scientific research, retarded industrial development and rendered the
country economically and militarily unprepared to withstand invasion.
Four years of war have vividly impressed on us the importance of
defense industries and caused us to make great efforts to advance industrial reconstruction work. Success will require unceasing con-
tinuance of these efforts. Reconstruction will not be achieved in a
day. China has lagged far behind the rest of the world in modern scientific progress. In the future there will be the increasing need of discover-
ing and training engineering talents, encouraging collaboration between
the business and technical sides of industrial enterprise, stimulating
the spirit of original research, and bringing into closer contact workers
in different fields of science. We must also seek academic and technical
cooperation in our relations with other countries. Progress in research
work will lead to greater efficiency in industrial enterprises. National
economy will benefit proportionately.

A telegram dispatched to the Tenth Annual Meeting of the Association of
Chinese Engineers held at Kweiyang, Kweichow, on October 20, 1941.

A nation in the world today depends for its existence as much upon its preparedness to defend itself as upon a high quality of national morale. The development of engineering theory and practice is an indispensable requirement of national defense, for without national defense no nation can exist. I have therefore said that we must put two great aims before us now: victory in resistance and, in reconstruction, absolute security in national defense. The equipment of all the armed services demands the skill of engineers in its production; communications and transportation unceasingly require it. A nation can in no respect be strong unless its engineers can constantly be pressing forward to fresh and greater achievements. National defense requires, as Dr. Sun taught, full and general realization of the importance of science and the acquisition of mechanical ability and aptitudes among our people.

The Government has issued its "General Scheme of National Reconstruction," and for the implementation of most of its provisions for the economic reconstruction of the country the whole-hearted cooperation of engineers will be indispensable. Dr. Sun's Plan for Industrial Development remains the most comprehensive and final statement of our national policy in this respect. Last year you organized a committee for the study of this Plan and the drawing up of minute, practicable projects. I am informed that some of the main points have already been sketched, and will be presented for discussion at this annual meeting. I am confident that this product of expert opinion will be a sound contribution to the groundwork of national defense and reconstruction. Nothing could be more valuable today.

Your Association was founded at the time of the birth of the Republic; the labors attendant on its growth have been contemporaneous with those whereby the Republic has been fashioned. It is noteworthy that a far greater number of men entering universities this year are taking courses in engineering; this is a reflection of a national change of attitude. It means that there will be no lack of recruits for the profession in future years, and to guide them in their service to the country is the mission of your Association. I feel confident that you will not fail to appreciate the significance of the hour and discharge your responsibilities to the nation and to the engineering sciences.

America's Chance to Strike at Japan

MORE than six months have passed since the first session of this Council, and during this time some of you have been on a tour of inspection in the war areas, some of you have been taking part in the work of the Kangting-Sichang Investigation Mission, some of you have been canvassing subscriptions to the national bonds, and others of you have been engaged in all sorts of economic, educational, cultural and relief activities in various places. Now you have gathered here from far and wide with the intention of devoting all your energies to the public good. This is a matter for profound gratification.

During this period the Government has been concentrating its efforts upon the development of local autonomy, financial adjustments, the general strengthening of national economy and the opening up of new lines of resistance. Detailed reports will be made for you to comment upon. In the present address I wish first of all to describe the supremely important and decisive phase upon which the War of Resistance and the international situation have now entered.

First. The most striking feature of events during the past six months has been the division of the whole world into two great camps, with the Nazi-dominated Axis countries aligned on the one side against the democratic nations on the other. The conflicts in the Orient and in Europe are now seen to involve one and the same issue. Solidarity of the forces resisting aggression had been materialized. The passage of the American Lend-Lease Bill, the heroic achievements of the Soviet armies, the progress made in coordinating defense in the Pacific, and President Roosevelt's repeated declaration of his country's determination to assist China, Britain and Russia,—all this is evidence of the genuine cooperation achieved by the democratic nations.

The past three months have seen the Japanese initiate negotiations with America only to proceed simultaneously to devote themselves to all manner of preparations for future acts of aggression. They have established a so-called "Headquarters of National Defense" at home,

Opening address before the Second Session of the Second People's Political Council on November 17, 1941.

while abroad in Indo-China and in Manchuria they have steadily increased the strength of their armies. The present Tojo Cabinet has announced its intention of "disposing of the China Incident and breaking down the encirclement of Japan by hostile powers" and of bringing to bear to that end "granitic resolution and lightning activity." Sufficient proof of the Japanese resolve to embark on a fresh campaign in concert with the Axis is to be found in the recent revision of the conscription law whereby men between the ages of 40 and 50 and those of third-rate physique are being called to the colors, and the increase of military expenditure to 3,800,000,000 yen for the next four months.

Second. Chinese resistance has greatly exhausted the enemy's strength. His losses during the period between the Shangkao campaign in April and the Second Changsha Battle in September were immense. His recent offensives against North Hupeh and Chengchow were on a very limited scale and brought him disastrous defeats. He has likewise been compelled to withdraw from many garrisoned points of the first importance. The war in China after more than four years has delayed Japan's scheme for attacks on other countries of the world. Germany has now been fighting with Soviet Russia for nearly five months and the European War is more than two years old. Had it not been for Chinese resistance Japan would certainly have seized the priceless opportunity to launch some predatory enterprise.

The Tojo Cabinet is now summoning up its courage to pierce the lines of encirclement and making a show of determination to strike at the Yunnan-Burma Road as the virtual beginning of southward expansion. A Japanese invasion of Yunnan would lead to attacks on Thailand, Singapore and other parts of the Southern Pacific region. The primary object would be to sever contact between the armies of resistance in China and the forces of the democratic powers without, as a necessary preliminary to further moves southward. China will naturally defend every inch of her territory and spare no effort to deal the enemy a blow hard enough to remove with his defeat the greatest obstacle to peace in the Far East. You will all be aware that the preparations for united democratic defense in the Far East are now complete. That happy circumstance is to be considered the fruit of China's four years of resistance. It is the achievement given the world by China's dogged efforts, by her resilient and selfless spirit, and in continuing to display that spirit we shall lend our full strength to the forces fighting aggression.

Third. As to the responsibility of Britain and America towards the Far East, I am sure they have no intention of dealing lightly with any one of the aggressors. The time is ripe for them to deal with Japan and they will not be diverted from their purpose by any such negotiations as those undertaken by Kurusu. My reasons for affirming this are as follows: (1) The Japanese massing of troops in Indo-China with the object of cutting China's lines of communication contravenes two of the principles declared by President Roosevelt and Mr. Churchill regarding the use and threat of armed force and the freedom of the seas and of trade.

(2) Japan has for ten years been violating her international undertakings and especially those of the Nine-Power Treaty, of which America is the leading signatory. She is not to be thought capable of deserting the principles that have determined the whole development of her national policy. Moreover by declaring herself the arsenal of the democracies America has signified her readiness to assert the cause of justice against the law-breaking ambitions of the aggressors. With Anglo-American military preparations in the Far East complete, she will all the more readily take action to that end.

(3) Despite all the honeyed words of the Japanese, America will not forget Konoye's assertion of last October, when he said: "If America cannot accommodate herself to the contentions of Japan and the Axis powers, there will definitely be war." Nor can America forget the words of Matsuoka: "If America persists in the attempt to maintain the status quo in the Pacific, there will be nothing for it but war." Again, Mabuchi, a spokesman for the Army, declared a month or so ago that Japan must break through the encirclement of the ABCD [1] bloc of powers and undertake a protracted war with Britain and America as the chief powers that compose the bloc.

(4) The long list of incidents that have occurred since the war in China began, such as the wounding of the British Ambassador, the sinking of the *Panay* and the insulting treatment of British and American men and women at Peiping, Tientsin, Tsingtao and Shanghai, have left no room for doubt of the intention of the Japanese to assail Britain and America in the course of their campaign of aggression in China.

I am therefore certain that compromise with Japan on the part of Britain and America is impossible both on grounds of interest and principle, while I am equally confident that they will not let slip the present excellent opportunity of discharging their moral responsibility for the defense of peace in the Far East.

Fourth. Whereas the Japanese dream in vain of the settlement of

[1] American, British, Chinese and Dutch.

"the China incident," I think it may rightly be said that now is the time when the powers fighting aggression can best, and most urgently ought to, liquidate "the Japan incident." Those powers command the strength of about nine-tenths of the world's population. In Russia the situation on the central front has been stabilized and the Nazi forces are at a standstill, confronted by unfavorable weather conditions. Britain has gained the mastery of the Mediterranean following successes won against the German and Italian naval forces. This winter is clearly a period that ought to be devoted to the smashing of Japan as a potential danger to the rear of the democratic forces in the world conflict. President Roosevelt predicts that 1943 will see the end of that conflict. I believe he has good reason for saying this.

It is unthinkable that the democracies should permit the Axis to threaten their rear and next spring see the Japanese launch an attack on Russia coordinated with a German offensive. Nor can they stand idle while Germany triumphs in the Near East and Japan strikes towards the Indian Ocean. A traditional maxim of the Chinese art of war is "first to crush the weakest member of an alliance of enemies." Japan is the weakest link of the chain of aggressor nations but if time is allowed her to recuperate strength and manoeuvre as she pleases the consequence may very well be eventual defeat for the democracies. Now is the vital moment and opportunity that must by no means be neglected. Britain and America are no doubt fully aware of the facts.

Japan is now resorting to blandishments and intimidation. Abroad, the Japanese militarists trample upon mankind's conceptions of justice and equity; at home they flout the rights of their own people. By such conduct they are simply courting destruction. The Japanese are now conscious of the fact that they are hemmed in on all sides and face imminent ruin. To continue in their reckless courses will inevitably bring them to disaster; their national existence can only be preserved by their complete abandonment of thoughts of aggrandizement in submission to the demands of justice and equity.

In doing so there would be two points of the first importance in the conditions to be fulfilled: (1) The abandonment of the policy of aggression, with the withdrawal of all forces from Chinese soil, including the Northeastern Provinces, and a similar withdrawal from Indo-China. Garrisons in the Northeast are equivalent to forces posted as a menace to Siberia and garrisons in Indo-China equivalent to forces posted as a menace to the Philippines and Malaya. In neither case are they to be tolerated. The never-changing aim of our resistance has been the total preservation of China's territorial sovereignty and the Japanese must realize that we shall never accede to its infringement by a single Japanese soldier remaining on our soil.

(2) Japan's detachment from the Axis alliance. The utter incompatibility of the aims pursued by the Axis powers and those opposing them necessitates for Japan's salvation her withdrawal from the Axis camp and the rejection of its aggressive principles and activities. Failing the willingness of the Japanese militarists to take this course there is nothing for it but their overthrow by the Japanese people. There is yet time for Japan to repent. She has now to choose between sincere allegiance or avowed opposition to the powers fighting aggression. There is no third course. The mind of those powers is irrevocably made up.

Finally, let all of you here at this session realize that the issue of our War of Resistance is one with that of the struggle between the forces of light and darkness throughout the world, a struggle now approaching its climax. In the Far East the forces of justice and brute force are about to clash in decisive combat. It is the moment for us to exert our greatest efforts. The enemy is intent upon the destruction of China and we upon her preservation. He would plunge the Pacific into the darkness of Hell, while we strive to make it a lighthouse for mankind. That being the nature of the task we have undertaken, we shall surely stint no effort or sacrifice to accomplish it.

IV
China Fights On with Allies
(1941-1943)

The Common Struggle Against the Axis

IN OBDURATE pursuit of their evil courses the Japanese have now, in concert with the Axis powers of Europe and in fulfillment of the undertakings laid upon them by the Tripartite Pact, suddenly attacked in dastardly and treacherous fashion our friends Great Britain and the United States, striking with the same piratical rapidity of the raid on Mukden ten years ago. In this way they have brought upon the Pacific the afflictions of war and exposed mankind to unprecedented losses and distress. You will be aware that the Chinese Government, has in the desire to vindicate international justice and preserve human civilization, formally declared war on Japan and at the same time upon Germany and Italy.

Since the invasion of the Northeastern Provinces by the Japanese our whole nation has been undauntedly striving and, during the past four years of war with resolution and steadfast devotion only the more marked. We set out to chastise the outrageous ambition of the Japanese, recover the territory lost to them, and by bringing about the downfall of this ringleader, check the scourge of aggression. Today the Japanese so far from repenting of their conduct have taken fresh steps towards the fulfillment of the abominable designs they share with the Axis powers. The democratic nations of the two hemispheres have now, however, arisen to act in unison, with the result that the world is divided into two clearly distinguished camps of the aggressors on the one hand and those who oppose them on the other.

Ours was the first country to suffer the inroads of aggression and also the first to assume responsibility for the vital task of putting bounds to the evil. Our faith is firm in the continuity of man's destiny and the indestructibility of his conceptions of equity. Nine-tenths of mankind are striving to defend justice, peace and the right to national freedom. The eventual overthrow of the aggressors is therefore a matter of certainty. Up to now our sacrifices have been made to the end of merely

A message to the Chinese people at home and abroad, and to the Chinese Army on December 10, 1941, following China's declaration of war on Japan, Germany and Italy.

driving the invaders from our own soil. Henceforth we shall be fighting shoulder to shoulder with Great Britain, the United States, Soviet Russia and other friendly nations in a united endeavor to suppress the enemies of civilization and establish lasting peace in the world.

The Chinese people, possessed of their heritage of five thousand years' civilization and the Three People's Principles designed to save both their own nation and the world, are now charged with a mission of unprecedented magnitude. Now our efforts will go beyond the aim of success for resistance and the restoration of our territorial sovereignty and also have the goal of speedy victory for the cause of justice in the world at large. But should our spirit slacken and the enemy be permitted to extend the term of his ill-doing indefinitely we shall fail not only all those who have sacrificed their lives for resistance but also our friends in the common struggle. In this momentous hour I expect of army and people ten times the strength of will displayed during the past years of war in the execution of the sacred duty that is now ours.

Citizens at home and abroad must keep in mind the greatness of the national genius that our sages and heroes have handed down to us and realize the supreme value that victory in resistance will have for the world, and how decisive for the welfare of future generations and of mankind our coming exertions will be. The foundation for victory has been laid, but the task before us is the more arduous in proportion to the vast conflict in which we are now engaged, the scale of the forces with whom we are allied and the immense vista of new significance added to our national fate. Henceforth we must be more severe in our self-respect and take a more serious view of our responsibility, each to the best of his ability and at his particular post of duty, fearless of all hardship and sacrifice and selfless in response to the extreme urgency of the issue that is to be decided.

Fellow-countrymen overseas are no less descendants of Hwang Ti, the progenitor of our race, than those at home, and it is for them wherever they may be to exert their great potential strength for the destruction of the common enemy and thereby add luster to the good name of their country. For our soldiers the present occasion makes a unique demand for their resolution and bravery in bringing fruition to the hard-won gains of a decade of warfare. The whole nation must advance with unfaltering determination to avenge the wrongs of this decade and deliver from outrage and injury those under the oppression of the enemy. At home the aim is the preservation of our territorial sovereignty as the primary aim of our resistance: in terms of world affairs we seek to vindicate international justice and win for our nation such renown as it has never enjoyed. From the limited scope of the beginnings of our enterprise we are moving towards the weightier implications of its final development.

Increase Our Fighting Strength

W E FIND this Session assembled within a few days of the beginning of the Pacific War launched by Japan. Chinese resistance and the world war against aggression have now merged into one conflict. China's position has consequently been very favorably affected. Looking back over the past ten years we recall that China first suffered from the enemy's attack and now after four years of furious combat has at last gained the comradeship of other peace-loving nations in the struggle against aggression. The story is one which is written on a glorious page of our national history. Every member of the Party should appreciate its significance and be inspired thereby. It must not be thought that the Revolution is yet complete or the national future without its perils; on the contrary, the present moment sees the country in the throes of a crisis which it will either survive or perish. If we do not achieve success in our revolutionary work, we shall meet with failure. When we think of our failings in the past and the heroic magnitude of the sacrifices made by our fellow-citizens and soldiers, we must redouble our efforts to continue our struggle that began ten years ago.

The work that faces this Session is of unusual moment. In a spirit of comradeship and with complete sincerity we must take stock of the errors of the past and devise measures of amendment. All outstanding unsolved problems must be given solutions and unfinished tasks carried to completion. At the same time, in relation to the immediate needs during this period of resistance and reconstruction there are two points to which our attention must be especially devoted. In the first place, we have to increase our fighting strength to a point that will enable us worthily to play our part as one of the powers fighting shoulder to shoulder against aggression. In the second place, a firm foundation for national reconstruction has to be laid. Now is the time to fix our fundamental policy of reconstruction on the basis of the general principles already established. These are two great aims for our work at this

An address delivered at the opening of the Ninth Plenary Session of the Central Executive Committee of the Kuomintang on December 15, 1941.

Session. We hope to arrive at satisfactory decisions through careful deliberations.

In order to increase our fighting strength it is necessary more fully to develop the total strength of the nation. This total strength may be expressed in the armed forces, in the political, economic, and social life of the country. During the past four and a half years of war, however, the results obtained in the political, economic and social spheres have not been ideal. A searching review of the situation reveals that the spiritual and material strength of the nation remains at least fifty per cent and possibly as much as eighty or ninety per cent undeveloped. Now that we find ourselves allied to other friendly countries in a common cause, it is inconceivable that we should continue in such slackness. Conscious of this, every Party member and citizen should rouse himself to new and more vigorous efforts. The survival of the nation depends upon whether our military, political, economic and social affairs can be directed along modern lines to yield their maximum strength. The modernization of the national life and its adjustment in all respects to wartime needs requires of us all a unanimous revitalization of our revolutionary spirit, and such increased efficiency in our work as shall assure the thorough execution of all the resolutions we shall arrive at here.

In this time of war we must not think to defer reconstruction. The war is for reconstruction, and reconstruction will contribute to our fighting strength. The present period of national awakening is singularly propitious for redoubled efforts in establishing the basis for the political system of the Three People's Principles and the Five Constitutional Rights. We have no immediate duty more important than that of carrying out the fundamental provisions of our policy in reconstruction along the lines laid down in Dr. Sun's Program of Reconstruction and our Program of Resistance and Reconstruction. Everything must be undertaken with a broad consideration of the fundamental issues; this is no time for short-sighted preoccupation with unessential details. On the one hand, we must set about adjusting the functions of existing organizations; on the other, we must observe the bearing of the present situation upon the basic policy and system now operative in military, political and economic affairs with a view to instituting necessary reforms. In this connection I have three points to make:

(1) *Building up the basis of national strength.* This is the most important of the tasks essential to reconstruction. You must all strive to train the people in the exercise of the four political rights in preparation for the institution of popular sovereignty. Progress with the new

system of *hsien* administration and the introduction of local autonomy to all grades of administrative districts must command your resolute efforts, to the end that after the war the country can proceed immediately to a system of government of the people, for the people and by the people.

(2) *Utilizing the country's talented persons.* For the purpose of achieving success in resistance and reconstruction the Party must draw into collaboration all non-Party men of ability who are loyal to the country and the Three People's Principles. Another point of great importance is the necessity of unifying the source of military and political authority; otherwise, if the attempt is made to assert authority independently of the Central Government the resulting disunity and disorder cannot but be highly injurious to the cause of resistance and reconstruction. Disloyalty to nation and people is intolerable in the eyes of every citizen, whether a member of the Party or not. All patriotic and gifted fellow-countrymen, however, are to be sought out and enlisted in the service of the nation. This is one of the indispensable lines of action we have to discuss at this Session.

(3) *Carrying total mobilization into a new stage.* The Central Government has been promoting General National Mobilization since the war began. The results of four years' work in this respect have not, however, been entirely satisfactory. Now we find ourselves ranged with other great powers of the world in the struggle against aggression and only determined replenishment of our strength can suffice to meet the great call upon it. How the nation's resources of all kinds are to be developed most effectively and how the social, political and economic standards prevailing in our national life are to be raised to a new level: these are questions this Session has to deal with. China is one of the most ancient, extensive, densely populated and potentially rich countries in the world. That after four years of resistance she is still so weak and backward is wholly due to our failure to develop our strength and concentrate our human and material resources. With the consolidation of the anti-aggression front, all the nations which compose it will have to achieve not only military coordination but also effective sharing and interchange of their human, and particularly, financial and material resources. If we can now exploit the potential resources of our land with foreign technical assistance, we shall certainly be victorious in war and successful in building the strong and healthy new China which was Dr. Sun's ideal.

I trust that this Session will also give its attention to the adjustment of administrative machinery and the simplification of legislation to suit the wartime needs. In those affairs which are the Party's own province we must be still more thorough in weeding out failings and developing our revolutionary spirit of sacrifice and taking all possible progressive measures. All of us here present must concentrate our powers of mind and spirit and decide upon the future policies and administrative procedure governing our Program of Resistance and Reconstruction.

One Half of the World's People

DURING my two weeks' stay in India I had the opportunity of discussing very frankly with the highest civil and military authorities as well as with my Indian friends questions concerning joint plans against aggression and the objective of our common efforts. I was happy to find that there was full sympathy and general understanding between us. My mission is now drawing to a close. On the eve of my departure I wish to bid farewell to all my friends in India and to thank you for the many kindnesses showered upon Madame Chiang and myself. The briefness of my stay has not permitted me to tell the Indian people all that I wished to say. I avail myself of this opportunity to address to them this farewell message. It is an expression of my high and warm regard and of long cherished hopes for India. It comes from the depth of my heart.

Since my arrival in this country I found to my great satisfaction that there exists among the people of India a unanimous determination to oppose aggression.

China and India comprise one half of the world's population. Their common frontier extends three thousand kilometers. In the two thousand years' history of their intercourse, which has been of a purely cultural and commercial character, there has never been any armed conflict. Indeed nowhere else can one find so long a period of uninterrupted peace between two neighboring countries. This is irrefutable proof that our two peoples are peace-loving by nature. Today they have not only identical interests but also the same destiny. For this reason they are duty bound to side with anti-aggression countries and to fight shoulder to shoulder in order to secure real peace for the whole world.

Moreover, our two peoples have an outstanding virtue in common, namely the noble spirit of self-sacrifice for the sake of justice and righteousness. It is this traditional spirit which should move them towards self-negation for the salvation of mankind. It is also this spirit

A farewell message to the Indian people on the eve of Generalissimo Chiang's departure for China on February 21, 1942, after a historic two-week visit in India.

which prompted China to be the first to take up arms against aggression and in the present war to ally herself unhesitatingly with other anti-aggression countries, not merely for the purpose of securing her own freedom, but also for the purpose of securing justice and freedom for all.

I venture to suggest to my brethren people of India at this most critical moment in the history of civilization that our two peoples should exert themselves to the utmost in the cause of freedom for all mankind, for only in a free world could the Chinese and Indian peoples obtain their freedom. Furthermore, should freedom be denied to either China or India, there could be no real international peace.

The present international situation divides the world into two camps, the aggression camp and the anti-aggression camp. All those who opposed aggression by striving for the freedom of their country and of other countries should join the anti-aggression camp. There is no middle course and there is no time to wait for developments. Now is the crucial moment for the whole future of mankind. The issue before us does not concern the dispute of any one man or country, nor does it concern any specific questions now pending between one people and another. Any people therefore which joins the anti-aggression front may be said to be cooperating, not with any particular country, but with the entire front. This leads us to believe that the Pacific War is the turning point in the history of nationalism. The method, however, by which the peoples of the world could achieve their freedom might be different from what it used to be. The anti-aggression nations now expect that in this new era the people of India will voluntarily bear their full share of responsibility in the present struggle for the survival of a free world, in which India must play her part. The vast majority of world opinion is in full sympathy with India's aspirations for freedom. This sympathy is so valuable and so difficult to obtain that it cannot be appraised in terms of money or material and should therefore by all means be retained.

The present struggle is one between freedom and slavery, between light and darkness, between good and evil, between resistance and aggression. Should the anti-aggression front lose the war, world civilization would suffer a setback for at least one hundred years and there would be no end of human suffering.

So far as Asia is concerned, the cruelties committed by the Japanese militarists are beyond description. The suffering and oppression, which have been the fate of Formosans and Koreans since their subjugation by Japan, should serve as a warning. As regards barbarities committed by the Japanese army since our War of Resistance, the fall of Nanking in December 1937 is a case in point. Over 200,000 civilians were massacred within one week. For the last five years the civilian population of Free China has been subjected almost daily to bombings from the air and bombardments by heavy artillery. In every place invaded by Japanese troops, men, women and children were either assaulted or killed. The young men and the educated people received their special attention with the result that men of intelligence and ideas have been tortured. Nor is this all. Institutions of culture, objects of historical interest and value and even articles necessary for livelihood, such as cooking utensils, ploughs, tools, and domestic animals, have been either forcibly taken away or destroyed. In places under Japanese military occupation, rape, rapine, incendiarism, murder, are frequent occurrences. Moreover they have with official connivance everywhere opened opium dens, gambling houses and houses of ill-fame in order to sap the vitality of the people and destroy their spirit. Such is the disgraceful conduct of the Japanese, the like of which is not found in countries invaded by other aggressor nations. What I have just said is but an inadequate description of the true state of affairs as reported by Chinese and foreign eyewitnesses.

In these horrible times of savagery and brute force, the people of China and their brethren people of India should for the sake of civilization and human freedom give their united support to the principles embodied in the Atlantic Charter and the joint declaration of twenty-six nations, and ally themselves with the anti-aggression front. I hope they will wholeheartedly join the Allies, namely, China, Great Britain, America and the Soviet Union, and participate in the struggle for the survival of a free world until complete victory is achieved and the duties incident upon them in these troubled times have been fully discharged.

Lastly, I sincerely hope and I confidently believe that our ally Great Britain, without waiting for any demands on the part of the people of India, will as speedily as possible give them real political power so that they may be in a position further to develop their spiritual and material strength and thus realize that their participation in the war is not merely aid to the anti-aggression nations for securing victory but also the turning point in their struggle for India's freedom. From the objective point of view, I am of the opinion this would be the wisest policy which will redound to the credit of the British Empire.

To the Flying Tigers, Salute

COLONEL CHENNAULT, officers and men: To be with you American volunteers here today, to observe your excellent spirit and to hear of your achievements fills me with delight and admiration. The American Volunteer Group of the Chinese Air Force has acquired a world-wide reputation for greatest courage.

It is three months since the Japanese, our common enemy, picked their quarrel with Great Britain and the United States. The splendid victories the Volunteer Group has won in the air are a glory that belongs to China and our ally, America, alike.

I have already communicated the news of your repeated successes to your Government and President Roosevelt. The record of what you have done shows that every one of you has been a match for thirty or more of the enemy. Your friends and relations will undoubtedly have felt boundless pride and elation to hear of your exploits. The blows you have struck at the Japanese have put you in the fore-front of the Allied forces fighting the aggressor. You have established a firm foundation for the campaign against his lawlessness which China and America are united to wage. You have written in the history of this world war a remarkable page, the memory of which will live in our minds forever.

As the Supreme Commander of the Allied Forces operating in the China theater of war, I am entertaining you today as my comrades-in-arms and on behalf of my four hundred and fifty million fellow countrymen I salute you, confident that you will continue together with all the Allied forces in Burma to display your valor until final victory is won over our common enemy.

Since you are under my command, I wish to impress upon you your identity with all the other men serving in the Chinese armed

A speech at a dinner in honor of the American Volunteer Group of the Chinese Air Force given by Generalissimo and Madame Chiang in Kunming on February 28, 1942, upon their return from India and Burma. Madame Chiang and Colonel Claire L. Chennault, Commanding Officer of the A. V. G., also addressed the gathering.

forces. Your lives are one with theirs and mine, your good name is one with theirs and mine. I act toward you as I act toward other members of the Chinese Air Force. I shall extend to those of your comrades who have given their lives the same mark of distinction and the same care for their families and children. For this I hold myself responsible. I trust that you will perform your duties free from any anxiety on this score. Your task is great. When victory is ours I hope to celebrate together with you our successful issue of the war in Tokyo.

Colonel Chennault's Response

Members of the A. V. G.: Never before in history do I know of any military unit such as ours having been accorded the honor such as comes to us tonight. No matter how many decorations we may have bestowed on us in the future I am sure we will never receive more honor than we have received tonight. For five years I have followed the Generalissimo to the best of my ability and I know him to be a leader of the highest principles and greatest determination. He is a leader who prefers death to compromise. He is a leader, not only of China, but of the entire Allied effort. It is easy for us Americans to follow such a leader.

In addition to Madame Chiang's work in aviation she is also the leader of all the women in China. The orphans and widows of China come to her either directly or through the agencies which she has set up and receive aid. To me, she is the mother of China.

During this time millions of Chinese soldiers have gone to the fronts and have been killed and seriously wounded. Orphans have been left in the ruins of their homes and in the fields. All of these needed aid and they have been given that aid as rapidly as possible. And now there will be thousands more to feed and educate, to receive medical attention.

One problem, of course, is to provide the money for this. It takes money to do all these things, probably less in China than elsewhere but even in China money is needed to buy these things. Madame Chiang's generosity is boundless. Her shoulders are always willing to take on additional burdens, but if money is lacking to provide the necessities her work must suffer. I would be unable to recite all that Madame Chiang has accomplished; however, one thing I have not yet mentioned. When the organization of this Group was first discussed in America I was asked for recommendations as to how it would be handled in China. The first thing that I insisted upon was that Madame Chiang should act as our chief staff officer; that Madame Chiang should serve as liaison staff officer between the Generalissimo and the Group. And although she has hundreds of activities that require a great deal of her time she consented to this because of her eagerness for China to have effective military aviation. So even though you are unconscious of the fact, Madame Chiang has been Honorary Group Commander and Staff Officer of this Group since its organization and I would like to present her tonight as our Honorary Group Commander.

Madame Chiang's Speech

Colonel Chennault, members of the A. V. G. and other friends: As your Honorary Commander may I call you my boys? You have flown across the Pacific in China's gravest hour on wings of hope and faith. For this reason not only does the Chinese Air Force but the entire Chinese nation welcome you with outstretched arms. The Generalissimo has already spoken to you of the fine and brave deeds you have done and he has called the A. V. G. the world's bravest air force.

I am very proud tonight that I have had a little share in making it possible for you to fight for China. When I think of the life-and-death struggle which China has passed through these last five years I have before my mind's eye the millions of our people who have been killed or wounded and others who had to flee from Japanese cannon, machine guns and bombers. I also see the rivers of blood which have flowed over our territory, the very life blood of China's fairest manhood. I think of the tens of thousands of our women whose honor has been violated by the Japanese and the hundreds of thousands of our little children who have been killed and maimed or else taken to Japan to be trained as traitors to their motherland.

And now you have come here to vindicate us. We have always been resolved to fight until final victory is ours but we lack the air arm which you are now providing. You have come to fight side by side with us. For this I wish to express our heartfelt thanks.

Colonel Chennault has taken an active part in Chinese resistance during the last five years. You boys know him personally. You know what an admirable commander he is and how very selfless. The only complaint I have against him is that he is never satisfied with his own work. I venture to say, too, that he also thinks that you ought to have more work regardless of how much you already have.

Colonel Chennault has just introduced me as Honorary Commander of the A. V. G. I think I am prouder of this title than any other title I've had, because I know that you are not only fighting with your bodies and your skill, you are fighting with your hearts and spirits. Just now Colonel Chennault brought to me two of your very fine comrades who have braved death today in the air. They forgot themselves entirely while fighting the enemy because they knew that although they might have to make the final sacrifice, their comrades would carry on the great work which the A. V. G. has set for itself. This spirit, I feel, is the secret of the A. V. G.'s successes.

I was asked a little while ago by one of my officers, "Madame Chiang, some of the A. V. G. pilots are shooting down so many planes that we won't have room enough on the wings for all the stars which they merit. What shall we do about it?" I told him, "We shall have to provide them with an additional pair of wings." And that is what we will have to do if you all keep up the score.

Although you are here in China, I am sure that often your minds and your hearts fly back to your loved ones in America, and for this reason I am glad that America is now realizing that China is not fighting for China alone but for America and for the whole world. You, in giving the best that is in you, are doing it for your own country as well as for China. Time and again your Commanding Officer has dinned into your ears the necessity for discipline. Hateful word, isn't it? Discipline in the air, discipline on the field, and yet without discipline we can accomplish nothing and I, as your Honorary Commanding Officer, am going to din more discipline into you.

I would go further than Colonel Chennault. I mean the discipline of your inner selves. It isn't enough to observe discipline only. We must have inner discipline so that we may have fully developed characters. However, I am not trying to make you little plaster saints and I am quite human enough to like interesting people, but I do want you boys to remember one thing: the whole of the Chinese nation has taken you to its heart and I want you to conduct yourselves in a manner worthy of the great traditions that you have built up. I want you to leave an impression on my people, a true impress of what Americans really are. I trust and I know that you will act worthily wherever you are in China.

Forgive me for speaking to you like that. Perhaps I should be very polite and say, "Boys, you are just grand. You are little angels with or without wings." But you are my boys. I can speak to you freely. I know that you will understand when I say that I hope every one of you, whether in the air or on the ground, will remember that you are China's guests and that everything you do will reflect credit upon the country which I love next to my own, America, where as you know I was educated and which I always look upon as my second home.

Colonel Chennault just now said something which rather embarrassed me. He spoke to you about my needing money to carry on relief work. I know that money is necessary, Colonel, but I don't want to rope you boys in tonight for this purpose. If I had this dinner would be very hard to digest so I didn't do that, but I do want to thank you for what you voluntarily contributed to the war orphans during Christmas. Please don't feel that you have to contribute now, that's one thing I beg of you.

Just one final word. War is not only a matter of equipment, artillery, ground troops or air force; it is largely a matter of spirit, or morale. When I came into this room I felt at once how very keyed-up you are. Now that you have been fighting for a few months you are full of enthusiasm and pep. That is a good thing, but the greater thing is to gather momentum as each day goes by and not let yourself be discouraged no matter what happens, because as you soar into the skies you are writing in letters of flame on the horizon certain eternal truths for the world to see: First, the indomitable courage of the Chinese people; Second, the indestructible spirit of the Chinese Army; and Third, the deathless soul of the Chinese nation. And so, whatever you do, wherever you are, remember that such is the China which you have come to assist.

I would like all of you to get up and drink a toast to the two great sister nations facing each other across the Pacific. They now have a bond of friendship and sympathy which serves us well in the crucible of war and which will serve us equally when victory has been won.

The Duties of a Vanguard

THREE years have passed since the Program of Spiritual Mobilization was issued. During these three years the nation has passed through many difficulties and immense changes have taken place in the international situation. By their resolute and tenacious resistance to the aggressor the Chinese people have caused the world to hail their spirit as a citadel of world peace and the enemy to realize the moral strength of that spirit as inviolable. Since the outbreak of war in the Pacific, China has no longer been resisting the Japanese singlehanded; she is now fighting shoulder to shoulder with all those other nations opposing the aggressors as her allies. She has become the sole base of Allied operations in Asia. Our responsibility has accordingly grown more onerous, and our task more difficult. Apart from our responsibility for the future of our own nation we are now charged with the mission of preserving human civilization and international justice. The spectacle of China's indefatigable and unflinching resistance has inspired the other nations allied against aggression with faith in their cause and stimulated the morale of all the countries of the democratic bloc. It is therefore more important than ever before that we should exert ourselves and rid our conduct of all indolence and negligence, which may now damage the interests of our allies as well as bring irretrievable ruin upon unborn generations of our own people. In initiating the struggle against the aggressors we assumed the duties of a vanguard, and we must continue to stand with rock-like firmness in the flow of world events. Such must be our present thought and purpose.

On New Year's Day I uttered a warning: "During the next few months vigorous activity on the part of the Japanese is to be anticipated and bad news may continue to come of the progress of operations in the Pacific. We must prepare ourselves for the worst possible situation that can arise. The shadow of Japanese aggression is now looming over the Indian Ocean and in time Burma and India may be threatened or even overrun." I made this prediction because whereas the Japanese had been

A message broadcast to the nation on the third anniversary of the Spiritual Mobilization Movement on March 12, 1942.

286

preparing and planning for over twenty years to carve up the resources of the Pacific, the friendly countries concerned, having pursued a policy of peace and good faith, found themselves off their guard and were bound to suffer initial reverses as a result. On the same occasion I explained: "We shall have to wait until, with the further extension of the fronts on which the enemy is fighting and the excessive demands upon his manpower involved, he experiences such embarrassment in maintaining his lines of communication that he is exposed to the danger of piecemeal destruction at the hands of the Allies. Then they will be in a position to inflict overwhelming punishment upon him and finally rout him decisively." That time is now rapidly drawing near, and the collapse of the enemy will soon begin.

The history of past wars is full of examples of early successes won by those who are disastrously defeated in the end. At the present time four of the largest nations in the world, China, America, Britain, and Soviet Russia are united in an alliance absolutely superior in resources of men and material to the Axis bloc. Our enemy has taken the evil course to make us his slaves; we for our part have made our aim the freedom and equality of status for our people. On his side the motive is self-seeking; on ours it is justice. Justice is always triumphant over greed. We must realize that for all his overbearing outward manner the enemy is inwardly disheartened, only because he knows he is making war without any just or upright cause. The more territory his soldiers seize the remoter seems the final goal of their campaign. If this is understood it will be realized that it is only natural for the enemy to make desperate or risky moves in his conduct of the war, but both the spiritual and material factors involved ensure his final defeat. With us time is of more importance than space, and at present it is for us to stand firm and steel our hearts to endure.

Let us now review the activities of the Spiritual Mobilization Movement during the past three years and ascertain to what degree they have come up to the standards we set ourselves. Have we done all possible to make up for our material handicaps? To what extent have we achieved a distribution of our resources suited to wartime needs? Many difficulties have certainly been overcome through the development of our national spirit, but we have yet to go far in developing it to the utmost. This national spirit has been formed through the care and teaching of sages and philosophers throughout the five thousand years of our history; it has penetrated so deeply into the life of our people that its strength is now like the irresistible flow of a great river. We must now employ this strength in generating and conserving material power. During the past

287

five years of war the international status of our country has been steadily improving; now we must strive further to exploit our strong points and remedy our weak points. Dr. Sun often emphasized the fact that an effective use of weapons depends far more upon the spirit with which men fight than upon the quality of the weapons. In making use of our material resources we must adopt an ordered and organized process, and in rendering our work efficient discipline and morale are the most essential factors. Spiritual mobilization is therefore the most urgent side of the actual prosecution of the war.

In the first place, we must give full play to our national tradition of inflexible resolution, which in the course of our history has produced so many glorious examples of devotion and courage and called forth the admiration of the world. This is a spirit of humility in time of success and fortitude in the hour of failure. We shall be shaken by nothing if we can maintain such a determination springing from inward conviction, making it the center for the concentration of our will and strength. We shall be prepared to do our whole duty in resistance and reconstruction in this vital stage of the war if we continue to manifest the ethical ideals that are our national heritage. China is called upon to furnish the world with a pillar of rectitude, founded upon those ideals, the philosophic basis for which our educationalists should interpret and stress in the teaching of the young. They must bring to the fore the historical continuity of Chinese ethical doctrines and the robust and independent view of life expressed therein. I have already pointed out to youth its obligation to carry forward the cultural movement based upon the Three People's Principles for the purpose of initiating the philosophy of national reconstruction. In the fifth paragraph of the Program of Spiritual Mobilization allusion is made to the need for a spirit of resilient and positive vitality. In educating the young every effort must be made to guard against tendencies to reckless, irrational and abandoned conduct and to cultivate a selfless patriotism and public-spiritedness. Haphazard and slothful habits of thought and life are to be displaced by preciseness and self-reliance. In this way we shall be applying our national philosophy to the actual needs of our time.

In the second place, we must develop the scientific side of national defense. As the existence of the nation depends upon defense, so does defense also depend upon science. We are nationally handicapped by our inadequate material provision for defense, and the chief reason for this is to be found in the small use we have made of scientific technique. Here the Movement has a remedy to offer; it provides for the mobilization of national ability for the purposes of research and investigation into scientific means of warfare. Modern weapons are constantly being improved upon and fresh devices to meet them are progressively discovered. Arms for attacking tanks, contrivances for protection against magnetic mines, detector apparatus in air defense, are all proof of the great part played in modern warfare by the inventive brains of scientists. It is imperatively necessary that our scientists and scientific strength should be mobilized and put at the disposal of the nation—at work, for instance, in devising substitutes for materials of which there is at present a lack. In the schools and throughout society we need the spread of scientific knowledge and technique, the increase of production by improved methods of production, and rapid measures of industrialization.

In the third place, we must make increased use of the competitive stimulus in encouraging rationalization and higher efficiency in production. However, the mere principles of division of labor and cooperation are not sufficient to ensure a satisfactory degree of success. A still more important condition is the development of an enthusiastic working spirit, good organization and efficient management. If the spirit cultivated is one of willingness good organization will follow naturally, and efficient management will come with good organization. These things mean the fullest possible employment of each man's energy and the fullest possible utilization of all resources, and to this end every man must be animated by a conscious and voluntary working spirit. I believe that the competitive principle is invaluable in stimulating such a spirit. In our ordinary everyday work we often feel too easily satisfied with our own standard, but in a competition satisfaction comes only with the greatest possible effort to outdo others and the standard is set by the best worker. In all branches of human activity throughout the world the motive for the intense devotion displayed in training and work usually comes from competition. We shall do best to introduce this element of competition into our endeavors in order to cultivate in all citizens a wholehearted, unselfish, vigorous, and joyful devotion to work.

In the fourth place, as a part of our preparation to wage a long-protracted war and cope with the worst possible of circumstances, we must put ourselves in readiness to encounter even greater hardships in days to come, for the world war in which we are now taking part has only just begun. We must on the one hand do all we can to expand production, and on the other restrict consumption. We must think of the great value which things not consumed by the individual can have if they are utilized for the purposes of resistance and reconstruction, and derive from this reflection a spiritual recompense for the material loss. In ancient times frugal living was associated with filial piety as a virtue. Now it is the nation which is the highest object of our loyalty or filial duty. Our country is one of great and rich natural resources and, if the most is made of them we shall find them fully sufficient for all our needs in times of war and peace. The guiding principle of our conduct must now be the exhaustive and effective employment of our human and material resources, for which the practice of thrift is one essential condition. The maximum effort in this direction will ensure us all against excessive deprivations.

I am sure that if we act on the four points I have here suggested we shall prove equal to all the difficulties we may encounter through the complete mobilization of our national strength, and especially of our spiritual strength. Let us entertain not the slightest doubt that we shall thus be able to drive out the enemy and establish a free and independent country. At the same time our own high morale will exercise a good influence over that of our allies, to the benefit of the common cause for which we are fighting. We shall do well now to think of our task as world salvation, rather than merely the salvation of our country. In spiritual mobilization is to be fulfilled this sacred mission.

Strike from Every Vantage Point

WHEN the enemy is on the very threshold of Australia, my thoughts are engaged not only by consideration of sacrifice and trials which you people will be called upon to endure; I think also of the lasting contribution which they are now in a position to make towards the vindication of the Allied cause. The task before you is difficult and your responsibility is tremendous. Not only will you be defending your own homes and hearths against a ruthless and powerful enemy, you will also be charged with the arduous duty of overcoming the enemy's attempts to consolidate his gains and cut the communications of the United Nations.

I am confident, however, that Australians, who have distinguished themselves on many battle-fields, will prove equal to the task. Do not let what the United Nations have failed thus far to achieve in other theaters of the war be a source of dismay to you. The earlier reverses should arouse in you as well as in the other United Nations a fierce determination and greater efforts. Experience has taught us that in resisting the Japanese who, even today, possess superior armaments, the people must be thoroughly organized and trained, not only for facing the shock tactics of the enemy without yielding ground, but also for striking and embarrassing the enemy from every point of vantage. This calls for daring, coordination, ingenuity and endurance, but I am certain our Australian comrades possess these qualities in abundance.

In the hours of stress, it is well to remember that the enemy is fighting not only against the combined forces of the United Nations but also against his most formidable foe—time. Every hour and every inch of ground denied the enemy is an achievement worthy of all the efforts and sacrifices that it demands.

In your bitter struggle against our common enemy, the entire Chinese nation will be wholeheartedly with you and I am confident that Australia will jealously guard her fine traditions and her people will fight as they have never fought before. I am confident that Australia will do more to act up to the important position which she holds today in the anti-aggression front.

A message to the people of Australia sent around March 20, 1942.

Morale Plus Equipment

MADAME CHIANG and I have gladly accepted the invitation of the War Department to send greetings to you, the American people. As I am speaking, bloody battles are being waged in the east, north, south and southwest of China. In these areas Japanese planes have been daily, relentlessly bombing our Army which has been gallantly fighting without air protection.

For five years China has stood up against Japan. We have fought with inferior equipment and with little more than bare fists. Though we are producing small arms we have not had the time nor the means to build up heavy industry. We lack airplanes, artillery and tanks. What has sustained us and made it possible for us to continue resisting has been the adoption of what I might term magnetic strategy which consists of attracting the enemy to the interior, bog him there, and hold him at bay by the more vital factor of morale.

As a realist I must point out, however, that morale, important as it is, is not sufficient in itself to win a decisive and final victory. It must be supplemented by mechanized equipment. Mechanized equipment by itself, however, is futile. Morale and equipment combined spell final victory. This truth can readily be seen when we consider how much the American Volunteer Group of the Chinese Air Force has been able to help us despite its ever slender resources. As Commander-in-Chief of the China Theater of War, I pledge you my word that, given 10 per cent of the equipment you produce in America, the Chinese Army will reap for you 100 per cent of the desired results.

In looking toward the future I would like every one of my listeners to realize that our Chinese people are convinced that the principles enunciated in the Atlantic Charter are not vague assurances and empty diplomatic phraseology, but that they are the underlying convictions to which the peace-loving people of America are dedicated. To my mind these principles should be applied, not only to America and Europe, but also to all peoples and races so that freedom, justice and equality may

A broadcast from Chungking to America made by Generalissimo and Madame Chiang on May 31, 1942, on the Army Hour program.

reign the world over. For all the principles and support, both moral and material, which the government and people of America under the leadership of President Roosevelt have given us throughout these five years of resistance, we wish to express our heartfelt appreciation.

Madame Chiang's Speech

You have just heard the Generalissimo's reaffirmation that in spite of the long years of war our conviction in ultimate victory is stronger than ever. I have one more word which I would like to utilize by pointing out to you an insidious example of enemy propaganda which has just come to my attention, and which I hope deceived no one. The plot is to sow dissension between us by announcing that China has plenty of arms and is now stalemating because she depends on America to win the war for her. I need not tell you that this is a malicious lie, fathered by those who wish to undermine our friendship. China has always proved loyal and will continue to fulfill her obligations. In the past she has never hesitated to divert her entire resources to the common cause. She does not hesitate now, nor will she hesitate in the future.

China has survived all kinds of wars because she has consistently adhered to certain moral principles. Those principles preclude her acting otherwise than in an honorable manner. The enemy has repeatedly made offers of peace to China and sought to assure her that the Western Democracies were making use of her as a tool, whereas Japan would cooperate with and consider her as an equal. The fact that we have unhesitatingly rejected those offers is proof positive that we have implicit faith in America's sincerity. We know that you are equally certain of China's sincerity. In oneness of purpose, in devotion to a common cause and cooperation, therefore, let us march forward, shoulder to shoulder, beneath the flaming banner of freedom to sure victory.

China's War, a World War

TODAY we commemorate the fifth anniversary of the beginning of China's armed resistance. The struggle of the Chinese Army and people against aggression has been in progress for five full years. The past year has, moreover, been a year of extraordinary developments in the world situation which will determine the final outcome of the war.

On this solemn occasion foremost in our hearts and minds must be the sorrowing homage we owe to all those who have nobly laid down their lives for the common cause. At the same time let us take this opportunity to express our gratification at the achievements of our allies. The present moment affords me also a fitting occasion to acknowledge China's appreciation of the gallantry of our Allied forces which are fighting shoulder to shoulder with us. To the governments and peoples of the United States, Great Britain, Soviet Russia, the Netherlands, Australia, India, Canada, Czechoslovakia, Poland, Mexico and others of the United Nations I express our warm thanks for the unfailing concern they have felt for us at every stage of our national trial. Their readiness to extend collaboration to China has been a constant source of encouragement to us.

You must realize, my fellow countrymen, that these five hard years of resistance comprise a record unprecedented in the annals of modern warfare. The war China is engaged in is unique not only as being the longest for the past hundred years but also as an example of a weak nation standing up against a strong. In this long and bitter conflict the unshakable solidarity of the Chinese people has demonstrated the greatness of their traditional spirit of independence. We have become the vanguard of the forces opposing aggression. The whole world recognizes our position as champion of international justice and understands the value of our spiritual strength.

The present war is a war between good and evil, between right and might. The difficulties and perils we have encountered have only served to give proof of the undaunted revolutionary spirit possessed by our

An address to the Chinese people on July 7, 1942, on the occasion of the fifth anniversary of China's resistance against Japanese aggression.

294

people. Through all these difficulties and dangers a sure path has been found and our efforts have not been in vain. The guidance we have derived from the noble principles of Dr. Sun Yat-sen's revolutionary teachings has enabled us to give this demonstration of the invincible and sustaining qualities of our national character. The moral ascendancy we have acquired is such that no force or knavery can ever shatter. It is the guarantee for our victory and an all-important factor in our reconstruction.

Today China no longer stands alone as she has stood for four and a half years. Our present position imposes greater responsibilities upon us. I desire today to impress upon you the weight of those responsibilities that fell to our lot in the present World War. You will, I trust, continue to do your duty with devotion and endurance.

China is charged with the duty of operating as the main fighting force on the Asiatic continent. That duty is laid upon us with the same urgency as the duty of America to deal in the Pacific with her first and most threatening enemy, Japan. The other allies such as Great Britain and Soviet Russia have each naturally a particular duty to perform in accordance with their respective geographical position. Each is keenly sensible of certain inalienable obligations. The naval situation in the Pacific, for instance, has developed in such a way as to expose American soil to a direct threat from Japan which was the first power to invade American territory, attack the American fleet and flout American prestige.

What we have seen of recent American action in the Pacific, the bombing of Tokyo and the engagements in the Coral Sea, off Midway Island and at Dutch Harbor has been sufficient indication that America is beginning to discharge her supremely important duty in the Pacific. That is to say America is bound to deal first with the enemy from which she has most to fear for the defense of her own soil and for her security as the arsenal of the Democracies and in order to carry out her mission of world leadership not only during the present war but also in post-war reconstruction.

You must be on your guard against giving credence to superficial speculation that Allied strategy and policy consider the Pacific War to be of secondary importance, that our allies intend to let Japan have her own way for the time being or even that there is no comprehensive Allied strategy and that there is no concrete organization to direct Allied efforts. All such talk leads to unjustified apprehension. In the near future the collapse of the enemy will be apparent—then the strategy, organization and strength of the United Nations will be properly appraised.

It is my hope that you, my compatriots, will depend upon yourselves to exert your utmost in the fulfillment of your sacred duty as citizens of China in the Asiatic theater of war. There must be full realization of the fact that both space and time were on Japan's side during her campaign in the South Seas. Her initial successes, however, are no reliable criterion of her real strength. In a number of broadcasts this year I have emphasized this point. Today my chief concern is to have you grasp the significance of the Midway Islands, Coral Sea and Dutch Harbor engagements in which the enemy met with sharp reverses, lost four out of her six newest aircraft carriers and two battleships. This blow marks the beginning of the decline in her fighting strength. Far greater defeats will rapidly overtake her, defeats that will mean the beginning of her final collapse. Here a single fact will suffice to show the weakness of Japan. The total tonnage of her naval and merchant vessels is scarcely more than five million tons. It will be impossible for her to maintain with so few ships the vast fronts over which she has spread her forces.

Meanwhile, the land, sea and air strength of the United Nations is daily increasing and already exceeds that of the Axis bloc. By the end of this winter Japan's strength will be only one tenth that of the Allies. I need not elucidate further the significance of this comparison. The final defeat of Japan will start on sea and will end on land. Her depredations in the South Seas will prove to be the prelude of her disaster. She is meanwhile plunging deeper and deeper into the morass of her continental adventure wherein for five years she has pursued a suicidal course dictated by our strategy. She is now beyond recovery. Our efforts will determine the speed with which she can be finally overthrown.

At this moment we are at the turning point in our War of Resistance. Patriotism demands of us sustained sacrifice. Irrespective of age or sex we must each contribute to the all-important task which when completed will bring victory and permanent security to a freed world.

A Friend From Distant Lands

I CONSIDER it a great honor to have the privilege to extend on behalf of the Chinese Army and people a most hearty welcome to our distinguished guest Mr. Wendell Willkie in this wartime capital.

We have an old saying—"Is it not delightful to have friends coming from distant lands?" Since the announcement of Mr. Willkie's proposed visit to China the Chinese Army and people have been looking forward to his arrival with great interest and eagerness. He shares with us the same aspiration and ideal. We are indeed happy to have him in our midst.

Our guest of honor comes to China as the personal representative of President Roosevelt. He is a farsighted statesman of high ideals. As Honorary President of the United China Relief, he has worked indefatigably for China's cause. We count him as one of our closest friends irrespective of personal acquaintanceship.

From his public utterances we know that he fully comprehends the long-cherished ambition of Japan for world conquest and the significance and importance of China's stubborn resistance in face of untold suffering. He has, moreover, a sympathetic understanding of the ideals which have inspired our War of Resistance and our work of reconstruction. The energetic and fruitful efforts he has made in America for aid to China have brought the Chinese and American people closer together, peoples who have built up their nations upon the same ideology. His present visit has moved us to redouble our efforts in order to fulfill worthily our responsibility as a member of the United Nations and to come up to the expectations of our allies and our good friends, among them our guest of honor, Mr. Willkie.

The forces of aggression are still at large. In order to deliver humanity from barbarism and darkness all peace-loving peoples must needs go through hardships and tribulations. Our distinguished visitor will see with his own eyes the wanton destruction wrought by the Japanese in China during the past five years. He will notice our optimism, our

A speech of welcome to Mr. Wendell L. Willkie upon his visit to Chungking, delivered at a dinner on October 3, 1942.

conviction and our determination to achieve final victory. He will not fail to see how in the face of immense difficulties we have been doing our utmost to increase our fighting strength and to carry on our work of reconstruction, how the Chinese Army and people are struggling for the attainment of our common aim and victory.

Mr. Willkie will, I venture to hope, let the Chinese people know more fully the concerted war efforts of the American Government and people so that they thereby be inspired to greater exertion for the common cause. If he discovers any shortcomings in the work in which we are now engaged, I hope he will give us his candid opinion.

The very simple reception of this evening is an inadequate manifestation of the warmth with which our four hundred fifty million people greet our distinguished guest, and great friend of China. There are present with us the representatives of the United Nations in China. This auspicious occasion is a token of the solidarity among the United Nations, of our determination to cooperate to the fullest extent, to fight on until we obtain ultimate victory and create a new era in the future world order. Now I ask you to join me in drinking to the health of President Roosevelt and Mr. Wendell Willkie.

Mr. Willkie's Response

I have come to China to pay homage not only to the Chinese people but to one of the truly great men of his time, your Generalissimo. This tribute I deliver to you personally as one American who has watched for years the struggle of China under his leadership. But I deliver it to you also as the representative of President Roosevelt and as the representative of the American people.

Your Generalissimo is one of the best known men in my country and one of the best liked. I think that most Americans like and respect him for two qualities. They see in him an aggressive spirit, the spirit of a man who is not daunted by difficulties but works ceaselessly to overcome them. And they also see in him, as they have come to know about him through our newspapers, our motion pictures, our radio, a man with a broad vision of the future, who believes in his heart that freedom and security are possible of achievement not only for China but for the whole world. I think I understand tonight more about this aggressive spirit than I ever did before.

I came to China not through what used to be called a "treaty port," but through the great and wealthy provinces to the west of here. I have lived and worked in the West of America and I know from first-hand experience the kind of aggressive self-confidence which is developed in pioneer regions by men who are not afraid to take chances, sometimes very grave chances, in pursuit of what they believe in.

Prediction is not my business, but I would be prepared to make a substantial bet that the confident, aggressive, determined spirit I have seen in Sinkiang and in Kansu and Szechwan and which the outside world knows about chiefly through the personality of your Generalissimo, is not likely to be stopped by floods, by earthquakes or by the Japanese.

Americans are no less interested in the Generalissimo as both a symbol and a leader of the great struggle for a better future in which we are all engaged. As you know even better than we in the United States, war is an expensive, ugly business. Its rewards must be great if mankind is not to perish by its own sword. The rewards of this war must be greater than those of any other war and they must be paid in the cash of freedom and security. The Generalissimo, working with the principles of Dr. Sun, has helped to launch the Chinese people on a great experiment in democracy, one in which the goals of self-government and liberty have not been lost sight of even in national crises where security, the security of the Chinese nation has been paramount. I like to think that not only China but the whole Pacific area and the entire world may emerge from this war with their faces set directly toward a larger experiment along the same line. It will not really be an experiment because we are confident that we already know the answer. We know that only liberty, real liberty of all peoples, is worth fighting for. We know that only security which means the right to live decently and well for all peoples can be a guarantee that we shall not have to fight these wars over again every generation.

Your Generalissimo stands in the very front rank among leaders of his time who have given this challenge to the world and who are struggling to fulfill it. I report to you as an ordinary American who loves China and the Chinese people that your leader is a great man not only among his own people but before the world.

I view this war as a great world struggle for freedom. It will not be won by timid souls. It will be won only by bold and courageous men who inspire their peoples to undertake and carry through bold plans. Timid souls can always find reasons for a delay in aggressively pushing through to victory. I have just visited the Mediterranean area, the Middle East and Russia, and now I am here in China. I toured the battlefronts of both Egypt and Russia. I talked with military officials, with government leaders and above all with scores and scores of people —regular people, simple people—and what I did learn from them, particularly from the ordinary citizen in whose intuitive judgment lies wisdom even for experts, was that the ordinary citizen from Cairo to Moscow to Chungking is a lover of liberty and wants action, action now. He feels the time has come for the United Nations in a great unison of effort to take the offensive everywhere. He is ahead of his leaders—this plain citizen of Africa, of Europe or Asia or America. He wants to get on with the war, he wants to get the job done. He no longer believes or fears the myth that Germany and Japan are invincible. It annoys him that much of the might of the United Nations stands idle awaiting action only on some future day. This ordinary citizen is ready now. He is the strength of the United Nations. His faith in the justice of our cause makes him a superman. We must all catch his infectious spirit of enthusiasm for an immediate slashing, courageous attack to enable us to sweep over the aggressor nations and on to a new world of victory with justice, freedom, equality and opportunity for all nations and all men.

Loyalty and Reciprocity

O N THIS solemn anniversary day every citizen should call to mind the arduous achievements of the Revolution in the past and render himself better aware of his own responsibility for its future progress. I wish on this occasion first to describe the moral basis for our national policy and existence.

For five thousand years the spirit of our national culture and tradition has been such as may be summed up in the phrases "loyalty and reciprocity" and "goodwill and love." Loyalty consists in performing one's duties to the very best of one's ability. Reciprocity is the will to think of the affairs of others in terms of one's own, to avoid doing to others what one would not have them do to one's self. Since we will not tolerate oppression and aggression from others we must refrain ourselves from oppressive or aggressive action in our dealings with others and discountenance such action throughout the world.

The aim we and our allies have set before us in the present war is freedom and security for humanity and its civilization. We are not concerned with the selfish interests of a single nation or country. In striking contrast with the ambition of the Axis to subject other races to the tyranny of one that claims superiority, our desire is to see proper importance attached to the interests of all races.

Resistance is an expression of our solicitude for the well-being of all mankind and our determination to make it possible for the world to enjoy genuine peace. It is also a demonstration of our faith in the Three Principles of the People. Of those principles the Principle of Nationhood is of especial importance at the present stage for while the existence of the nation remains in danger the application of the other two principles will depend upon our success in applying the first.

The Principle of Nationhood requires of us the deliverance of our nation and also the endeavors to obtain equality of status for all other nations. Our national tradition of "goodwill and love" impels us to this concern for the interests of other countries. Dr. Sun in asserting these

A Double Tenth message to the nation delivered on October 10, 1942, to mark the founding of the Chinese Republic thirty-one years ago.

tenets as a national creed believed that the world can attain to lasting peace and order only through the development of this spirit of goodwill and love. The object of his revolutionary work was as much world salvation as national salvation. The goal of world unity he envisaged consists in equal enjoyment of the goals of independence and freedom by all peoples without distinction of color or power. Being engaged in this just war for the assertion of right against might we must prepare in collaboration with our allies to devise means of making sure that there shall be no repetition of this disaster in the future. Our duty for the present remains to exert our best effort in our own defense and national rehabilitation.

I turn next to national reconstruction and the main principle we must keep sight of in all we do to that end. The qualities it demands of us are industry, frugality and conscientiousness which it happens are qualities peculiarly characteristic of our people. We must lay fresh emphasis upon their importance. On several occasions this year I have urged upon my fellow countrymen the necessity of conforming their ways of living to the exigencies of wartime and carrying into full effect the provisions of the National Mobilization Law.[1] Today, however, there is still insufficient evidence of the social atmosphere of urgency and energetic devotion to duty which we require. We must have a livelier sense of the gravity of the emergency and the realization that life in wartime must necessarily be one of hardship. We must be prepared to endure privations for the sake of the great undertaking of national rehabilitation. We must all bestir ourselves to bring all our activities into line with the provisions of the National Mobilization Act.

All those with technical ability must make their contribution to its full implementation. The individual must practice thrift in his personal life and go about his work with enthusiastic and scrupulous attention to the public interest. The hardships of the fighting men at the front should be considered the standard by which behavior elsewhere is to be judged. Their sacrifices should be the measure of what is required of all citizens. If this maxim is obeyed the country will be in no danger of falling short of the aims of reconstruction.

[1] The National Mobilization Act was promulgated on March 29, 1942, to regulate wartime conduct and promote greater war effort.

National and Allied Cooperation

WHEN our last plenary session was held in November of last year the Pacific was threatened with imminent outbreak of war. Since the subsequent beginning of the Japanese campaign of aggression in that ocean, China, in the company of her allies, has become the most important member of the forces fighting on the continent of East Asia. She is no longer the singlehanded protagonist of the cause of our own independence. Her fate is one with that of the whole world. Our responsibilities and the scope of our operations are now far more extensive than ever before.

The battles fought in China during the past year have made it clear that we have already passed from the defensive to the offensive. We have achieved indubitable results in all our military measures of preparation for a general counter-offensive despite the great difficulties of the situation we have had to face.

In the initial stage of the Pacific War the Japanese seemed borne along by a wave of good fortune. Since June of this year, however, they have met with a number of sharp reverses in the Coral Sea, off Midway Island and at Dutch Harbor. Their naval and air strength has been steadily declining and recently in the Solomons and New Guinea where the Allies have not yet fully developed their offensive there have been unmistakable signs of the enemy's exhaustion. The Japanese militarists have called upon their people "not to underestimate" Anglo-American strength. They have announced that the present moment is not opportune for the commencement of reconstruction in the South Seas. They have emphasized the need of preparing for a war of long duration. They have appealed for greater sacrifices. Although Soviet Russia is now engaged in fierce fighting with Nazi Germany she has in no way relaxed the vigilance she maintains on her eastern frontier. As the result of the failure of the German offensive in Russia and the stabilization of the British position in northern Africa the Japanese have had to abandon their plans for northern expansion

An address before the inaugural meeting of the First Plenary Session of the Third People's Political Council in Chungking, October 22, 1942.

and a junction of forces with Germany. The future presents to them a spectacle of fathomless uncertainty.

The past year has been especially memorable for the change it has seen come about in our relations with other powers. Despite the damage done to our means of communication with the outside world by the loss of Hong Kong and Burma the circumstance has done much to bring about fuller collaboration between China and Great Britain, the United States, Soviet Russia and her other allies. But we are also opening up fresh routes of communication and we have achieved genuine military coordination. A great deal of the financial and material assistance at our disposal has resulted. Our allies have come to appreciate the effectiveness and importance of our resistance and to understand better the moral significance and aims of the war we have been waging for so long.

A still deeper cause for gratification is to be found in the announcements made by the British and American Governments on the Double Tenth of their intention immediately to abrogate their extraterritorial rights in China, and enter into negotiations with a view to making all relevant adjustments in their relations with the Chinese Government. There will, therefore, be no occasion to wait until after the war for the abolition of extraterritoriality. The gratitude we feel and the encouragement we have derived are inseparable from an added sense of our great responsibility. We are fully aware that since our allies have accorded us equality of status it stands to reason we shall rightly be expected to bear up a share of the war burden no less heavy than theirs.

There are four points of vital importance in the present situation. (1) The power of the Axis having passed the zenith of its development is now on the decline. Its final defeat is a matter of certainty. (2) The war will be of long duration and a conclusion is not to be looked for within any short period of time. (3) The rapidity and volume of Allied war production are such that victory is assured to the cause of the nations fighting aggression. (4) The present conflict will issue in a thoroughly conclusive decision and the post-war world will undoubtedly be one wherein all nations can live in freedom and equality of status one with another. The moral prestige of the nations which have contributed most to the victory will be correspondingly high.

The chief features of our efforts henceforth must be "endurance and conscientiousness." We shall be able to sustain those efforts only by conscientious striving toward a total victory. The war in China is already unique for its length and after more than five years the privations with which we are afflicted are nothing to be surprised at. We must

304

rouse our energies and summon up the maximum of our national strength to meet the difficulties to be overcome. Trepidation or unwillingness to make sacrifices will rob us of the fruition of our past exertions.

Modern warfare is by no means merely a matter of military operation. Economic affairs stand together with them in the first rank of the factors of importance. The implementation of the National General Mobilization Legislation and the advancement of economic policy will therefore have an immense influence on the course of the war. If we fail to mobilize our manpower to effect complete economic control, to stabilize prices, to adjust production and distribution, repeated successes at the front will not free the nation from its peril.

Let us take note of the way in which America, whose national strength is greater than ours, after less than a year of war has already instituted full economic control and mobilized her manpower to an astonishing extent. She has recently announced that the lower age limit for military service has been changed from twenty to eighteen. In China, however, there is still a lack of spontaneous enlistment in national military and labor service. There is still extensive waste of manpower and inadequate restriction of consumption. We have not succeeded in establishing fully effective control of commodities and prices. To a considerable degree social life is as lax now as in peace time since many merchants have taken selfish advantage of wartime conditions to profiteer and enrich themselves. Enthusiastic patriotism is widely absent among the people and habits of self-seeking and neglect of the public interest remain as obstacles to the success of the Government's economic policy.

If this state of affairs continues the prosecution of the war will be seriously impeded. The Government is determined, however, to effect complete application of National General Mobilization, to exercise comprehensive economic control in order to stabilize the national economy and to override all obstructions in its course to those ends. The help of persons of influence in society is required if satisfactory progress is to be made in this respect and the good offices of your Councillors and those of local county and provincial councils can prove invaluable in bringing about the desired effect.

I trust that Councillors will bear in mind the following four points in providing leadership for the people and assisting the Government:

First, an attempt must be made to correct the prevailing tone of social life and promote the practice of all necessary principles of conduct in time of war. This means stimulating frugality and a sense of urgency, reprehending indolence and preventing extravagance.

Second, prices must be stabilized for this is fundamentally necessary to the strengthening of war economy. For the success of all restrictive measures imposed, the investigation of marketing and distribution conditions, the detection of illicit practices, the facilitating of transportation, the control of commodities and the application of the rationing system, your leadership is needed.

Third, in concentrating the nation's resources it is essential to make the people understand that wartime financial policy is founded upon revenue from taxation, subscription to public loans, the collection of land tax in kind and the promotion of savings. Consequently the enthusiastic support of the people must be had for the effective imposition of direct taxation, the soliciting of subscriptions to war bonds, the compulsory purchase of materials of war, the limitation of high incomes and the control of profits and rates of interest. Only on this condition can the issue of currency be kept within proper bounds and a firm foundation for the national livelihood be secured.

Fourth, the conscription of manpower for military and labor service will, it is to be hoped, be supplemented by the promotion of voluntary enlistment and the prevention of evasion and abuses. The system of stage transportation must be further expanded to employ more fully in this way the labor power of the people. The utilization of spare time in labor service on the part of young students and professional men is also to be urged, women encouraged to devote their energies to productive activities and all other means sought to bring out total manpower to bear in resistance and reconstruction.

This assembly follows closely upon the promised abolition of extraterritoriality by Great Britain and the United States and our country is being watched by the world with fresh interest. This should stir our Government and people to a more positive awareness of our responsibilities and invigorate our resolve worthily to advance the cause of the United Nations.

306

From Equality to Ideal Unity

FOR ten days this session has been sitting and all you Councillors have been unsparing of your energies by night and by day in deliberating upon military affairs, foreign policy, internal administration, finance, economy and education. You have dealt with present problems and plans for future improvements and have arrived at a great number of concrete and detailed resolutions. You have especially concentrated your attention upon means of strengthening the war effort, mobilizing manpower and resources and controlling prices. In order to facilitate and expedite the application of the National General Mobilization Act and wartime economic measures in general, we have resolved to set up within this Council a committee for the advancement of economic mobilization. Henceforth we must unanimously proceed to do all we can to inspire our fellow countrymen with the determination to fulfill the duties of citizenship in time of war in such a way that the national policy may be completely carried out and final victory won.

The present session has been conducted in an extremely practical and factual spirit. It has been pervaded with an exhilarating atmosphere of determination to meet growing difficulties with redoubled resolution. I wish now to make some remarks in which I shall express the hopes I entertain regarding your future work.

One of the deepest causes for gratification we and our fellow countrymen find in recent events is, of course, the abolition of the unequal treaties. In this respect there is nothing specific to report at present but I wish to stress the importance of the fact that Great Britain and the United States should have spontaneously made this proposal with such sincerity of intention that an entirely satisfactory outcome of the negotiations is already assured us in principle. I believe the essential thing at the moment is how after we have gained equality of status with other nations we are to exert ourselves and not fall short of our allies' expectations of us or fail worthily to play the part of a modern and

An address at the closing ceremony of the Third People's Political Council, October 31, 1942.

independent nation. Consider how momentous an episode in the history of the nation is this deliverance from the shackles that have bound it for a hundred years. All of you here today from the oldest to the youngest member have without exception grown up out of a period of repeated national humiliations.

Dr. Sun Yat-sen, Father of the Republic, made it his great aim in his revolutionary leadership to secure freedom and equality of status for China among the nations of the world. The Principle of Nationhood had first to be applied before obstacles to the solution of problems involved in the application of the Principles of Rights and Livelihood could be removed. The vindication of our national honor has been the unvarying demand of the whole Chinese people, alike of those who were and were not actually concerned with the work of the Revolution. Now the way is open to that goal and the occasion calls for a proper sense of its unique importance on the part of every citizen.

Let us look back over the history of the nation's sufferings since the establishment of the Republic and to the time of the Northern Expedition that put an end to the civil wars waged by the militarists. In 1927 the world began to understand China and if it had not been for troubles at home and menace from without the unequal treaties would have been abolished long ago. Half of the obstacles were due to mischief done by the Japanese imperialists and half to pretexts founded upon our own lack of unity. The present success is the result of more than five years of war. Now we must go on to display with firmer solidarity the greater effort our full comprehension of the stages by which the Revolution has been advancing and concentrate our will and activity upon victory in resistance and the complete application of the Three Principles of the People. This is the first point I hope you will endeavor to bring to your fellow countrymen's notice.

Having now attained equality of status with our allies and other nations of the world, we must shoulder the responsibilities this age has laid upon us. The nation is responsible not only for its own interests but also for those of the world. No difficulties or sacrifices must deter us from the fulfillment of our duties as one unit of the forces of the United Nations and after the war we must be prepared, as a progressive and free nation devoted to the cause of justice, to do all that is required of us in collaborating with those nations to recreate world order and effect the deliverance of mankind. China is the largest and most ancient of Asiatic countries but it is not for us boastfully to talk of her right to a position of "leadership" among those countries. In the spirit of the saying "All men are brothers" we shall rather regard it as our responsibility to treat the peoples of Asia, like all suffering and oppressed humanity elsewhere, as equals to help and support. Recognizing equality as the highest guiding principle of international affairs, we shall do well neither to underestimate nor overestimate our own importance and dignity. It is precisely Japanese militarism with its ambition of dominating Asia under the pretense of organizing a "Co-prosperity Sphere for Greater East Asia" that constitutes the universal enemy we are determined to crush.

We have been fighting this War of Resistance with purity of motive and consistency of principle—not for any selfish purpose but for the salvation of the world through first saving ourselves. Toward Asia as toward the whole world we wish only to do our duty to the exclusion of any lust for power or other desires incompatible with the moral dictates of love and benevolence that are characteristic of the Chinese national spirit. The aim of the Revolution is, so far as the interests of China herself are concerned, the restoration of her original frontiers and in regard to the rest of the world a gradual advance of all nations from the stage of equality to that of an ideal unity. Such is the full extent of our desire. Every citizen should take stock of his country's position.

The Washington conference [of 1942] made China one of the four main powers and that was an expression of the high regard in which our allies hold us, yet the degree to which our national reconstruction and strength are inadequate in comparison with other powers must fill us with a sense of unworthiness. With the continual and fierce development of hostilities we must go about the discharging of our responsibility toward the world by building up our own strength and intensifying our preparations for a general counter-offensive. In the present period we must stand firm, permit ourselves no vainglorious thoughts or rashness and never slacken in our vigilance. This is the second point I would have you Councillors impress upon your fellow countrymen.

In all matters relating to efficiency in military operations and administration both your unreserved advice and assistance are needed by the Government. The nation has not yet in many respects met fundamental requirements for the implementation of its war policy. There is no uniform standard of knowledge pervading among the people and this is one very undeniable difficulty and shortcoming. We must make a searching review of our national circumstances, devise practical measures, coordinate our efforts and proceed fully conscious of the indivisibility of our interests, to reinvigorate our national strength by urging the whole people to exertion in the common cause. The nation's affairs should be regarded as indistinguishable from the individual's. The failings of the nation or of individual citizens, should make us all equally ashamed. We must convert indifference into enthusiasm, negative attitudes into positive, get rid of irresponsibility and replace the tendency to blame others by willingness to cooperate with others.

The future status of our nation can have no resemblance to what it was in the past. Our intelligentsia and men of influence in society cannot therefore any longer maintain that posture of complacent aloofness they so often affected in the past, for now the nation needs their services. Their fellow citizens need their instruction and guidance, and youth their leadership. What I trust you will do is positively to make yourselves responsible to the nation and people by providing enthusiastic leadership in the work of cultivating new political and social tendencies and eradicating the bad old habits of insincerity, display, indolence and dilatoriness. Every citizen must realize that the status we have now acquired is the fruit of fifty years' revolutionary endeavor and five years of war. It might be lost as easily as it was gained with difficulty.

If we cannot bring to the fore the virtues of energy and thrift for which our people is renowned and cultivate habits of endurance and conscientiousness but continue to present the spectacle of disunity described in the phrase "a tray of loose sand," each man for himself, false to others and self-deceiving, we shall never be able to give our society or our nation a place in the modern world. It will reject us and if we cannot overcome the aggressor who is the final obstacle of our national rehabilitation we shall have wasted our former toil and generations of our people yet unborn will be enslaved.

The reform of our social modes of thought and life is the essential means to national salvation. We must rouse our fellow countrymen to awareness and circumspection that they may avoid all activity and thought that conflict with the process of modernization, all feudalistic provincialism and sectionalism that undermine the authority of the Government. The nation must be led solely to value the unique opportunity it now possesses of restoring its pristine glory and demonstrating the spirit of selfless devotion to the universal good which is the salient feature of its cultural tradition. There must be a rebirth of that spirit such as will enable us to fight and to build with success. This is the third point I have to recommend to you as a keynote of your activities as leaders of your people.

The recent war situation is more favorable than that of any other time when the Council has met. We can perceive the coming of the dawn both of victory in war and success in national reconstruction. The problems of the future will, however, be numerous and the crisis through which the Revolution will yet have to pass confront us in anticipation. The recovery of full health and vigor in a country afflicted with so many maladies as ours has been, will not be so easy a matter as some may suppose.

The fate of the nation is now in the balance. We must look to ourselves for the strength to win survival for our country. Its destiny will depend upon men of our generation. We must not allow any particular set of circumstances to affect the fixed conception of our mission. Only by a great devotion to the cause can we act up to the achievements of these years of war and carry on the unfinished work of the Revolutionary martyrs.

One of the most important duties of you Councillors who are about to return to the localities from which you have come will be the expediting in all ways that lie within your power of national mobilization and the work of the committee for the advancement of economic mobilization. These are days in which the nation's hopes are high and in which at the same time the weight of our duties is constantly growing. I trust that you will all strive your utmost in that national service that is yours.

From Men's Oldest Parliament

I DEEM it a great pleasure to have the privilege of extending to you on behalf of the people of China a cordial and hearty welcome. We have been looking forward to your visit with eagerness and we are all the more delighted to have you with us because this is, I understand, the first time that the British Parliament—the oldest representative assembly in the world—sends an official mission abroad.

You have come from afar after an arduous trip to bring us a message of goodwill from your great nation, to acquaint yourselves and take back with you the hopes of the future of our people regarding your people and to strengthen the bonds of comradeship between us. Your mission is on everybody's lips and your presence cannot fail to be a source of encouragement and inspiration to the Chinese Army and people.

We Chinese have a saying, "To see even only once is better than to learn from a hundred reports"—which is equivalent to your "Seeing is believing." From your own observation you will not fail to notice the deep appreciation of the Chinese Government and people for the moral and material assistance you have rendered them in their struggle.

We are sincerely touched by the widespread sympathetic interest of the British people in our ordeal and by the innumerable tokens of sympathy as manifested in the incessant efforts to enlist support for our cause. The present United Aid to China Fund, the recent renunciation of extraterritoriality and related rights, and the visit of your mission itself are to us additional proof of Great Britain's friendship for China.

I hope that you will gain a true picture of the severity of our trials and tribulations in these five long years, the grimness of our determination to prosecute the war to total victory and the firmness of our faith in the ultimate triumph of the common cause to which our people have dedicated themselves.

For several years we fought alone against aggression in this part of

Speeches of Generalissimo Chiang and members of the British Parliamentary Mission at a banquet given by the Generalissimo in their honor on November 11, 1942.

the world but never for a moment did we lose faith in the ultimate outcome of our resistance against aggression for as one of our ancient sages, Mencius, said, "He who has a just cause receives aid from many quarters." How true these words ring today.

Now that our two countries and the other United Nations are intimately bound together in a common cause and a common destiny it behooves all of us to cooperate to the fullest extent and I know we are equally resolved to do it—not only in the prosecution of the war but also in the building up of a saner and happier world.

Response of Lord Ailwyn, member of the House of Lords

May I express on behalf of the British Parliamentary Delegation our most grateful thanks to Your Excellency for your very kind welcome to us here this evening and for words with which you have been good enough to address us.

The British people were not slow to realize the importance and the significance of Your Excellency's request that a Parliamentary Mission should visit this country. They were, too, greatly pleased at the interest and satisfaction expressed in messages from China welcoming this visit. It is as Your Excellency has said a unique event—the first of its kind, I believe, in British Parliamentary history—and we are very proud to find ourselves here as members of this mission.

We were delighted with the warm and enthusiastic welcome which we received on our arrival at Chungking yesterday and we shall not fail to tell them at home of the kindness extended to us both in the matter of our reception and in the thought and consideration given to our comfort and welfare for the term of our visit.

Before leaving London we were received by His Majesty the King who charged us with the delivery to His Excellency the President of the National Government of a personal letter of greeting from His Majesty. We were further entrusted with two personal letters to Your Excellency, one from our Prime Minister Mr. Churchill and the other from the Lord Chancellor of Great Britain and the Speaker of the House of Commons. We have been happy to carry out these duties and we have had the honor of delivering these letters today.

Your Excellency, we have come to China with the keenest anticipation. We hope to see all that it is possible to show us of the great and valiant work of the Chinese people and of the Chinese Army under the inspiring leadership of Your Excellency through nearly five and a half years of epic struggle. Nor do we forget the noble work and high courage of Madame Chiang Kai-shek, some of the results of whose labors up and down the country we shall also hope to see. We should like, if you will permit us, to tell you something of the British war effort and of our inflexible will and determination not to sheath the sword until out of this welter of bloodshed and suffering there emerges a world purged once and for all of the forces of evil which now beset the peace-loving peoples of the world.

May I express once more to Your Excellency our deep sense of gratitude for this great privilege which is ours of visiting your great country and for your kind hospitality to us this evening.

Response of Mr. J. J. Lawson, member of the House of Commons

We count it a privilege to visit your country at a time when China and her people have won the admiration of the world by their heroic and long-sustained stand against a cruel and powerful enemy. It is not only a privilege but a very great honor to come at the invitation of your Government to represent the Parliament of Great Britain.

Two of our members are Conservatives, one is a Liberal, one is a Socialist. But whatever our political views, however we may differ, we have one strong bond of unity today, and that is rooted in the view of the British people and its Parliament, to utterly destroy the Fascist enemy in Germany and Japan.

To that end the whole life of the people of Britain is dedicated. In times of peace we never had more than fourteen million industrial workers. Since the war we have turned twenty-three million men and women to the production of armaments out of a population of forty-six millions. In addition we have sent millions into the armed forces and great numbers to civil defense.

It can be truly said that today in Britain, apart from the very old and very young, everybody is engaged in the common struggle with the enemy. You in this land were the first to meet the onslaught of cruel men upon the decent peace-loving people of the world. You met the attack with a courage and fortitude which has gained for the Chinese people the gratitude of the Allied Nations. We are proud to be standing side by side with you.

When the old lost sense of security is restored by victory I trust that the friendship welded by the fires of war may enable us to work together for the establishment of that permanent peace in which new triumphs of culture will be achieved and new depths of human friendship sounded among the nations of the earth.

China's After-War Aims

THE political testament of the Father of our Republic, Dr. Sun Yat-sen, began with the reminder to his followers, "The Revolution is not yet achieved." Even after the National Revolution succeeded in overthrowing the warlords and unified China in 1927, we have continued to characterize our Government as a Revolutionary Government.

Critics asked, now that you have established a Government of all China, why do you persist in calling yourselves a Revolutionary Government? What do you mean by Revolution?

The answer is that what we mean by Revolution is the attainment of all three of Dr. Sun's basic principles of national revolution: national independence, progressive realization of democracy, and a rising level of living conditions for the masses. When victory comes at the end of this war, we shall have fully achieved national independence but will have far to go to attain our other two objectives. Hence our claim that ours is still a Revolutionary Government which means no more or less than it is a government dedicated to attaining these other two objectives.

Insisting on national independence for all peoples, Dr. Sun's vision transcends the problem of China, and seeks equality for all peoples, East and West alike. China not only fights for her own independence, but also for the liberation of every oppressed nation. For us the Atlantic Charter and President Roosevelt's proclamation of the Four Freedoms for all peoples are cornerstones of our fighting faith.

For many centuries Chinese society has been free of class distinctions such as are found even in advanced democracies. At the core of our political thought is our traditional maxim, "The people form the foundation of the country." We Chinese are instinctively democratic, and Dr. Sun's objective of universal suffrage evokes from all Chinese a ready and unhesitating response. But the processes and forms by which the will of the people is made manifest, and the complex machin-

A message to the eleventh annual New York Herald Tribune Forum on Current Problems delivered on November 17, 1942.

ery of modern democratic government cannot, I know to my cost, be created overnight, especially under the constant menace and attack of Japanese militarism.

During the last years of his life Dr. Sun devoted much of his forward thinking to the economic reconstruction of China, and nothing, I believe, so marked his greatness as his insistence that the coming tremendous economic reconstruction of China should benefit not the privileged few but the entire nation.

The absence of a strong central government capable of directing economic development, the bondage of unequal treaties trying to keep China as a semi-colony for others, and above all the jealous machinations of Japan, all these greatly retarded the economic reconstruction to which the National Revolution of China is dedicated.

But the end of the present war will find China freed of her bondage, with a vigorous government and a people ardent with desire to rebuild their country. I feel the force of this desire as a tidal wave which will not only absorb the energies of our people for a century but will also bring lasting benefits to the entire world.

But the bright promise of the future, which has done much to sustain us during our grim struggle with Japan, will cruelly vanish if after paying the price this second time we do not achieve the reality of world cooperation.

I hear that my American friends have confidence in the experience of men who have "come up the hard way." My long struggles as a soldier of the Chinese Revolution have forced me to realize the necessity of facing hard facts. There will be neither peace, nor hope, nor future for any of us unless we honestly aim at political, social and economic justice for all peoples of the world, great and small. But I feel confident that we of the United Nations can achieve that aim only by starting at once to organize an international order embracing all peoples to enforce peace and justice among them. To make that start we must begin today and not tomorrow to apply these principles among ourselves even at some sacrifice to the absolute powers of our individual countries. We should bear in mind one of the most inspiring utterances of the last World War, that of Edith Cavell:

> "Standing at the brink of the grave, I feel that
> Patriotism alone is not enough."

We Chinese are not so blind as to believe that the new international order will usher in the millennium. But we do not look upon it as visionary. The idea of universal brotherhood is innate in the catholic nature

316

of Chinese thought; it was the dominant concept of Dr. Sun Yat-sen, whom events have proved time and again to be not a visionary but one of the world's greatest realists.

Among our friends there has been recently some talk of China emerging as the leader of Asia, as if China wished the mantle of an unworthy Japan to fall on her shoulders. Having herself been a victim of exploitation, China has infinite sympathy for the submerged nations of Asia, and toward them China feels she has only responsibilities—not rights. We repudiate the idea of leadership of Asia because the "Fuehrer principle" has been synonymous for domination and exploitation, precisely as the "East Asia co-prosperity sphere" has stood for a race of mythical supermen lording over grovelling subject races.

China has no desire to replace Western imperialism in Asia with an Oriental imperialism or isolationism of its own or of anyone else. We hold that we must advance from the narrow idea of exclusive alliances and regional blocs which in the end make for bigger and more terrible wars, to effective organization of world unity. Unless real world cooperation replaces both isolationism and imperialism of whatever form in the new inter-dependent world of free nations, there will be no lasting security for you or for us.

A New World Built on Christian Love

TODAY is the birthday of Christ, a day of universal joy. I am quite sure that if you were in your own country, you would be able to celebrate Christmas in an even more festive mood. On my part, it is indeed a great pleasure and honor to have you join me in celebrating Christmas together.

Five years ago China, unprepared and under-equipped though she was, resolutely took up arms in defense of herself against the Japanese militarists. But it was my firm conviction from the very beginning of our resistance that the final victory would belong to us. It was also my belief that all democracies sooner or later would join hands in a common effort to exterminate brute force and deal a blow to the aggressor nations. Just as our ancients said that those who are in the right will receive aid from many quarters while those in the wrong will find little sympathy, we now have thirty-one countries united in arms and fighting shoulder to shoulder for justice and peace. This proves the truth of the Chinese saying and proves also that my vision has come true.

The present world line-up may be said to be divided into two blocs. On the one side are aligned thirty-one peace- and justice-loving countries which, united in purpose, find their fighting power daily increasing as they struggle for the freedom and preservation of humanity. On the other side are grouped Germany, Italy and Japan, three ambitious totalitarian states which, bent on extending their territorial domains, have swallowed up weaker nations one after another and which have cherished the ambition of partitioning the world.

But it must be noted that this Axis camp is fighting for an unjust cause and is solely guided by a policy of utter treachery, ruthlessness and barbarity. That being the case, how can they stand up against our allied and righteous armies? Consequently, it is a foregone conclusion

An address to several hundred Allied military representatives and officers and men of the Allied armed forces stationed in the Chinese wartime capital, who were guests of Generalissimo Chiang Kai-shek at a Christmas Day program on December 25, 1942.

that the final defeat of the Axis bloc is inevitable, just as the ultimate triumph of the United Nations is a thing that admits of no doubt. The United Nations are fighting entirely for international justice and human freedom. This coincides with the principles of the late Dr. Sun Yat-sen's *San Min Chu I* and when translated into action, it will also mean the realization of the spirit of love of Christ.

It is my firm conviction that out of this war, the thirty-one United Nations will be able to reestablish the world on the basis of equality and mutual assistance and will also be able to build up a new world order of genuine peace and happiness. Such a new world order must be created on the foundation of love as preached by Christ. Therefore, at this Christmas, amidst the raging of a world conflict, I sincerely pray to Jesus Christ, the Prince of Peace, for the early arrival of our common victory so that the world may be delivered from the ruthless oppression of the three Axis countries, Germany, Italy and Japan, and that the conquered peoples now living under their domination may sooner obtain their liberation and freedom.

As the Commander-in-Chief of the China War Theater, I wish the United Nations an early victory and our Allied officers and men happiness and good health.

New Treaties: New Responsibilities

ON Oct. 10 last year the United States and Great Britain voluntarily announced their relinquishment of the special rights they had long enjoyed in China under unequal treaties. Yesterday in Washington and in Chungking our Government signed new treaties of equality and reciprocity with these two nations.

Fellow countrymen, just a century before the American and British announcements, the Manchu Dynasty concluded the first of China's · unequal treaties with foreign powers. By fifty years of revolutionary struggle and five and a half years of war and sacrifice, we have transformed an inglorious anniversary into an occasion of national rejoicing. Today marks a new epoch in China's history and today Britain and America have lighted a new light to guide man's progress on the road to equality and freedom for all peoples.

By their actions our allies have declared their basic war aim—to sustain the rule of human decency and human right—and have proved their high ideals and lofty purposes. From the United States we have received an especially gratifying, complete and unreserved agreement to the hopes and aspirations expressed by our Government. From the action of our allies every one of the United Nations must draw new courage for the fight. The aggressor nations may observe and doubt.

But we should all understand that freedom and independence are prizes to be won only by our own efforts. I have often said to you, my fellow countrymen, "We must be self-reliant before we can be independent; we must be strong before we can be free." Before the Republic of China can be independent and free the nation must be strong. Before our soldiers and our people can be worthy citizens of a China, independent and free, they must be self-reliant and ready for hard tasks. By abolition of the unequal treaties our national responsibility has only been increased. We should meet the new responsibility with a still keener resolve to do our duty.

A message to the people and the army of China on the occasion of the signing of the Sino-American and the Sino-British treaties for the relinquishment of extraterritorial rights in China, January 11, 1943.

320

This is no time for arrogant conceit or self-satisfaction with the little that has been accomplished already. If we fail to make China independent, free and strong, if the nation we build is impotent to do its share for the general welfare of mankind, then what we have gained will soon be lost. When the war ends our task will not be done. We must continue as we have begun or we shall sink back into dependency and our children and our children's children will live out their lives in bondage.

China's destiny, in truth, is the heavy burden which has been placed upon the shoulders of our generation. To safeguard the broad lands bequeathed to us by our forefathers, and to ensure to our posterity liberty and well-being, we must resolve this day to acquit ourselves loyally with self-reliance, without shirking, and in harmony with one another.

We can see already the first signs of coming victory in this world war against world aggression. The time of the enemy's defeat is near at hand. There are some who assume that China's destiny will be easily decided at the conference table after victory has come. There are others who believe that the outcome is certain and that China may easily participate in the fruits of future victory without present struggle. These men are wrong. The time to decide the destiny of our nation is now. The choice is plain before us. Are we to be masters in our own house or are we hereafter, as in the past, to obey the voice of others? At such a time there is no room for procrastination or lethargy or doubt. From this moment we must work still harder and bear without complaint still greater privations than we have done in the past five and a half years of war. There is no other way to succeed in the great task which fate has laid upon us.

Fellow countrymen, until today we could rightly assert that unequal treaties with foreign powers had hindered and prevented our efforts to build a nation. The unequal treaties emplanted among us disunity, economic backwardness and social chaos. They taught our people a sense of inferiority which we could not overcome. They encouraged a mood of weak surrender by which too few were shamed. Even today we are without the self-confidence or moral courage which should be ours. But now that the unequal treaties have been abolished their influence is also gone. Henceforth, if we are weak, if we lack self-confidence, the fault will be ours only. Habits learned in the bad times of our nation's dependency may still survive. With one mind and one will we must weed them out and we must rally together around the

321

standard of the Three Principles of the People to defeat our enemy and reconstruct the country that we love.

Success in our long struggle is at last in sight. Together we must go forward believing the teachings of the Father of the Republic, applying the Three Principles of the People and supporting our National Government. As one man we must do our duty, living the hard wartime life and doing all that is necessary to be done. As one man we must fight and as one man we must work to lay the foundation of the better China of the days of peace.

Fellow countrymen, this is the period of our golden opportunity. It is our good fortune to see on this day the final casting off of the bonds of the past and to begin on this day a new and more hopeful stage on the long road to independence and freedom. As I urge you on this day to intensify your struggle, I urge you also to remember the best traditions of your nation in dealing with other nations friendly to China. Their citizens will now enjoy the protection of our laws. Toward them we must be friendly and courteous. Formerly what passed as friendliness and courtesy on our part was nothing but capitulation and humiliation. Now that the unequal treaties have been abrogated we are on an equal footing with Great Britain and the United States. An independent China has become a real friend of these two nations. In our relations with other people we Chinese have always been guided by the principles of propriety and righteousness. Therefore, in our future relations with friendly nations we should be more courteous and friendly than ever before. Look to the lessons of the past. Keep before you always the beacons of *Li, Yi, Lien* and *Ch'ih* [propriety, righteousnes, integrity and conscientiousness]. March forward with a common purpose until we can join our allies in building a better world as we have joined with one another to build a better nation.

Fellow countrymen, I greet this memorable day with deep confidence and ardent hope. I pledge my utmost effort for the future as you must pledge yours. From the bottom of my heart I thank you all for your courage and endurance in these hard years. We have gone through much together, you and I.

I offer heartfelt tribute to the memory of the martyrs of our great cause and I salute the victory that is to come.

Long live the freedom and independence of the Republic of China.

Long live the success of our national revolution.

Long live the Three Principles of the People.